Redefining
Realness

Redefining
Realness

My Path to Womanhood,
Identity, Love & So Much More

JANET MOCK

ATRIA BOOKS
New York   London   Toronto   Sydney   New Delhi

ATRIA BOOKS

A Division of Simon & Schuster, Inc.
1230 Avenue of the Americas
New York, NY 10020

First Atria Books hardcover edition February 2014

ATRIA BOOKS and colophon are trademarks of Simon & Schuster, Inc.

For information about special discounts for bulk purchases, please contact Simon &
Schuster Special Sales at 1-866-506-1949 or business@simonandschuster.com.

The Simon & Schuster Speakers Bureau can bring authors to your live event. For
more information or to book an event, contact the Simon & Schuster Speakers
Bureau at 1-866-248-3049 or visit our website at www.simonspeakers.com.

Interior design by Jill Putorti

Manufactured in the United States of America

10   9   8   7   6   5   4   3   2   1

Library of Congress Cataloging-in-Publication Data

Mock, Janet.
  Redefining realness : my path to womanhood, identity, love & so much more/ by
Janet Mock. — First Atria Books hardcover edition.
      pages   cm
  1. Mock, Janet. 2. Transgender people—United States—Biography. 3. Racially
mixed people—United States—Biography. 4. Gender identity—United States—Case
studies. 5. Self-actualization (Psychology)—Case studies. I. Title.
  HQ77.8.M63A3   2014
  306.76'8—dc23   2013047625

ISBN 978-1-4767-0912-3
ISBN 978-1-4767-0914-7 (ebook)

For Aaron,
who loved me because of myself,
held me accountable to my truth,
and became home

You become strong by doing the things you need to be strong for. This is the way genuine learning takes place. That's a very difficult way to live, but it also has served me. It's been an asset as well as a liability.

—AUDRE LORDE

Redefining *Realness*

Author's Note

This book is my truth and personal history. I have recalled facts, from events to people, to the best of my ability. When memory failed me, I did not seek answers in imagination. I sought clarity through conversations with those who've shared experiences with me. When my recollection of events varied from theirs, I sided with my memory and used their voice, often direct quotes, to contextualize events.

Many people featured in the book gave me permission to use their names; others I changed or labeled with an initial to protect their privacy, whether they were guilty, innocent, indifferent, or somewhere in between.

As for terminology, I prefer to use *trans* over *transgender* or *transsexual* when identifying myself, although I don't find either offensive. I do not use *real* or *genetic* or *biological* or *natural* to describe the sex, body, or gender of those who are not trans. Instead, I've used *cis,* a term applied to those who are not trans and therefore less likely to experience the misalignment of their gender identity and assigned sex at birth—a matter we do not control, yet one that continues to frame who is normalized or stigmatized.

Finally, though I highlight some of the shared experiences of trans women and women of color throughout this book, it was not written with the intent of representation. There is no universal women's experience. We all have stories, and this is *one* personal narrative out of untold thousands, and I am aware of the privilege I hold in telling *my* story. Visit JanetMock.com for more information, resources, and writings.

Introduction

I was shopping for dresses I didn't need at a vintage store near my apartment when I read the e-mail that changed my life. It was May 13, 2011, and the message—titled "Drum roll please . . . *Marie Claire*"—contained a three-page PDF of what would become known as my "coming-out story." "I hope you like it," the editor of my profile wrote. "We are very pleased with it. Very proud of it."

I downloaded the file on my iPhone and read the article for the first time, seated on a curb outside the boutique. It was a brisk and sunny Friday in the East Village, one of those days that hadn't decided what season it wanted to be. My palms were moist and my heartbeat was hasty as my eyes glided across twenty-three hundred words written by journalist Kierna Mayo. I read the article three times from the same spot on that cold cement. After each reading, I was moved but strikingly detached.

It was a stranger's story to me. It belonged to some brave girl who defied all odds, crossing sexes, leaving her past behind, making it to *People* magazine, and living to tell her story in a major women's magazine. I found myself applauding this heroine for embodying the do-it-yourself bravado that Americans celebrate. Although the facts correlated with my life, the story belonged to *Marie Claire* through the reportage of Kierna. The profile was a compilation of a series of meetings, phone calls, and e-mails from the past few months that disclosed one aspect of my identity: I am a trans woman, or, as *Marie Claire* put it, "I Was Born a Boy." The fact remains that the girl in that article didn't resonate with me because it wasn't really *my* story.

When Kierna approached me back in 2010, only the people closest to me knew I was trans: my family, my friends, and my boyfriend. They were people I trusted, who nurtured me, with whom I was intimate. I took Kierna's call because a friend to whom I had opened up told me I could trust Kierna. This friend was the same person who had disclosed to a well-known journalist what I'd shared with her in confidence. Regardless, I was not ready for the vulnerability that comes with public openness when I spoke to Kierna at age twenty-seven. During our conversations, I withheld parts of myself and details from my journey (partly because I was unpacking my own shame; partly because I needed to save those details for my own story). As a result, the girl in the piece seemed untouchable, unscathed, a bit of an anomaly.

I was reluctant to open up to the world for the same reasons I had been afraid to reveal myself as Janet to my mother and siblings at thirteen, to wear a dress through the halls of my high school, to tell the man I loved my truth: I didn't want to be "othered," reduced to just being trans. I struggled for years with my perception of what trans womanhood was, having internalized our culture's skewed, biased views and pervasive misconceptions about trans women.

Growing up, I learned that being trans was something you did not take pride in; therefore, I yearned to separate myself from the dehumanizing depictions of trans women that I saw in popular culture, from Venus Xtravaganza's unsolved and underexplored murder in *Paris Is Burning*, to the characters of Lois Einhorn (played by Sean Young) in *Ace Ventura: Pet Detective*, and Dil (played by Jaye Davidson) in *The Crying Game*, to numerous women exploited as modern-day freak shows on *Jerry Springer* and *Maury*. Let's not forget the "tranny hooker" credits seen everywhere from *Sex and the City* to every *Law & Order* and *CSI* franchise. According to the media, trans women were subject to pain and punch lines. Instead of proclaiming that I was not a plot device to be laughed at, I spent my younger years internalizing and fighting those stereotypes.

I don't want to be seen as one of them, I told myself a number of times as I grappled with making the decision to tell my story publicly. I remained silent because I was taught to believe that my silence would protect me, cradle me, enable me to have access, excel, and build a life for myself. My silence and my accomplishments would help me navigate the world without others' judgments and would separate me from the stereotypes and stigma.

As I remained silent, though, I became aware of the fact that behind these limited media images and society's skewed perceptions, there were *real* girls out there. I knew these girls. I'd grown up with them in Honolulu and passed them on the streets of New York. These girls and women were not given the same opportunities and concessions with which I'd been blessed. They were dismissed and dehumanized, which made an overwhelming majority of them vulnerable to the harshest treatment, exclusion, discrimination, and violence. These women stood at the intersections of race, gender, class, sexuality, and personal economy on the margins of our society. Despite my attempt to remain separate and be the exception, the reality was that I was one of these women.

I had to be honest with myself about the totality of my experiences, and opening up to the world—even if the story disclosed only a facet of my journey—was a gift. It wasn't a gift just to the hundreds of women who've thanked me for stepping forward; it's the greatest gift I've ever given myself. In the three years since I read that PDF on the curb, my story has been embraced by people from all walks of life. I've had the opportunity to share space with folks around the country, speaking about my experiences of privilege and oppression, my mission to be unapologetic about the layered identities I carry within my body, and reclaiming the often erased legacy of trans women's survival that enabled me to thrive as a young, poverty-raised trans woman of color. I exist because of the women who came before me, whose work, lives, and struggles I've greatly benefited from. Whether it was 1966's Compton's Cafeteria riots or the Stonewall uprisings of 1969 or the daily battles against policing, exiling, violence, and erasure, trans women—specifically those from the streets with nothing to lose—always resisted. My foremothers have role modeled, through their lives and work, the brilliance of anchoring yourself in marginalized womanhood.

The responsibility that comes with being visible is a duty, one I'm still growing comfortable with. I have been lauded as a voice, a leader, and a role model. I know intimately what it feels like to crave representation and validation, to see your life reflected in someone who speaks deeply to whom you know yourself to be, echoes your reality, and instills you with possibility. That mirror wasn't accessible to me growing up. It was an utterly lonely place to be. So when a girl with tears in her eyes embraces me and tells me "I want to be like you when I grow up" or "Reading your story has given me hope" or "You're my hero," I understand the gravity of her statements.

My story has shown that *more* is possible for girls growing up like I did. I'm proud of that, yet I struggle with being held up as the one who "made it," as an exception to the rule. For years, exceptionalism was a bandage I proudly wore to make me feel worthy. I felt validated when people stated that I was *exceptional* or *unique* or that I was not the norm. Basking in these proclamations, I soon realized something was amiss: If I'm the exception, the so-called standard of success, then where does that leave the sisters I grew up with on the streets of Honolulu who didn't "make it"?

Being exceptional isn't revolutionary, it's lonely. It separates you from your community. Who are you, really, without community? I have been held up consistently as a token, as the "right" kind of trans woman (educated, able-bodied, attractive, articulate, heteronormative). It promotes the delusion that because I "made it," that level of success is easily accessible to all young trans women. Let's be clear: It is not.

We need stories of hope and possibility, stories that reflect the reality of our lived experiences. When such stories exist, as writer and publisher Barbara Smith writes, "then each of us will not only know better how to live, but how to dream." We must also deconstruct these stories and contextualize them and shed a light on the many barriers that face trans women, specifically those of color and those from low-income communities, who aim to reach the not-so-extraordinary things I have grasped: living freely and without threat or notice as I am, making a safe, healthy living, and finding love. These things should not be out of reach.

Having "made it" leaves me with survivor's guilt. I often go home after delivering a keynote or appearing on television and pull the lashes from my face, pile my wild curls atop my head, and face myself. I'm bare and vulnerable, looking at myself exactly as I am, not how I hope to be perceived, and asking: *Why me?*

Redefining Realness is my attempt to extend that nakedness and vulnerability to you. It is about those parts of ourselves that we silence every day; those parts that we all store away in boxes deep within, where they gather the dust of shame that clouds us. In this book, I aim to open those boxes, display their contents, and be accountable to my truth. This process was gradual and challenging, one in which I had to excavate answers within myself for some tough questions: Who am I, really? How does that answer contribute to the world? How do I tell my story authentically without discounting all the facets and identities that make me? Can I resolve my personal history with sexual abuse, body image, self-love and sex, as well as unpack my relationship with womanhood, beauty, objectification, and "passing"? I hope this book offers clarity and pushes you toward beginnings and conclusions of your own.

My ultimate goal with *Redefining Realness* is to stand firmly in my truth. I believe that telling our stories, first to ourselves and then to one another and the world, is a revolutionary act. It is an act that can be met with hostility, exclusion, and violence. It can also lead to love, understanding, transcendence, and community. I hope that my being *real* with you will help empower you to step into who you are and encourage you to share yourself with those around you. It's through my personal decision to be visible that I finally see myself. There's nothing more powerful than truly being *and* loving yourself.

They sat there in the fresh young darkness close together. Pheoby eager to feel and do through Janie, but hating to show her zest for fear it might be thought mere curiosity. Janie full of that oldest human longing—self-revelation.

—ZORA NEALE HURSTON, *THEIR EYES WERE WATCHING GOD*

NEW YORK, 2009

I thought about telling Aaron on our first date. That moment in the back booth of that Brazilian restaurant in the West Village when my head rested in the space where his chest met his armpit. He smelled like sweat and cilantro and looked a lot like that one thing I yearned *and* feared: intimacy.

He was looking at me, his brown eyes studying mine. *Can he see me?* I thought.

"I see the little girl in you," Aaron said, seemingly surprised by his discovery. "Will she play with me?"

I wanted to tell him then. He was the kind of charming I couldn't resist blushing at and scolding myself for being moved by. I knew I was slipping away from my own barricades of insecurity and into a more honest nook. But decades of internalized shame about my past and its relation to my present couldn't be undone by mere charm and romantic projections. It would take something special, outside of myself, to unwrap me. I had an instinct that Aaron was something special.

We had met only days earlier, the night before Easter Sunday 2009, at a Lower East Side bar called La Caverna. It resembled a cave—on purpose—and was spritzed in pungent hopefulness and perfumed desperation, the official scent of most of my single Saturday nights in Manhattan. *Maybe tonight he'll walk through that door,* I heard the resounding chorus of women sing. They were lured to the city by the unattainable glamour and girlfriend-ships of *Sex and the City* or the navel-gazing of *Felicity,* the ones who flocked here to be among the achievers, who fled the tiny towns they were born into in hopes of growing up into starter offices and enviable wardrobes and a one-bedroom with the Channing Tatum of their reality. Maybe I'm projecting my dreams here.

Gratefully, the three slightly spilled martinis I consumed pacified my longing for all of this and much more. Pop beats filled my head as my booty and voluminous hair, draped over my bare shoulders, bounced on the dance floor. In this swaying mass, no one's past mattered. Every person's only requisite was to keep moving. I twirled and twerked to Kelis's "Milkshake," my gold-tinted curls bobbing around my face. I felt the brightness of my wide, toothy smile and the ampleness of my cheekbones, a feature given to me by Mom, and the prominence of my forehead, inherited from Dad. My pointed widow's peak draped a thick tendril over my right eye, shaded in bronze eye shadow and framed by an arched brown brow.

I was soon stopped in midorbit by the sight of a man. *Fuck, he's hot!* was my first thought. His skin was the color of sweet toffee, the kind that gets stuck in your teeth. He had shiny black wavy hair, just long enough to run my fingers through, and that indistinguishable ethnic look that one could take for Dominican or Brazilian or some kind of swirly black. He looked dangerously yummy, with sly brown eyes, one of which was punctuated with a horizontal scar that matched the mischievous curve of his smirk. His beauty—birthed out of my mental sketch of Mr. Hypothetical Husband—led me to commit to sleeping with him if the night led us to a bed.

He said hey, and I said hey back.

"I'm on my way to the bathroom, but will you be here when I come back?" he asked.

I nodded while flipping my curls to the other side of my face: my go-to "My Hair Is Real I'm So Flirty and Effortless" move. He returned a few minutes later with that same smirk. "Take a walk with me," he said, nodding toward the exit.

"I don't even know your name," I said.

"If you come with me, maybe I'll tell you," he said, pointing toward the exit.

I rolled my eyes and smiled as we walked out the door.

He led me a few blocks away to a fluorescent-lit twenty-four-hour coffee shop called Sugar's, where I ordered a latte, he a coffee, and we shared an unsatisfying cinnamon roll and people-watched during pauses in our conversation. It was during those pauses that I heard whispers from deep within myself that told me he was *the one*. This notion was also apparent in the steadiness of his gaze as I spoke, in the tranquil curve of this one curl resting just so on his forehead, in the way his face lit up when he found pleasure in something I said, in the ease of his name, Aaron.

In two early-morning hours, you can learn a lot about a person who's open enough to share himself. I listened as Aaron told me about his grandparents' wheat farm in North Dakota, which served as the setting of his childhood, and how he moved to Maine with his mother, spending his adolescence on the basketball courts with visions of Michael Jordan leaping in his mind. He told me he was a dog trainer who longed to make films and to have horses of his own someday. As he spoke effortlessly about the details of his life, I wondered if it really was that simple to tell your story. It took effort for me to talk to strangers, even more to men. I self-consciously traded similar details that matched the weight of intimacy he was clearly aiming to build with me. I told Aaron that I was from Hawaii and had moved to New York four years ago for graduate school. I told him I got paid to write about celebrities and that when I grew up I wanted to write stories that matter.

"What do you mean by *matter*?"

I said I didn't know.

"Yes you do," he said, sipping his coffee and lifting a brow. He was challenging me. He saw beyond the pretty, which I had relied on during many first meetings with guys, aiming to remain a mystery, to remain unseen because being prettily invisible allowed me safety. His cocked brow signaled that he wouldn't be afraid to know the real me.

"I write about famous people, about when their new movies come out, what they're wearing on the red carpet, who they're dating and having kids with," I said. "Those things don't *really* matter. Yeah, it's fun, but there are stories I want to tell and don't know how to yet."

I felt I'd said too much in the comfort of late-night intimacy. Insecure, I shifted my focus away from Aaron and into the emptiness of my mug and onto the clock above the espresso machine, which pointed to a bit after three A.M. We decided to split a cab, which slowed across the street from his apartment, lit by the lights of La Esquina's taco stand.

I stared at Aaron. I wanted him to kiss me. He leaned in and pressed his cheek to mine and whispered good night in my ear. As the taxi pulled away, I watched his boots stomp across Kenmare Street and soon read his text: "You're a complete pleasure."

I had yearned for true love ever since my junior year of high school, when I read *Their Eyes Were Watching God* in Mrs. Chun's English class. Zora Neale Hurston wrote that Janie's "soul crawled out from its hiding place" when she met Tea Cake. I wanted to come out of my hiding place. I wanted a love that would open me up to the world and to myself. I wanted my own Tea Cake who wanted all of me. I draped myself in all of these expectations when I arrived for my first date with Aaron a week after our rendezvous at the coffee shop.

I spotted him through the windows of the New Museum, all six-two of him. He wore a black T-shirt, jeans, and rustic brown boots, which reminded me of North Dakota and horses and steadiness. The skin of my armpits stuck to my leather jacket's lining as we leaned in, our cheeks reconnecting. "Shall we?" he said, flashing the tickets to the exhibit.

The first floor acted as an icebreaker. I told him I didn't care for supermodern art, whatever that meant, arguing that displaying the contents of a woman's purse was not art. He smirked as I spouted my opinions about the exhibit, which included a woman sleeping on an all-white bed, a "performance" that drew a crowd. I giggled inappropriately at the sight of intent onlookers tuned in to this unmoving, sticky-haired blonde. After a couple of glares from fellow museumgoers, we excused ourselves to the second floor.

In the stairwell, Aaron grabbed my waist. I was standing two steps ahead of him. "I think it's time we kissed," he said.

It was an invitation, one that didn't fit my itinerary for our date. I imagined that he'd kiss me when he said good-bye, under the glowing gaze of the moon and my neighbor's twinkling lights and the sound of the city cheering us on. Not in the daylight with these brighter-than-white walls and the reflective metal rails. It was too sterile, too open, too early.

When I looked around to see if anyone was there to witness this impending kiss, Aaron laughed at me. I must've seemed about thirteen, like a girl contemplating taking a drag from a friend's cigarette.

I leaned forward, placing my lips to the heat of his. We fit, the cleft of our mouths meeting and the pressure of his deep pink lips against mine.

"Now that that's out of the way, I can concentrate on what you're saying," he said, smirking. His charm threw me, and immediately I wondered if he had a girlfriend at home, because there was no way this man was available. I didn't know how to be truly happy. I had to cope with it by dismissing it, by forecasting its inevitable end. My belief system operated on the notion that the good things in my life were a universal hiccup where doom surely loomed. Happiness was fleeting and accidental; goodness wasn't in the cards for a girl like me.

Video installations boomed on the next floor, allowing me to work through my awkwardness about the kiss during the final pieces of the exhibit. I squeezed my right hand into my left, my lifelong tell of nervousness, the same way I would when Dad focused on me as I searched for an answer to one of his probing questions. I felt out of control, as if I had crossed a threshold into fast-forward, no-turning-back closeness with Aaron. Getting close meant intimacy, and intimacy meant revelations. Sensing my discomfort, Aaron suggested we take a walk.

We headed west on the movie-set-ready blocks of Bleecker Street as the sun descended over this second island that I call home. Girls in printed frocks and summer maxis passed us, making me feel even more out of place in my leather jacket on this spring day.

"Let's play a game," Aaron said after a quiet couple of blocks. "We'll ask each other questions back and forth. The only rule is that you have to answer the question. Wanna go first?"

My first question for him was the one I'd been asking myself since we met: "What are you afraid of?"

It didn't take him but a few seconds to answer. "You," he said, looking down at the gum-spotted pavement. "Because I told myself I would commit this year to me, not a girl, not a relationship. See, I'm a relationship guy."

Hearing him say that being in a relationship was part of his identity, in an age when men were believed to be afraid of commitment, had me feeling like I was in an episode of *The Twilight Zone*. This was not what years of watching Carrie Bradshaw skip around the city had taught me.

"I'm most comfortable in relationships," he continued, "but they distract me from myself. So my answer is simple: I'm afraid of you because I'll break my commitment to myself."

I was taken aback by his openness, which a part of me, from the world I'd grown up in, received as weakness. Aaron seemed available to the world because he knew, somewhere deep within himself, that the world was available to him. He probably never had to fight for anything, I thought. He probably had people in his life who listened to him, who waited with a grilled cheese sandwich on the table when he got home from school. He probably had *that* kind of childhood on the farm.

While I stood in judgment of a life I never had, the pressure of the date, of the kiss, of what was to come, left me. I didn't have to say anything about my past, I assured myself, because he didn't even want a relationship.

Then he took my hand, placing my fingers in between his. "Okay, it's my turn," he said. "And I'm going to steal your question."

I'm afraid you won't love me once you know me, I wanted to say. Instead I led with another truth: "I'm afraid of getting too close to anybody."

We stayed in each other's company until dinnertime, when we kissed and cuddled to the sounds of Portuguese lyrics at a Brazilian restaurant, the one where he said, *I see the little girl in you.* I wished I could see her. She didn't have the chance to just be, to frolic, to play.

She was the wrong kind of girl. I let him gaze at her and knew that this night was the beginning of love: I knew right then that he saw me like no one had before, and there was no turning back from this kind of closeness. I let him see that vulnerable, wide-eyed girl inside me, and I kissed him until the dusty stained-glass lantern dimmed to darkness and the soft samba melodies silenced.

We said good night for the second time on the corner of East Fourth Street and Bowery after he showed me how to salsa and I giggled while moving my hips. The pressure of his hand on the small of my back told me it was okay to let him lead me.

In the coming weeks, Aaron and I took a nighttime stroll through Central Park; heard my intellectual girl-crush, Zadie Smith, talk about writing at my alma mater, New York University; licked ice cream cones outside Lincoln Center; saw a bad romcom during the Tribeca Film Festival; and had our first sleepover.

When Aaron arrived at my place—a ground-floor studio fitting my full-size bed, desk, and TV—he came bearing gifts: *The Artist's Way* by Julia Cameron and two red tension balls. "I figure they'll help you relax and write," he said.

We watched my favorite relationship movie, *The Way We Were*, and discussed my love of Katie and my longing to be with someone who'd push me as much as Katie pushed Hubbell. Eventually, we kissed our way into my bed, and these kisses were freedom kisses— uninhibited by my self-conscious, overthinking tendencies. We gradually bared our bodies to each other, with my legs spread, my body yielding to him. He touched me like I had never been touched before, and I trusted him to see me. Just as I let my guard down, I put it back up, like a reflex, and he returned to the pillow beside me.

After a moment's pause, I studied his face: His eyelashes crowded the edges of his lids, creating a sweeping, almost epic frame on his knowing brown eyes. I wondered if this man next to me, the one I had let touch, taste, and smell me, was ready to really know me. What does it mean to truly know someone, to claim that you're ready, ready to love a human being, not just a sketch of all your fantasies come to life? I wanted him to see *me*. My internal utterances must've manifested themselves into movable energy, because he smiled, widening the scar beneath his right eye like a pencil mark I would make in a book to note something significant. I moved my middle and index fingers across the jagged line.

"I got that when I was twelve or thirteen, " he said, reaching back two decades to tell me a story about a boy running away from someone without care or caution. He'd snagged his face on a low-lying tree branch. The remnant of that carefree moment was forever on his face. "You know, I've never told anyone that before," Aaron said, traveling back to bed from that North Dakota emergency room.

I felt privileged but wondered why he'd chosen to tell me, out of all the people he'd known in his life, all the people he had loved and those he thought he had loved. Why was I worthy? And wasn't that the question I'd asked myself the entire time: *Why me? Why did you choose me in that bar? Why did you take me to that coffee shop and not just fuck me and discard me? Why did you tell me in dozens of little ways that I am special?*

He couldn't answer those questions because he didn't really know me, just like I did not really know him. But he was trying to be known, offering many of his life's stories and memories since our meeting. It's in these moments, in bed, in the dark, when you share and create new memories, that a relationship is built. I was holding on to everything I had not to be fully known; if he knew me, then this would end. The mere thought of it ending overwhelmed me, and he saw it, using his fingers to wipe away my tears.

Days later, I listened to a message from Aaron: "Hey, just calling to see what you're up to tonight. Nothing? Great. Come over. I want to talk to you."

My stomach ached when I heard the message. I felt past the lightness of his message to its weight. His call was in reaction to my crying in bed. I scolded myself for being vulnerable in front of him. Something in his voice told me that he knew. He *had* to know.

When I arrived at his apartment—a three-bedroom share without a living room—I sat on his bed as he closed the door behind him. Aaron's bedroom was a ten-by-ten space, softly lit by a lantern that illuminated remnants from our three-week courtship: a flyer from the exhibit; two pairs of movie stubs; and a photo of us from one of our dates. In it, my curls were a harsh yellow, shocked as a result of the previous day's highlighting session. Despite the frizz, I appeared pleased standing next to Aaron, who looked just over the photographer's shoulder. "You make a perfect pair," the man had said after fanning our Polaroid to dry. I remember Aaron thanking me with a kiss for indulging him in the touristy act.

Now I placed one of his pillows between my legs to shield myself. I knew from his expression that I was the one who was going to talk tonight. I looked into his eyes one last time and saw that he was anxious: He didn't sit down in his own room. I realized then that he had something to lose, too, with what I had to say. There was a dream in him that could be wrecked by my revelation.

I had presented Aaron a distorted me, and I couldn't give him me while wrapped in secrets—stories I've never told. They trap you, and you become so wound up in your own story, in the pain inflicted on you in the past that you've worked hard to keep at bay, and the people and actions and all the things you've been running away from, that you don't know what to believe anymore. Most important, you lose touch with yourself: The self you know, the you deep inside, is obscured by a stack of untold stories. And I had been groomed to believe that they were all I had in this world, and the keeping of them was vital to my survival.

I felt I had endured enough. From some cavernous place, I reached inside myself and grabbed the courage to take a long trip back to a place I never thought I'd revisit. I took a deep breath and exhaled. "I have to tell you something."

Part
One

The world's definitions are one thing and the life one actually lives is quite another. One cannot allow oneself, nor can one's family, friends, or lovers—to say nothing of one's children—to live according to the world's definitions: one must find a way, perpetually, to be stronger and better than that.

—JAMES BALDWIN

Chapter *One*

I was certain the sun's rays would filter through the legs of the table under which I slept and Grandma Pearl would wake me from my fold-up mattress with the scents of margarine-drenched toast and hot chocolate. I knew my sister Cheraine and her best friend Rene, a towering Samoan girl with waves flowing down her broad back like lava, would walk me to school, the heels of our rubber slippers smacking the warm cement. I was certain my first-grade teacher would part her coral-lacquered lips to greet me with a smile as I carefully placed my slippers in the blue cubbyhole labeled *Charles*. I was certain that when it was time for recess or bathroom breaks, we would divide into two lines: one for boys, the other for girls.

I was certain I was a boy, just as I was certain of the winding texture of my hair and the deep bronze of my skin. It was the first thing I'd learned about myself as I grew aware that I existed. There was evidence proving it: the pronouns, the penis, the Ninja Turtle pajamas, the pictures of hours-old me wrapped in a blue blanket with my eyes closed to the world. When they opened and I began learn-

15

ing the world, my desire to step across the chasm that separated me from the girls—the ones who put their sandals in the red cubbyholes labeled *Kawehi*, *Darlene*, and *Sasha*—rose inside of me. The stature of this faint desire, whose origins I can't pinpoint to a pivotal *aha!* moment, grew taller and bolder despite the cues, rebuttals, and certainties of those around me, who told me through a slightly furrowed brow or a shake of the head that even attempting to cross that void was wrong.

When I look back at my childhood, I often say *I always knew I was a girl* since the age of three or four, a time when I began cataloging memories. No one—not my mother, my grandmother, my father, or my siblings—gave me any reason to believe I was anything other than my parents' firstborn son, my father's namesake. But it was my very first conviction, the first thing I grew certain of as a young person. When I say *I always knew I was a girl* with such certainty, I erase all the nuances, the work, the process of self-discovery. I've adapted to saying *I always knew I was a girl* as a defense against the louder world, which has told me—ever since I left Mom's body in that pink hospital atop a hill in Honolulu—that my girlhood was imaginary, something made up that needed to be fixed. I wielded this ever-knowing, all-encompassing certainty to protect my identity. I've since sacrificed it in an effort to stand firmly in the murkiness of my shifting self-truths.

I grew to be certain about who I was, but that doesn't mean there wasn't a time when I was learning the world, unsure, unstable, wobbly, living somewhere between confusion, discovery, and conviction. The fact that I admit to being uncertain doesn't discount my womanhood. It adds value to it.

The first person I ever valued outside of my family was Marilyn, whom I met in kindergarten. She lived in the same two-story building as Grandma Pearl, in Ka'ahumanu Housing, the public subsidized complex in Kalihi that was the setting of all my early memories in Oahu. Marilyn had a stick-straight bowl haircut and a wide gap between her front two teeth that didn't prevent her from smiling. She was the first person with whom I had things in common: We were the same kind of brown—like whole wheat bread— because we both came from brown people (I was Hawaiian and black, while Marilyn was Hawaiian and Filipino); we both lived with our maternal grandmothers; and we both loved playing jacks, hopscotch, and tag. We were always barefoot, the khaki-colored bottoms of our wide, flat feet turned black from the earth. When we wore ourselves out, we'd rinse our feet with the hose in her grandmother's front yard and rest on the ground under the clothesline, the moist grass pressed into our backs. The wind blew around us, making the floral dresses that hung above us dance, swaying like hula dancers. Humidity was in the air, and so was fragrance: Tide detergent and gardenias and lunchtime rice. The sun's rays filtered through the clothes and touched our skin in shifting patterns. Marilyn looked unblinkingly at the sun, glowing and dark, like a shiny copper penny I'd pick up on my way to school.

"Truth or dare," Marilyn said as I lifted my back from the grass. I see myself in my favorite McDonald's T-shirt, the light-blue one I wore in my first-grade school photo.

"Dare!" I said over Grandma's birds of paradise that peeked over her bushel of tea leaves.

"Okay, you see dat dress ova dea?" Marilyn boasted in her Hawaiian pidgin, pointing at a pink muumuu with a mustard and white hibiscus pattern that hung on her grandmother's clothesline. I nodded. "I dare you for put dat on," she said.

"Ho, that's so easy!" I said, standing up, reaching for the dress.

"No, I not done!" Marilyn scolded. "You gotta put it on, den run across the park, all a way to da rubbish cans and back."

The dress flowed forward in the wind toward my destination. I half contemplated the trouble I could get into for dirtying a clean dress, but chickening out on a dare was not an option. Truth or dare was more than a game; it was our way as kids to learn intimacy and trust. I trusted that Marilyn wouldn't ask me to do anything drastic, and she trusted that I wouldn't tell any of her truths, like the time she'd told me she had a crush on Keoni, the husky boy who smelled like Uncle Toma's dirty socks.

I pulled the dress down by its ruffled trim, producing a synchronized snap of wooden clothespins. As I slipped it over my small frame, the puffed shoulders rested at my elbows, and the hem circled me like a puddle of water.

"Ho, your grandma this big?" I laughed in fuchsia-clad hysteria, and Marilyn's gap-toothed grin joined mine.

Hiking up the dress, I looked diagonally above us at Grandma Pearl's front porch. She wasn't in the yard or in the kitchen, so I figured she wouldn't see me. I clenched the fabric in my fists. Stepping out from Marilyn's yard, I felt the warmth of the cement on my bare feet as the heat of the early-afternoon sun spread across my body.

Checking Grandma's front door one last time, I sprinted across the sidewalk. I felt lovely in the muumuu, which flirted with my skin as the Oahu trades blew moist kisses at me. At the trash bin, I did a little Paula Abdul move to my inner DJ's spin of "Straight Up" for Marilyn's delight. She mimicked me from across the parking lot and waved for me to hurry back. Running toward her lawn, I galloped and grinned with the glee of soon-to-be achievement. Just as my feet touched the grass, I heard my eldest sister, Cori, cackling from the balcony. "Grandma! Come look at Charles," she screamed teasingly, her long, straight black hair and blunt bangs blowing in the wind.

A bit ruffled, I picked up the pace and prayed that if God let me get the muumuu back on the line without Grandma seeing me, then I would never wear a dress again. With each step, the fabric felt heavier, confining my ability to get out of the dress swiftly. I felt silly under Cori's gaze. The joy that I had experienced mutated into transgression.

"Charles, getcha fuckin' ass ova hea!" Grandma shouted at me, though my sister's laughs lightened her bark. "Now!"

Grandma Pearl was the first woman to make an impression on me, my first example of what a woman was supposed to be: strong, dutiful, and outspoken. Her voice was harsh from years of talking to her own six children and her children's children. She didn't edit her language for anyone and was unapologetic about cursing regardless of the age of her company. Grandma penciled her absent eyebrows onto her prominent forehead in an arched line only when she felt like it. She rarely left the house without a bright red lipstick and a light mist of hair spray on her curled salt-and-pepper bangs. She smelled of baby powder, which gave her dark brown skin an ashy appearance under her collection of patterned silk shirts.

I was sensitive to Grandma's presence at all times, checking in often to ensure that I was never in her way. "Be a good boy for Grandma, yeah" were Mom's parting words when she dropped me off on Sunday nights. Despite Grandma's toughness, she made me feel there was no other place I should be but in her apartment.

I can still feel the sting from her strong hand smacking my behind as I ran past her to the lanai, where I sat on a blanket, hoping she wouldn't follow. Grandma's lanai was my sanctuary where I hung out as she cleaned, scrubbing to the staticky rhythm of Hawaiian music playing from her silver clock radio. The lanai was outfitted with pillows, coloring books, a secret stash of Smarties, and a pair of sumo action figures, the only dolls I didn't get yelled at for playing with.

I loved the feel of their silky ponytails, which I ran my fingers through for what felt like hours until Mom dropped by after work. It was the weekend, which meant I stayed with Mom and her boyfriend in Pearl City, a twenty-minute drive from Grandma's in Kalihi. Through the screen door, I saw Mom kiss Grandma and Cori, who was thirteen at the time. Mom's visits were a nonevent to my other sister, Cheraine, who had spent the majority of her eleven years at Grandma's.

"Ma, guess who got caught wearing a dress?" Cori, ever the gossip, reported to Mom as she made her way to the living room couch to rest her feet. Mom, in her blue skirt suit with white piping, looked at me as I side-eyed the conversation, pretending I'd heard nothing.

"Charles was outside skipping in a muumuu like some Mary!" Cori said. "I caught him, and Grandma whacked him one good one."

"Hi, honey," Mom greeted me as I slid the screen door open, rolling my eyes at Cori while she continued cackling from the kitchen table.

"No roll your eyes at me for I pop dem out of your head!" Cori said, standing up from her chair.

"Enough already," Grandma chimed in from the sink. "Just be happy Papa never catch him."

The women in our family used Papa as a looming threat. I don't remember him reprimanding any of us. Grandma was the one to be feared. Papa was the giver of money. He smelled of Drakkar Noir and watched Westerners from his La-Z-Boy and gave me a dollar every time he came home smelling of beer from the bar, his go-to spot after driving the street sweeper. I usually spent it at the Manapua Truck, Hawaii's version of an ice cream truck, named after local pork buns, where a man in a van sells greasy noodles, crunchy wontons, and a variety of candy and chips.

Cori walked out the front door, probably to go hang with her boyfriend, the Filipino Cheraine and Rene said she was skipping school to fool around with. At the time, I remember Cori and Cheraine being much older than they really were because they were so independent; their lives barely intersected with Mom's. I didn't question why they were not with us on the weekends in Pearl City as I sat next to Mom in the living room on a wicker love seat with floral seat covers.

I often felt dirty when Mom came to Grandma's straight from work, all perfumed and hair-sprayed. Her hair was long, dark, and straight, like vintage Cher, whom she resembled, especially in her teen years, with big brown eyes, olive skin, high cheekbones, and thin lips she painted pink. Her growing belly was out of place with her long, lean frame.

"Want to tell me what happened?" Mom said, wiping my eye with her saliva-moistened index finger. Her breath never smelled good as it dried on my face, but I felt cared for when she did that.

"I pulled a dress off the clothesline," I whispered, afraid Grandma would hear me from the kitchen and rebut my testimony. "But I put it right back."

Pushing my short curls from my forehead, Mom smiled. "I don't think Grandma scolded you for taking the dress, even though you shouldn't touch stuff that's not yours. You're not supposed to wear dresses."

She wasn't reprimanding me. She was just telling me the way things were, the way she'd learned the world. In her learning, what I did by openly expressing femininity as her son was wrong and, in effect, from Cori's cackle to Grandma's smack, taught me that my girlhood desires were inappropriate. Resisting and hiding my femininity would keep me from being laughed at by my sister, being hit by my grandmother, and being lectured at by my mother.

These women believed they were raising a boy child, and boys do not wear dresses, according to the rules of Western culture's gender binary system, which is rigidly fixed between two poles (boy and girl; male and female; man and woman; masculine and feminine) for all people depending on assigned sex (based on the appearance of one's genitals at birth). This system proclaims that sex is determined at birth; gender is based on your sex assigned at birth; no variation exists in sex or gender; you should not change your sex or gender; and you should act according to your assigned sex and its correlating gender-appropriate behaviors.

My family subscribed to this rigid belief system. They were unaware of the reality that gender, like sexuality, exists on a spectrum. By punishing me, they were performing the socially sanctioned practice of hammering the girl out of me, replacing her with tenets of gender-appropriate behavior. Though I would grow up to fit neatly into the binary, I believe in self-determination, autonomy, in people having the freedom to proclaim who they are and define gender for themselves. Our genders are as unique as we are. No one's definition is the same, and compartmentalizing a person as either a boy or a girl based entirely on the appearance of genitalia at birth undercuts our complex life experiences.

In my adulthood, Mom nonchalantly told me she wasn't surprised about my becoming her daughter. "You were just always like that. Very sensitive, very mischievous, too smart for your own good, and always into my things," she said, reminiscing about my early childhood, particularly the time her earring landed me in the emergency room.

Mom and Dad were still married at the time. Living with them were Cori and me and our brother, Chad, a year younger than I. Cheraine didn't come with us when we moved to Long Beach, California, my father's new naval duty station. She stayed with Grandma and Papa in Hawaii. At age three, I was playing with my mother's jewelry and placed one of her earring backs in my ear. The backing wasn't secure, so it slid inside my ear, beyond a finger's reach, and as a result of the discomfort, I screamed. I can still hear the suction from the tube the doctors put down my ear, which pulled out the gold pretzel-shaped backing, and I can still taste the sweet vanilla ice cream I got to eat for a week.

These stories of my early expressions of femininity echo many people's lived experiences with exploring, experimenting, and expressing gender. I've read and heard stories of trans people from all walks of life who remember playfully exhibiting their preferred gender behaviors and roles at age three or four without anyone's prompting. Some were given freedom to explore their inclinations; the majority were discouraged from experimenting outside their prescribed gender roles and behaviors. This contributes greatly to self-image, how people learn gender, and the path they'll eventually choose into adolescence and adulthood. Children who behave in line with their prescribed gender roles are *cisgender* or *cissexual* (throughout, I will use the prefix *cis*, which means "on the same side of," while *trans* means "across" or "on the opposite side of"), a term used for people who are not trans and more likely to identify with the gender that correlates with the sex they were assigned at birth. Most cis people rarely question their gender identity because the gender binary system validates them, enabling them to operate without conflict or correction. This makes it difficult for the majority of people—including parents of trans youth and those close to trans people—to grasp the varied identities, needs, and determinations of trans people.

Mom wasn't a disciplinarian; that role was reserved for Dad, a boiler technician in the Navy whose booming voice filled our house with reprimands about why his son was playing with earrings. He admits now that he took it upon himself to change what he believed to be my "soft ways."

"I didn't want to see it, man," he admitted. "I tried to be tougher on your ass. I thought I could fix you."

It would take decades for my father to realize that I didn't need fixing, and he should have been more focused on his marriage, which was plagued by infidelity, failed expectations, and youth. Mom was twenty-two when she met Dad at a nightclub on the Pearl Harbor naval base. She was partying with a coworker and was actually into one of Dad's Navy buddies. I don't know how she ended up talking to Dad, but I'm sure he was the pursuer, his gold tooth shining under the neon lights of the dance floor. Mom didn't tell Dad that she had two little girls, products of her first marriage to her high school sweetheart, who at the time was in prison for theft. When Dad met Cori and Cheraine, who were five and three at the time, Mom told him they were her nieces. "I feel so bad about that," Mom later told me. "It was easier to pretend that I was unattached, carefree. But your dad wasn't innocent. He had his own baggage."

Mom was referring to the three kids Dad had left in Dallas when he joined the Navy after high school graduation. They had three different mothers, each of whom thought Dad was *her* boyfriend. One gave birth to a green-eyed boy in January 1979; the second welcomed a son that February; and the third had a baby girl in April 1979.

"Your daddy was wild, man," Dad said, chuckling over fathering three children at only eighteen.

With the contents of their baggage displayed, Mom became Elizabeth Mock, marrying Charlie Mock III in May 1982, with my sisters serving as their flower girls at the Foster Botanical Garden in downtown Honolulu. Mom said her father wasn't too thrilled that she was marrying a black man, but she didn't care what he had to say because Dad made her smile and she knew that his military career would allow her to see the world and take her away from Hawaii, which she desperately wanted to flee. After I was born the following March, Mom (pregnant with Chad), Dad, Cori, and I moved to Long Beach. Dad kept his promise of taking Mom away from Hawaii, but monogamy just "wasn't his thing," Mom told me.

I had firsthand experience with Dad's dalliances. I was four at the time, and it was just the two of us on his motorcycle, his true love back then. I was under the impression that we were heading to the toy store, but we jumped off his bike in a neighborhood that didn't look much different from ours. Though it wasn't military family housing, it was similar in the sense that it had a cookie-cutter aesthetic.

Dad, in his camouflage fatigues, didn't knock on the door to this two-story town house. He didn't even say hello when we walked in. Guiding me to a faux leather couch that made too much noise for furniture, Dad placed a box of Golden Grahams and a remote control in my hands. A woman who smelled of smoke and drugstore perfume soon appeared from the staircase. She was the color of Cheerios and had crinkly hair that looked like waffle batter fresh from the griddle. She told me her name was Dara and said I could help myself to strawberry Pop-Tarts. I was fighting the desire to be easily pleased.

Dara hugged Dad, and I took notice of how he touched her. It mirrored the way he touched Mom, and that made me want to spit out my cereal. When Dad followed Dara up the stairs, I knew this was just between the three of us. Dad didn't tell me to hush; he didn't hold his index finger up to his mouth or wink at me in code. Instinctively, I knew Mom wouldn't hear a word about the Dara detour—at least, not from Dad or me.

Months later, Chad and I sat on our parents' water bed in our pajamas. Though the bed rippled under us, the night was still and filled with the sound of sorrow. Dad's eyes were wet. He hovered over the bed with his right arm across his chest and his left hand over his mouth. The sight of him prompted me to tears. Seeing my father cry was a shelter-shifting moment: I felt unsafe and exposed. Cori was seated on the floor, just a few feet away from the bed, holding a hand towel to Mom's wrists, which she had cut as a cry for help, an intervention of sorts to save her marriage after hearing about Dad's affair. I remember the silver threads of the monogrammed M struggling to shine through the blood it had soaked up.

Mom had straight bangs that veiled her large eyes, heavily lashed and thinly lined. She was so pretty and didn't even know it, as Dad described her. She had a sweet, soft voice and smiled with her mouth closed, which lifted her lips and emphasized her already prominent cheekbones. If you didn't know her, you would think she was bashful and amiable, and you wouldn't be wrong. But she had a fire in her lit by a string of disappointments, and it is her sorrow that permeates my bedroom memory of Mom on the floor.

Recalling this in pieces feels like a betrayal of my mother. It negates the kind, soft-spoken, perfumed visions I associate with my childhood memories of her. I have photos of us surrounded by flowers and sun, and another of Mom applauding me as I blow out the candles to my birthday cake. Her head is level with mine, and she looks happy to celebrate another year in my life. Those weightless images don't flick in the View-Master of my memory bank when I recall my parents' marriage; it's always the scene of Dad sobbing, Cori with the blood-soaked towel, and Mom, defeated, bleeding on her bedroom floor.

It's the only memory I have of my parents in the same room. Mom told me later that there were other women and other suicide attempts. Dad told me she was possessive and wasn't afraid to confront his other women. It would take decades for those disparate early memories of my parents to fuse: Dad's secret visits to Dara; Mom's anguish slashed through her veins; Dad being kicked out shortly thereafter. Mom said that Chad and I spent a lot more time at Dad's mistress's town house than I remember.

"While I was at work, you guys were at her house playing with her kids," Mom told me, and she wasn't wrong. Years later, when I was well into adulthood, I finally met my youngest sister, the product of Dad's affair with Dara. She showed us a video of Chad and me at a playground with her other two half-siblings, in which Dad and Dara's voices call out our names from behind the camcorder.

When our parents split, Mom returned to Grandma's house with me, Cori, and Chad. Dad protested that he wanted his boys back, and they agreed that Chad would live with him; I'd stay with Mom. Chad, whose skin was as yellow as the corn bread on the Jiffy box, says he remembers crying every time he saw a plane in the California sky, hoping I was on it to be with him and Dad. I imagined his big black eyes swollen with tears as he looked up in hope.

Selfishly, I wasn't mourning our separation, because I had Mom all to myself. I was the baby now. Being beside Mom as she read her paperbacks and snacked on canned tuna spread over Hawaiian soda crackers and crunched on cups of ice—that was home. But Mom wasn't all mine for long. She soon found another man, one she moved in with, leaving me at Grandma's.

Sitting on Grandma's couch, I meditated on Mom's belly, which carried my baby brother. I was excited to have another sibling and assumed that, with his birth, she would get a place big enough for all of us. When Jeffrey was born in August 1989, Mom and Dad made plans to send me to Oakland to be with Chad. "We never should've separated the two of you," Mom later told me.

The seven-year-old in the adult me can hear the silent outbursts. *What about you and me? What about us?* But I knew the answer to my unspoken protests: Mom was moving on, starting anew, and in order to fulfill the promise of new love, she had to discard her past. Like Cori and Cheraine, who were initially denied by my mother when she met my father, I represented her past, a remnant of her failure. Mom needed to travel light, so she sent her baggage to Oakland in 1990, and I wouldn't see her for another five years.

Chapter *Two*

I learned to ride a bike without training wheels atop a hill in an Oakland-area park. I was just seven years old and terrified of Dad's accelerated cycling method. Chad stared Dad's challenge in the face and excelled.

"There you go!" Dad applauded. "That's how you do it right there."

Hovering over my seat, I watched Dad clapping and smiling his starry smile as Chad made that steep hill his bitch. He was pedaling fast while our father's gold-toothed grin broadened, as if those pedals were a jack that lifted Dad's entire pleasure and pride system.

"Hit the brakes, baby!" he shouted when Chad reached the bottom of that grassy mount, conquering his first solo ride.

Placing his hands on my handlebars, Dad leveled his face to mine. I could see him rummaging his mind for the words to coax me down that hill, something he never had to do with Chad. There was a natural ease in my father's interactions with my brother that was nonexistent in our relationship.

"Just start off slow. And once you feel yourself going faster, press this right here," he said, pointing to the hand brakes that controlled my back tires. "You got it?"

I didn't hear much of what he said because I was lost in his tooth. The artistry of it, that is. I wondered how the dentist had cut the gold to fashion the shape of a star, an ode to the Dallas Cowboys, whose plays and wins and losses were discussed like philosophy, Chad being Aristotle to Dad's Plato.

I shook my head.

"What?" he asked, stunned by my refusal. "You just saw your brother do it. It ain't *that* hard."

"I'm not scared or anything like that," I lied. "I just think I will fall."

"You think I'd put you in danger?" he asked. I wondered if this was a trick question. It had been only a few months since I'd moved from Hawaii, and already I had been forced to swim, throw a spiral football, share a house with strangers, and now ride this bike that I hadn't even asked for.

"Boy, answer my question," he continued. "Do you think I'd put you in danger?"

I shook my head.

"Well, stop being a sissy and get your ass down that hill!" he said as Chad rolled his bike up to where we stood. I could see the excitement drain from his face as he traced Dad's speech. I hated that I took the fun out of things for him. I often imagine what Chad's childhood would have been like if our parents had kept us separated. He probably would have had a ball: baseball, basketball, dodgeball, and the holy grail of football. I can see Chad and Dad being heckled by Raiders fans when the Cowboys came to town; Dad studying Chad's form as they played catch; and Dad teaching Chad flamboyant ways to triumphantly slam a domino. Instead, Chad dealt with reality: his older sibling breaking down during an afternoon bicycle ride because he was such a sissy.

Sissy became one of the first epithets thrown at me with regularity. My father would say "Stop being a sissy" with the same ease as he'd say "I love you, baby!" *Sissy's* presence in my life helped numb me early on to harsher words that would soon be hurled at my body, from *freak* and *faggot* to *nigger* and *tranny*. When I was younger, I would protect myself by rebutting with the playground mantra, "Sticks and stones may break my bones, but words will never hurt me!" As my adoration for words deepened in adolescence, I grew to feel that mantra was a well-meaning lie, a pacifier meant to temporarily soothe the hurt and pain of such violent words. I now know that epithets say more about the user than the target, and I believe Maya Angelou, who says that "words are things" and that "someday we'll be able to measure the power of words." Words have the power to encourage and inspire but also to demean and dehumanize. I know now that epithets are meant to shame us into not being ourselves, to encourage us to perform lies and to be silent about our truths.

To my father, I was a sissy, and he tried his hardest to squash my femininity the only ways he knew how: intimidation and fear. He seemed to believe that if Chad enjoyed the bike ride, then I should also enjoy it. Chad was held as the standard of acceptable boy behavior; I grew aware of the fact that I negated that standard, and I internalized that on a deep level. I thought that something must be wrong with me because I didn't enjoy the things Chad did, the activities that Chad took on with such ease and little debate. The constant friction between my father and me led me to not like him. I would focus on the loudness of his voice, the aggressiveness of his actions, the argumentative nature of our conversations. As he compared me to Chad, I found myself comparing him to my mother, whose gentle, calm presence was in sharp contrast to his. The crux of our conflict lay in the fact that we each couldn't be who we wanted the other to be.

"If you don't go down that hill, I swear I'll buzz your hair when we get home," Dad said.

That threat, one Dad often wielded to put me in my place, gave me all the courage I needed to ride that bike. An actual haircut would cause irreparable damage, cutting the girl right out of me. With the sound of clippers buzzing in my head, I took a deep breath, rested my feet in the pedal loops, and began riding downhill.

"You can do it!" Chad said.

This isn't so bad, I thought as I descended. I didn't know what I'd been so afraid of. It was a nice day in Oakland, in the seventies, the same warmth of Hawaii without the humidity. I had been with Dad for a few months, and my memories of Mom were fading and enlarging and being replaced all at the same time. She was like a dream. I had fantasies of her picking me up from school and taking me back to Hawaii or even just to a movie, something like *Look Who's Talking* or *Honey, I Shrunk the Kids.* It all seemed unlikely, since she barely called after the first few months. I blamed her new baby, her boyfriend, and the Pacific Ocean that separated us.

My maternal thoughts couldn't keep up with the pace of my ride. The acceleration made me flustered and fearful, and Dad's instructions about the brakes left me. In a panic, I began to cry and kicked my feet out of the pedal loops and spread my legs wide, hoping they'd keep me balanced and reduce my speed. I was sure Chad and Dad had lost sight of me from their mount. Soon I was approaching a busy intersection outside the perimeter of the park. I whipped into a sharp turn on the sidewalk and crashed into a mailbox. I was shaking with fear that I would get whipped, fear that I had ruined my new bike, and fear that my father would cut my hair.

"Boy, you damn near gave me a heart attack," Dad panted, picking me up from the cement. "You could've run straight into traffic. You all right?"

I nodded, burrowing my wet face into his neck. Chad reached his arms around me from behind, which sandwiched me between the guys who were now home.

We lived on the top floor of a yellow two-story house on a hill. The house was shielded by trees that shut out the sight and sound of patrons from the strip mall across the street. Our backyard was trimmed with some kind of wild berry bushes along the far gate. Chad and I would eat the warm red berries, which tasted like sugar and bitters and a hint of dirt. We'd pop them in our mouths until our lips and tongues and lazily brushed gum lines were stained pink and our stomachs ached from the acidic sweetness.

It was at this same gate that Chad and I lit a bunch of ants on fire. I put a lollipop in a cereal bowl to attract an army of ants, and as they worked their way around the stick, I lit matches, one by one, striking and throwing them into the bowl. We watched the ants scurry around the melting red lollipop. Chad held a cup of water nervously while standing watch to make sure no one caught us. I initially wanted to fill the bowl with alcohol but couldn't reach the bottle in the medicine cabinet, and figured the ants would drown before I could burn them. Unfortunately, our downstairs neighbor caught me with the matchbook and told our father what we were up to, prompting Dad to give us our first whipping, which involved Chad and me stripping down to our underwear.

Dad punctuated each of his words with a lashing of his belt: "What'd (SMACK) I (SMACK) tell (SMACK) y'all (SMACK) 'bout (SMACK) playing (SMACK) with (SMACK) fire (SMACK)?"

I refused to cry during my whipping because I felt it gave Dad satisfaction to see me whimpering from his lashing. It was the same satisfaction I felt when I saw the ants scurrying away from my

matchstick, an exhibition of my own power. My refusal to acknowledge the pain only made my whipping longer. My brother antici-
pated the pain, crying before the belt even struck his light-skinned
behind. Afterward, I told Chad that I hated Dad, clutching my tear-
soaked pillow. "You shouldn't say that," he said in between his own
sniffles.

When I wasn't playing with fire, Chad and I watched television
from the moment we got up until we lay back down on our bunk beds.
We fixed our attention on cartoons (*Doug, The Ren & Stimpy Show,
Rugrats*), sitcoms (*Clarissa Explains It All, The Fresh Prince of Bel-Air,
Family Matters*), and late-night fare (from reruns of *I Love Lucy* and
Diff'rent Strokes to *The Arsenio Hall Show* and *In Living Color*). The
kids' shows we watched were filled with precocity and sentimental-
ity, which I was equally attracted to and disgusted by. If Clarissa, the
babies on *Rugrats*, or Steve Urkel got reprimanded, there was always
a lesson that tied up conveniently at the end of the show. Unlike a
sitcom, life's lessons weren't always clear-cut, and discovering them
often took longer than thirty minutes.

Our home belonged to Dad's girlfriend, Janine, and her teenage
son, Derek. Janine seemed to be built of bird bones that looked incapable of having once carried Derek. She was a slow-moving woman
who slid her feet, spreading her coconut-oil scent throughout the
house. She had large eyes, similar to Diana Ross's, that were childlike, making her look all the more vulnerable. She lived with diabetes
and underwent a strict dialysis routine that shuffled her in and out of
doctors' offices and clinics. It wasn't out of the ordinary for Janine to
be away from the house for chunks of time and for Chad and me to be
left with Derek as Dad slept with Janine in the hospital.

When Janine's health was stable, I clung to her as a stand-in
mother figure who handled me with care, giving me the nurturing
and feminine influence I craved in Mom's absence. I sought solace

in Janine's gentleness and her demure smile and her hair routine. I'd spend evenings seated atop the back of our sofa, she on the cushions in between my short legs. I'd part her hair with a fishtail comb and lather her khaki-colored scalp with herb-infused conditioning oil. If Dad was around, he'd sit in judgment of my femininity with a clenched jaw as I greased Janine's scalp to the comforting, sweet sounds of Anita Baker singing, "Don't you ever go away, it'll always be this way . . ."

Derek's father had left when he was just a baby. This house was the only home he'd ever had, and he'd shared it with his mother up until two years before, when Dad and Chad moved in. Derek and Dad seemed to stay out of each other's way, having only Janine in common. You'd think something as intimate as living together would have bonded the five of us. Instead, I always felt like the yellow house was Derek and Janine's home and that Dad, Chad, and I were temporary boarders, squatters. A sense of homelessness looms over my memories there.

Dad had a home in his heart with Janine, and Chad, Derek, and I merely cohabitated because our parents had a bond, though we had independent relationships with one another. Dad and Chad and I were family. Janine and Derek were family. Dad and Janine were romantic partners. Chad and Derek were Nintendo competitors. Janine and I were feminine comrades. Derek and I went unformed for months, but we found our way through the darkness.

Derek had a high-top fade, like Kid in *Kid 'n Play*, and usually paid us no mind because of our age. Chad soaked up any attention Derek threw his way. They played Nintendo together and watched basketball games on TV. Derek was a guard on his freshman basketball team and wore Karl Kani and Cross Colours. I gave him props for style but disliked him when his friend Rob came over. Rob had a belly that hung over his saggy jeans, and he wore a herringbone necklace that was supposed to be gold but was turning silver and green from rubbing against his neck-fat folds. Rob enjoyed barking orders at me and nicknamed me "The Fag One."

The first time he said it, Chad looked at me all wide-eyed to see what I'd say. I said nothing, nodding to him that it was okay. He continued to play Mario Bros. with Derek, and soon we became desensitized to "The Fag One." I took the name-calling with ease because 1) I was under the illusion that I deserved it because it was probably true; and 2) part of me felt guilty for not being a better big brother to Chad. He liked boy things, and I did not, but Derek and Rob did. They were the stand-in big brothers Chad deserved, the kind I couldn't be. While the guys played games or watched sports, I'd sit in the room quietly, trying my best to go unnoticed.

At the time, Dad drove a city bus, the only job I remember him having. I beamed when he'd sit next to me at the kitchen table wearing his AC Transit uniform, mirroring the childhood photos I have of our family, which show Dad in his Navy fatigues and Chad and me with our diapers on; surely Mom was behind the camera. He looked like a man with a plan and purpose.

He brought that sense of order to the kitchen table every weekday afternoon, helping us with our homework, the first thing we were required to do when we got home from school. With an Oreo in my mouth, a pencil in my hand, and Dad serving as what I believed to be an all-knowing source to my second-grade assignments, I basked in the ease of our interactions. Homework became neutral territory for my father and me. We were allies there, in the same way that he and Chad seemed to be teammates.

"You always gotta be a step ahead," he would say to me with a wink after explaining long division when my class was just learning basic division.

I believe Dad's diligence with my homework was his means of

bonding with me, and his coaching took me beyond the classroom's agenda, helping me excel in school while instilling a sense of structure and discipline and confidence. With Dad teaching me to do the work every day, I felt that nothing in a classroom could conquer or deter me except my talkative manner and undying need to be told I was exceptional.

When my teacher asked our class what we wanted to be when we grew up, my classmates chose respectable occupations. There were a dozen doctors, lawyers, and basketball players, countless cops and rappers, and a few firemen and teachers, but there was only one standout. "When I grow up, I want to be a secretary," my sassy eight-year-old self proclaimed. I knew my peers were weary of me raising my hand with the right answer, even in this subjective challenge.

Despite liking the way the word *secretary* rolled off my tongue and the number of syllables it boasted, proving my intellectual prowess to my peers, I chose it as my grown-up job because I understood it to be a woman's job. In nearly all the films or series I watched, I noticed that every man of importance had a secretary, an attractive, efficient keeper of his schedule. *That's* so *me,* I thought, attracted to the elementary hyper-feminine, submissive depiction of womanhood—a sharp contrast to the masculine world where I lived with my father. In reflection, I roll my eyes at my youthful understanding of gender roles (the man in a position of power, the woman his servant), how limited my views were. Little did I know that I actually wanted to be Clair Huxtable. It's a testament to how pervasive these images were—accessible to even a second-grader—and how these flawed and limited views of what was expected and encouraged of men and women shaped my understanding of what was possible. Thankfully, the idea of womanhood that I reached for in adolescence and adulthood was one that came from a place of internal power and accountability to one's own dreams as opposed to aiding a man in the pursuit of his dreams.

"Does everyone know what a secretary is?" our teacher asked the class, holding a knowing glance in my direction as my peers shook their heads. "Charles, can you please explain to the class what a secretary does?"

"A secretary sits outside an important man's office and takes care of things for him, like what time he needs to be at a meeting or the name of his new client, or types letters for him," I said. "So if you're going to be a doctor or lawyer, you're going to need a secretary."

"Very good," she said. "Everybody give Charles a hand."

As everyone applauded, I knew I was a hit. This was what made me love school: recognition. If you did well, if you excelled, then the system rewarded you, and I liked being rewarded.

That day I went home with a note for Dad. I jumped from my seat at the kitchen table when I heard him at the front door. When he came in wearing his blue uniform with his cap in hand, I handed him the note, which I was sure praised me. But Dad's face curdled, as if Ms. Johnson's note were sour. It was an exasperated look I had seen before. It mirrored Grandma Pearl's expression after seeing me prancing around in that fuchsia muumuu a few years earlier.

"You want to be a secretary, is that right?" Dad said, tiredly unbuttoning the top of his starched shirt.

I knew from his tone that the right answer was no. I didn't want to lie, so I remained silent as he lectured me not in long division or vocabulary but about what boys do in the world versus what girls do, how boys run and girls skip, how I was everything I shouldn't be. My father's rebukes were meant to be preventative, to stop whatever seed was growing inside of me. He looked at me quizzically, as if for the first time, because of a note from a stranger, what he had seen in me was now real. Someone else had seen it, it went beyond our own home, and he needed to stop it. I knew he wanted me to straighten my limp wrists and stiffen my hips as I walked, and lower the register of my playground wailing. Self-consciousness and shame about being different blossomed, and I learned to be more careful, more practiced, more aware.

I've heard parents say all they want is "the best" for their children, but the best is subjective and anchored by how they know and learned the world. The expectations my father had of me had nothing to do with me and all to do with how he understood masculinity, what it meant to be a man, a strong black man. My father welcomed two sons into the world, and one was feminine and needed fixing. Using my childlike lens, I felt Dad was against me, consistently monitoring me and policing my gender. I've come to realize that he simply loved me and wanted to protect me, even from myself. He was grappling with fears that involved my safety and how my outward femininity would make me a target of bullying, teasing, and other dangers that he felt lay ahead. My adult understanding of my childhood with my father doesn't erase the effects of his policing. I felt his gaze always following me, making me feel isolated as I quietly grappled with my identity. The loneliness and self-consciousness from these exchanges made me vulnerable in a way I wasn't able to recognize until decades later. This recognition cast a new light on one pivotal evening with Derek.

I don't remember where Dad went or why Chad wasn't playing Super Mario Bros. on the carpet in front of the living room television. It was just the two of us: Derek lay back on the brown microsuede recliner, and I sprawled out on the matching couch. We sat in silence for about an hour, watching TV, before he interrupted the programming. "This is boring, huh?" he asked.

"I guess," I said, watching him pull the lever on the chair to lift himself up.

"Let me show you something," he said, grabbing my ankles. His touch felt foreign. I was irritated because I did not want to engage in any kind of roughhousing. I had seen him wrestle with Chad, and they'd be on the ground in a human pretzel for what felt like an eternity before Chad would bow out.

He pulled me off the couch by my ankles and I said "Ouch" as my butt hit the carpet. I'd found that the more I complained about physical activity, the less energy I had to exert.

"Awww, did I hurt you?" he asked with a sweetness in his voice that mimicked a Jodeci song. "I didn't mean to."

Derek was rarely mean to me, but he wasn't exactly sweet, either. My presence was tolerated, so to hear this tenderness in his voice threw me off, like the touch of his hands on my ankles.

"I'm okay," I said, resting my weight on my knees, which dug into the carpet.

"Promise I'll be gentle." He smiled. "Let me show you a move. Get on my back and put your right arm around my neck."

I did so and was quickly back on the ground. This time I didn't complain. I relished Derek's single-focused attention, and we jostled until he conquered me, lying over me while my belly and the side of my face touched the carpet. My legs were spread slightly, and I remember my feet meeting his knees. Peering back up at him with my left eye, I could see him smiling, and I was happy he was having fun with me. It was a first for us, a breakthrough in our relationship.

Then I felt him holding his breath; there was a stiffening, a tightness in his torso. He let my wrists free and placed all his weight on me. I felt his hips moving and a growth in what I simply called his "privates" at the time. His breathing grew heavier through his nose, and my thoughts raced faster than the beating of his heart on my back. I couldn't see his face anymore. The TV screen flickered as he began digging his groin against my pajama-clad back.

Derek thrust faster and harder, and my cheek dug deep into the abrasive fibers of the carpet with each push. Derek didn't pet or caress me. He didn't say a word. He just kept grinding as his breaths filled the silence around us. Then he jolted and stood up and walked away. I heard water splash against the ceramic sink in our parents' bathroom.

I lay in that spot for minutes, not lifting my cheek from the carpet. I didn't know what this was. I had no words then to describe the "moves" he had shown me. I was certain that they were to remain in the darkness of the living room and that I had asked for it because I didn't play video games, because my wrists were perpetually limp, because his friend called me "The Fag One." *This is what happens to sissies,* I thought. *If Dad finds out, you're going to get whipped for acting like a girl again.*

Unsure of Derek's return, I peeled myself off the living room floor. In our bedroom, the sounds of Chad's snoring and *I Love Lucy*'s laugh track from the tiny TV on our dresser lulled me to sleep.

Chapter *Three*

I'm your boyfriend now, Nancy!" Freddy Krueger said, his tongue ramming through the receiver of Nancy's phone.

I watched his slimy tongue attack Nancy's earlobe with my mouth buried in my palm and my eyes peeking through the gaps between my fingers. *A Nightmare on Elm Street* reran often, especially on Halloween or Friday the thirteenth, and I was both enamored with and disgusted by Freddy's antics. There was no scarier villain to me. Freddy stayed with me for years because he had a sense of humor, an actual charm that made me chuckle, even though he was a predator, a pedophile who took away a young person's ability to dream.

The predator in my early life expertly blended good and bad qualities. Derek knew what attracted me and wielded that knowledge to target me. My inclinations made me all the more vulnerable to him, and my vulnerabilities made me easy prey.

Derek had me exactly where he wanted me the morning after our interaction on the carpet. As on all other mornings, I ate Cap'n Crunch in my plastic cereal bowl across the round kitchen table from him. As on all other mornings, Derek ignored the sound of me slurping the sugary-sweet cereal milk. But our silence felt irregular. Derek, chewing on the two eggs he'd scrambled to top a piece of burnt toast, was no longer just my father's girlfriend's son. He was no longer a fifteen-year-old basketball player. He was no longer my kind-of brother, my live-in babysitter, the guy who sent us to our room when we complained about him not sharing the TV. He looked different than he had on all other mornings because he'd opened a door inside of me that could no longer just be shut.

Through the view from that opened door, I noticed how pointy his dark brown ears were and how the angles were symmetrical with his rectangular haircut. I noticed his thin plum lips, his protruding hazel eyes, features he shared with his mother, Janine. I noticed his long, thin fingers and the way they curved around the edges of his toast. I had seen his features before but never taken note of them because Derek held no significance to me. Now he was the manifestation of a secret I wasn't equipped to keep.

Derek dragged me across a threshold out of childhood. Before he grabbed me by my ankles and opened that door, I had jumped double Dutch and played jacks and stolen packets of Nerds that jiggled in my pocket as I walked out of the corner store during beer runs for Dad. I had run away from scraggly stray dogs and rubbed my knees raw by riding my skateboard on one knee.

Now that door was cracked open, creaking on its hinges, and I didn't know when or if I should walk through it. My world shifted when Derek wrestled with me on that carpet. It wasn't the wrestling or the grinding; it was the foreplay that had me yearning for his return, that planted a craving in my belly. As I would later experience, Derek had petted me, held me, spoken softly to me, and I liked the attention, the closeness, and the intimacy. I liked the fact that this well-dressed teenager who had all the latest tapes and outfits liked me. It was his attention, his wooing, that shifted my focus. And that was what I later learned that predators have in their arsenal of affections: They are able to make an isolated, outcast child feel special. Derek made me feel special when no one else was around, and especially when no one else validated the girl-child inside of me. Derek treated me like a girl, I thought, so I understood him to be my only ally, and my ally wouldn't do anything to hurt me.

It took me years to recognize, label, and acknowledge Derek's actions as molestation. I made excuses for him, from blaming my femininity to blaming his age. He was young, so he didn't know any better, I often thought. But blaming myself and making excuses for Derek didn't allow me to uncover the facts about child sexual abuse.

I later learned that the majority of sexual abuse offenses are committed by people who know the victim, including immediate or extended family members: a neighbor, coach, babysitter, teacher, or religious leader. According to the U.S. Department of Justice and the Crimes Against Children Research Center, over a third of all sexual abuse against children is committed by a minor. These statistics show a commonality between my experience and that of others who know and trust their abuser, who may be another young person. Though I now have empathy for Derek and am aware of his emotional immaturity, that doesn't negate the pain his actions inflicted on me over those two years in my childhood.

Just a few nights after our first interaction on the carpet, Derek returned to me in the soothing darkness, shaking me awake in my twin bunk bed. "You up?" he said, framing his words with a smile, one I returned as he held out his hand. I took it, and he led me across the hall to his bedroom. I could hear Chad's snoring from behind Derek's closed door.

He took off his shirt and boxer shorts, and for the first time I saw him fully erect. It was the length of a Barbie, with the girth of two dolls. I stared at it as he lay down in bed. This was a penis, not his *privates* or a *thing* or *dingaling*.

"Come here," he whispered, and I followed him, fully clothed, under his sheets.

I could hear his steady heartbeat from his chest as if I held a cup to a closed door, listening to the secrets inside him. I felt chosen. So when he unlocked my linked fingers and put them around his penis, I did not protest. He led my clenched hand up and down, slowly moving the skin over his muscle. Once I got the groove, he said, "You should kiss it for me."

Apprehensive, I went under the covers and placed my lips on it. Then he told me to open my mouth. Soon his hands pressed the sides of my face, guiding my head up and down. I imagined it to be a Tootsie Pop. I had a pile of wrappers in my room, hoping to find one with a star so I could redeem it for a free lollipop. I had a hard time breathing as Derek moved his pelvis up and down, crushing the top of my head with a forceful palm. Then my mouth was full of what tasted like warm, spoiled ice cream and Brussels sprouts. I spit it on his stomach.

Derek reached for his boxers, wiped himself, and told me to go back to bed, to walk softly and keep his door open. That door stayed open for me for nearly two years. Blowing him became my nightly chore. When Derek shook me awake and guided me to his crotch, he didn't say much because he'd trained me to be numb, to be silent, to act on autopilot. I was a child half asleep, but my sense of obligation to him overpowered any exhaustion I felt. It was my duty to make him feel good.

As a survivor of sexual abuse, I developed a belief system that shaped how I viewed myself: *I can gain attention through sexual acts; my worth lies in how good I can make someone else feel, even if that*

means I'm void of feeling; what I do in bed is shameful and secret, there-
fore I will remain in the dark, a constant shameful secret.

Derek didn't command that I tell no one, that I keep what we did
in his bed a secret. He knew I wouldn't talk because I kept myself a
secret. The fact that I was feminine and wanted to be seen as a girl
was something I held close. I was prime prey. He could smell the
isolation on me, and I was lured into believing the illusion that he
truly saw me. I was a child, dependent, learning, unknowing, trusting, and willing to do what was asked of me to gain approval and
affection.

I blamed myself for years for *attracting* Derek. That I, the victim,
had *asked* for it. As I write this, it sounds ridiculous, but as a survivor
of sexual abuse, I have to forgive myself for how I coped and how I
learned to see and internalize the abuse. I didn't take into account
that because I was different, I was more likely to be at risk of sexual
abuse. Being or feeling different, child sexual abuse research states,
can result in social isolation and exclusion, which in turn leads to a
child being more vulnerable to the instigation and continuation of
abuse. Abusers often take advantage of a child's uncertainties and
insecurities about their identity and body.

Derek took something away from me when I was only eight years
old and left me with a lifetime of murkiness surrounding issues of
intimacy, sex, pain, love, boundaries, and ownership of my body.

By the time I was ten, when Derek grew tired of me, I found
myself wanting to fill the void that his absence created. That was
when I began acting on crushes. Junior was a kid who lived across
the street from us. He was kind of an asshole, at twelve the eldest in
our playgroup, and the only one who had underarm hair, which you
could see through his dingy rotation of tank tops, stained yellow at
the pits.

We produced dramatic reproductions of domesticity in ongoing games of house, where I demanded the coveted role of mom. It was during these games, with Junior serving as my husband, that I felt most myself. I had creative license to free my hair from its rubber band and lightly order my children—Chad; Maddy, a frizzy-haired girl with whom I was close; and her half-sister, Aisha, who wore the same pair of denim cutoffs daily—to run to the corner store for groceries and swish my hips as I served my family Now & Laters and Mambas for dinner. When our play children ran errands, I had Junior to myself on the grass. It was an innocent crush that flourished under the guise of husband and wife. He would rub his open palms against my hair. My budding attraction to Junior would surface in words: I would repeat movie lines that I'd heard girls say to boys, things that made them act silly, like "I love you." "I wish you were really a girl," he once told me during one of our make-pretend sessions.

Though Junior was a few years older and could easily dominate me in a fight, I was smugly confident in my premature sexuality. What we once fulfilled by lying on the grass side by side quickly escalated to something more adult. Junior kissed me in the back of our house by the berry gate, where no one could see us. It was my first kiss and awakened me to sexuality in a way that my nights serving Derek never did. Junior's unexpected kiss made me feel out of control, so I knelt in front of him and unzipped his jean shorts. He did not object when I tugged down his briefs and pulled him to my lips. My knees dug into the cool brown dirt and the air-conditioning vents roared, silencing Junior's moaning. I made him feel good, and it felt good to be in control, or so I thought.

I knelt in front of Junior only a handful of times, but after each tryst, he made sure to point out that he wasn't gay because he didn't do it back. As kids, we understood gay to be bad, a label denoting weakness. Junior was fine with accepting the blow jobs as long as he wasn't the one being labeled, as long as we were pretending to be other people, as long as I kept quiet about our interactions. Even then I didn't consider either of us gay; we both saw me as a girl in this context of our sexual playing, and there was nothing gay about girls sleeping with boys, I reasoned.

These trysts and my resulting questions about my gender and sexuality isolated me from my brother, who I felt could never understand me. I was blinded by an illusion that had me convinced that I was much more adult, more worldly, than Chad and thus had to carry burdens he could never grasp. Still, a part of me wanted him to understand me. Despite my isolation and uncertainty, he was my brother, and I looked forward to the routine of our evening communion, sleeping just a few feet away from each other.

"Hey," I whispered one night after clicking the television off. "You still up?"

"What's up?" he said, popping his head down to face me in my bunk.

"I feel like someone else sometimes," I told him. "Like different from you and other boys."

"I know that already," he said, flashing his missing-toothed smile. "You don't like boy things."

"I guess I just wanted to tell you," I said as he returned to his pillow. Though I didn't have the words then to define what was going on and who I was, a part of me feared that Chad would look at me differently, and not love me anymore.

Years later, Chad told me he had "some memory" of Derek "touching" me in "some strange way." He said, "I wasn't fully sure if he was molesting you or not. I was too young," and apologized for not doing something about what he'd apparently witnessed. I was struck that he carried guilt about something he couldn't have done anything about. How ridiculous does it sound for a seven-year-old kid to say he wished he'd done something about the abuse his eight-year-old sibling faced? "I wouldn't say that was one of the big reasons why you 'turned,'" he said. "I can't think of another word, but you know what I mean. It was always in you, and I knew you weren't happy with being who you were when we were younger. You wanted to be a girl."

I was apprehensive about writing about being molested because I feared others would make the same link Chad made, pointing to the abuse as the cause of my being trans—as if my identity as a woman is linked to some perversion, wrongdoing, or deviance. What must be made clear is that my gender expression and identity as a girl pre-dated Derek, and my expression as a child made me vulnerable and isolated, an easier target for Derek.

Gender and gender identity, sex and sexuality, are spheres of self-discovery that overlap and relate but are not one and the same. Each and every one of us has a sexual orientation and a gender identity. Simply put, our sexual orientation has to do with whom we get into bed *with*, while our gender identity has to do with whom we get into bed *as*. A trans person can be straight, gay, bisexual, etc.; a cis gay, lesbian, or heterosexual person can conform to expected gender norms or not; and a woman can have a penis and a man can have a vagina. There is no formula when it comes to gender and sexuality. Yet it is often only people whose gender identity and/or sexual orientation negates society's heteronormative and cisnormative standards who are targets of stigma, discrimination, and violence. I wish that instead of investing in these hierarchies of what's right and who's wrong, what's authentic and who's not, and ranking people according to these rigid standards that ignore diversity in our genders and sexualities, we gave people freedom and resources to define, determine, and declare who they are.

Chapter *Four*

I look back on tailored lawns fronting freshly painted houses and teenage boys in white tank tops flaunting burgeoning biceps who push mowers and pull rakes. I see Chad and me in crisp back-to-school outfits and unscuffed shoes, soles not worn to the ground, as we walk so fresh and so clean three blocks to homeroom. I see Dad, his waves brushed on point and his uniform, starched to crease, beaming at the stage as I accept the "class leader" award at an assembly.

I won many awards in the third grade, but Dad didn't see them until I placed them beside the living room TV, the most visible spot in the house. The reality was that Dad had stopped wearing his uniform long before. We had a front yard that was rarely mowed or watered. We got crisp back-to-school separates—a pair of jeans, a pair of shorts, and T-shirts we swapped to create more outfits—that we wore year-round until they were worn and outdated. I outgrew my jeans, the hems hovering over my ashy little ankles, at the same time I outgrew the illusion of stability that's supposed to accompany childhood.

One afternoon in 1992, I went to my room during homework hour to grab something from my desk. Through a crack in our bedroom door, I saw Dad sitting at the desk attached to the side of our bunk. His back was hunched over, too big for the rickety chair, which resembled dollhouse furniture. White vapor misted around his head. *Maybe he's sneaking a smoke of his Newports in our room, since Janine hates the smell in the house,* I thought. But it didn't smell like cigarettes, and I knew this wasn't for me to see. I was tiptoeing away from the door when Dad turned and looked straight at me. His eyes were wide, the pupils taking over his already dark brown irises. He pinched a charred glass pipe between his left thumb and index fingers, and a wrinkled piece of foil laid open on our desk.

"Why you sneakin' around?" he said. "Get in here."

I sat down on my bunk with my legs hanging over the wooden drawers. I looked down at my scabbed knees, blackened by skateboarding.

"Chaaaaaad," Dad yelled, pushing the door open so his voice would carry through the hall and living room to the kitchen, where Chad was surely daydreaming about playing outside.

Chad wore an apprehensive smile when he entered our bedroom. I could tell that he thought I had gotten us in trouble, and we were in for a long lecture that would shorten his outside time. Chad sat next to me on my bunk and took in the foil and the glass pipe and what looked like small shavings of Ivory soap. Dad's next action stuns me now in recollection. He brought the pipe to his chapped lips with his left hand, like he would a glass cigarette, and lit it with his right. The glass became cloudy with the vapor that went into him. He exhaled and released the white from his plum lips. Chad and my eyes grew large. This was against everything we heard at school. We were products of D.A.R.E. (Drug Abuse Resistance Education), programmed since we'd learned our ABCs and 123s to "Just Say No," with graffiti on our school walls proclaiming, "Crack Is Wack!" We were instilled with the hope that if we just said no and got an education, we could avoid the pitfalls of our community and, apparently, our own home. I bought into this dream wholeheartedly. It was all I really had, besides Chad. The dream I clutched to my chest was a black-and-white world where drugs were poison and the people who did them were poisonous.

"You see how goofy I look?" Dad said with the pipe in his hand and the vapor diminishing around him. "You see how silly I'm acting?"

I actually did not see any silliness; all I could think about was how weak he was. The strongest man I knew, my father, was smoking crack from a pipe in our bedroom, and he had the audacity to do it in front of us. I didn't understand addiction as a disease, so I saw my father as weak. His search for pleasure and power in a pipe made him pathetic. His eyes still follow me now. They were these black balls of nothingness, like looking into an empty well with no sunlight above you.

I was not attached to this man who smoked crack, and I was tempted to raise my hand, as if we were in show-and-tell, and ask him how he felt and whether his body tingled. I equated his inhalation to the burning of mouthwash at bedtime. I wondered if he burned on the inside. I also wanted to ask how he could do this to Chad. I was naive enough to think that I could handle this. Looking at Chad, with his head down and feet pointing into the carpet, I knew he had seen too much. In that moment, I realized that Dad meant more to Chad than he meant to me. For my brother, Dad was an all-knowing hero who could do nothing wrong. That was how I felt about Mom. But as with the heroes of childhood, you realize they're make-believe characters, and the qualities you so admired in them were magnified through your obstructed lens of adoration.

"Don't ever do this," Dad said with a hint of defeat in his voice. "Go on and play."

Chad left his worship in that room, and I left behind any illusion of safety. If Dad was all we had, the only person looking out for us, then we were all alone.

"Listen! If I ever catch you guys doing this," he said, lifting his empty eyes to meet Chad's wet ones, "I'mma whop your asses."

When I recalled this pivotal moment to my father years later, he said simply, "Your dad doesn't lie."

By 1992, we'd been in Oakland for two years, at what I know now was the height of the crack epidemic, which enveloped our already struggling neighborhood like the rising fog that covered the Golden Gate Bridge during those misty mornings. Some of my classmates were reportedly born addicted to cocaine, mislabeled "crack babies" by the media before their parents even got the chance to name them. We all teased one another incessantly, as kids do, about whose mama smoked crack. "Yo mama" jokes were all the rage ("Yo mama smoke so much crack, she . . ."), and we'd blame anyone's shortcomings on a mother's crack smoking. Our teasing mirrored chants of the kids in the Dogs' hit song, "Your Mama's on Crack Rock," in which a little girl is teased by kids chiming about her mother's "tricking" to get money for crack. The song ends with the girl pleading, "Mama, please stop, 'cause they pickin' at me."

Rarely were there images of fathers strolling the streets for a hit of exhilaration. We definitely saw men in filthy clothes around our block, but they didn't belong to anybody. Besides, none of my friends in our predominantly black neighborhood had a father. Before seeing Dad take a hit from the pipe, I thought crack was a "yo mama" problem, not a "yo daddy" problem.

My closest friend, Maddy, had a white father she had never met. The rumor was that her mother was her married father's dark secret, a macadamia-nut-colored woman with curly hair that matched Maddy's. I loved Maddy because she was smart and kind and had an open capacity for compassion that I envied. Once Maddy's half-sister, Aisha—who favored her mom, all sharp lines and angles anchored with almond-shaped eyes—yelled at Maddy, "Mama don't care 'bout us. All she cares about is her glass dick." Maddy, with tears welling up in her downcast eyes, whispered to Aisha, "You shouldn't say that. She can't help herself."

My feelings for my father didn't come close to empathy. What little that remained, I disposed of when I heard John, our neighbor, call Dad a crackhead.

Dad worked well with his hands and had a passion for cars, and John's champagne-colored Cadillac, with a matching leather interior that smelled of lemony oil, was Dad's adopted baby. At the time, Dad had a green Volkswagen Bug. He never complained about the size or its horrendous vomit color, but there was no hiding Dad's love of that Caddy. "This is a car right here, man," Dad said to himself, giggling, while changing the oil one day.

He babied John's car as if it were his own. It was Dad's "I've made it" marker, a sort of black man's dream, trumping white picket fences, Girl Scout cookies, and lemonade stands. Dad's care for John's car— the washing, the waxing, the tune-ups, and the oil changes—were a gracious act, in my perspective, one of friendship and passion. I was unaware that John and Dad had their own arrangement.

Dad was sweating under the hood of the Caddy on one of those sunny days in California that a kid born in Hawaii and living in Oakland took for granted. Everyone was outside. John wore a brown and beige silk shirt that draped over his rotund belly. He was bald on top of his head, with hair on the sides—he looked like Uncle Phil from *The Fresh Prince of Bel-Air*, and he had the same air of superiority, which showed in the volume of his voice. Only his should be heard.

As Dad tinkered on the Caddy, I sat on a patch of grass between the driveway and the street, where Chad and Maddy and Aisha were playing. Dad was on one side of me, under the hood, and on the other side was John, standing with a man who looked at Dad suspiciously. His sideways glance captured my focus because I recognized that I looked at my father the same way. I was the kind of child who, as Dad said, "can't stay out of grown folks' business," so my interest was piqued.

"How much you pay Charlie?" the man asked John.

I had to stop everything inside of me from saying that Dad did not get paid to tend to John's car. He was no one's employee; he did it because he was John's friend and he loved the Caddy as if it were his own.

"He loves that car, man," John said, calming my defenses. I knew he knew my father and appreciated his work. "But," John continued, "I feel sorry for him, you know. He's a crackhead. I give him twenty bucks here, another there."

I turned my head toward Dad, who was polishing away at a rim. Beads of sweat ran from his hairline to the lines of his forehead as he bobbed his head to a tune only he could hear.

In one instant, Dad was . . . a crackhead. Just like Maddy and Aisha's mom, ashy and antsy, circling the dudes in do-rags who hung outside the corner store. I realized then that I'd held on to a shred of hope regarding Dad; he was still a hero to me, if flawed. Rationalizing him and the glass pipe, Dad smoked crack, but he was not a crackhead; it was just something he did. To do something didn't define you, I thought.

I saw Dad through a dusty lens that distorted our relationship, as tarnished as his pipe. He was no longer just our father; he was his own person, with an identity and label and body separate from his relationship with us. He was someone who was judged outside of the lens of fatherhood, outside of our connection. When he was in the streets, he was not Dad. He was Charlie the crackhead.

I vividly remember the routine sight of a baby girl wearing a soiled diaper, playing with an equally dirty doll on her lawn. No parent or sibling in sight. She would just cry and cry and cry. No one asked, "Where's her mama?" Her wailing became the background vocals to our double-Dutch anthems, kind of like the barely heard baby yelps in Aaliyah's song "Are You That Somebody?" In addition to the baby girl, I saw stray dogs and crack vials on my way to school. But crack's reach went beyond those vials we skipped over. When Maddy's mom, who would beg the boys on the corner for "some stuff," passed away of AIDS complications, I hugged my friend good-bye: Maddy and Aisha moved to San José to begin a better life with their mother's sister.

An overwhelming feeling of envy spoiled my friendship with Maddy and Aisha because they spent all their lives with their mother. Even if she was flawed, at least she chose to be there with them. I yearned for mine, but Mom existed only in scant memories and dreams of her saving us from the dark cloud that hovered over us. These ideals of my mother contrasted with the reality of Dad, who was an anomaly, a single black father amid a gaggle of equally strug-gling single black moms. I was not able to recognize how unjust our circumstances were until I was well into adulthood and compared them with the experiences of friends who had relatively minimal ex-posure to trauma. My first sight of "normal" parent-child relations didn't come until I moved to New York in my early twenties. Both of my roommates had parents in town to set them up, to buy them underbed storage, and to assemble their Ikea desks. I came alone with a thousand dollars or so in savings, student loan checks on the way, luggage bought by Auntie Lisa as a graduation gift, and $150 in pocket money that Mom held for me.

I saw one of my roommates' father slip her a wad of cash; she said, "Thanks, Daddy," while her mom looked on with moist, swollen eyes. I had never felt so lonely as I did that first day in my tiny room in the

East Village with a bed I bought on Craigslist and a Kmart dresser I assembled alone with my iPod buds in my ears. My normal was loneliness and isolation and independence. I depended on myself. I had a family, people I came from, shared experiences with, and checked in on. But they could do nothing for me beyond the love and care and good wishes they sent my way. I grew resentful in adulthood about my parents' lack of planning. I became so used to being alone and depending on myself that I didn't know how to ask for help.

As a kid, I had no idea that we were poor because our friends looked like us. We were all outside playing while our parents were inside smoking their pipes. We all had about three outfits, dingy shirts, high-water jeans, and matted hair. I didn't have a subscription to *Highlights*, wasn't able to order books from the Scholastic catalog, and never bought school photos. I don't have a single image of myself from the second grade to the sixth, the years we lived with Dad. If not for Janine, I don't know how we would've survived those Oakland years. She was a single mother who took us on when we needed her most, when she had little to give herself or her own son. She was the one who gave us candy money, who mended our wounds when we fell or fought, who took us to Payless to replace our shoes when the soles began flapping.

No matter how much I adored and appreciated Janine, I couldn't make her better. Her body was too weak to continue fighting, and Dad was unapologetic about his lack of care. "You know your dad is selfish," he chanted with a dissonant chord of defeat and defiance, completely at ease with his shortcomings. I disliked his lack of reciprocation.

Dad was charming and energetic. He was the kind of guy who would break out and dance if "his song" came on. "Ooooh, this my jam here," I remember him saying, putting our car in park at a red light, opening his door, and making the street his dance floor. That sense of endless amusement is what led women to fall so quickly. It was what made me love my dad while also rolling my eyes at him. Looking back, I can't distinguish which parts of him were fueled by drugs and alcohol and which parts were not. I don't know what *before* looked like. His lectures became tangent-filled, disjointed. He often lost his point and would be easily distracted by imaginings of some perceived slight from me. "Boy, why are you looking at me like that? Don't look at me. Look at your hands," he'd say. Seconds later, he'd rebut, "Why aren't you looking at me? Boy, look at me when I'm talking to you."

I began avoiding him, even forging his signature in jagged all-caps print on report cards and permission slips for field trips for Chad and me. I didn't want to bother Dad in the mornings; I didn't want to wake him. I felt that the more he slept, the less time he'd have to search for drugs.

Despite the hardship, there were happy times, too, like the time Dad embraced me and told me he was proud of me after I got my ass kicked by the neighborhood bully in defense of Chad, or a vomit-laden car ride home from the Santa Cruz Beach Boardwalk. It was just Chad, Dad, and me, the only time I ever saw the Pacific Ocean from California. I remember the smell of salt in the air from the bright blue water and the sweet taste of cotton candy and sticky caramel between my back teeth from the glossy candy apples. We rode the Pirate Ship, the Sea Swings, and the Ferris wheel. Dad was clear and present that day. His eyes were bright, and he strolled with a steady calm that relaxed me.

I looked over the rail bridge that crossed the San Lorenzo River, and I thought that maybe we were crossing over, maybe there was better in store for us, maybe there'd be more days like this, maybe this was the beginning of good fortune. Chad and I flanked Dad as we walked over the wooden tracks of that old bridge. I could tell Chad wanted to run across the bridge, but I was worried that one false move and I would slip through the gaps in between the tracks and fall into the river.

"Y'all are all I got, man," Dad said. "Y'all give my life purpose. Wherever I go, y'all go with me." He didn't say it sentimentally; he said it as a fact. His love for us was undoubtedly a fact. I had a father who loved me. This was a gift I wouldn't fully appreciate until I fell in love in my twenties.

On our way home later that afternoon, I threw up in the backseat of the car. I was scared I would get yelled at for being so greedy and eating too much. "Your eyes are always bigger than your stomach," Dad often scolded me. He pulled over at a car wash and cleaned up my mess without saying anything mean. It's still one of the top five moments of my life.

Chapter *Five*

Ve all fulfill our quota of misfortune at some point in our life.
This is what I believed as a ten-year-old. It was a belief system of my own creation, part of a silent theory based on fairness and balance. I believed that some reached their quota early and advanced to a life of access and abundance, while others had beginnings filled with open doors and opportunities until they were met with their share of misfortune. This theory helped me cope with the foreboding darkness of Oakland. I held on to the hope that fortune would soon knock on our door.

Instead, when Chad opened our front door one night in 1993 as we watched TV, misfortune fell on our living room carpet in the form of a wounded Derek, who'd been shot just blocks away from our apartment. Blood trailed down Derek's bare legs, peeking through the fabric of his shorts. Chad's high-pitched screams launched me off the sofa and into our room, where we huddled together in our closet. I remember thinking the shooter was following Derek and would find us. This fear diminished when the red lights of the fire truck crept into our room, and Dad came home stunned by the blood in the foyer and the tears in our eyes.

I don't remember hearing gunfire that night, a common occurrence in our neighborhood, one that startled me the first few times I heard it until I wrote it off as a car backfiring, another common sound. Derek survived three gunshots, an apparent case of mistaken identity, according to Dad, who said the gunman—one of the guys who stood outside the corner store—told Derek, "Sorry, man, you ain't the one," then ran off into the streetlamp-lit night.

Those streetlamps are the last things I remember about the yellow house on the hill, the one shrouded by trees, the one Dad, Chad, and I ran away from a few months after Derek returned home on crutches. In early 1994, in the middle of the night, we boarded a Greyhound bus to Dallas, Texas, Dad's hometown. He refused to let us say good-bye to Janine, fearful that she'd guilt him into staying. Dad cut people off quickly, moving on from relationships with little care or accountability. I don't know what became of Derek or the kids on my block like Junior, and I was sad to hear from my father only a few years ago that Janine passed "a while back" from kidney complications after years of dialysis. Dad didn't make the three-hour drive to attend her funeral in Houston, where she had relocated a few years after we left Oakland.

He later told me that running away was the only way he felt he'd get out of Oakland alive. He was running away from the violence that was so close to home and the pipe that was his constant companion. Dad called our bus ride "an adventure," one where he played spades with Chad and we ate all the barbecue-flavor Corn Nuts we wanted, stinking up the bus.

Sitting on my knees, I followed the lines on the highway as we rode for thirty-six hours from Oakland to Los Angeles and Phoenix to El Paso and finally Dallas, where the city was in a joyous uproar over the Cowboys' back-to-back Super Bowl wins in 1993 and 1994.

Sunday dinner at my grandparents' home in a suburb of Dallas, the same neighborhood where Dad and his four younger siblings came of age, was a day of food, family, and football. Grandma Shellie ruled the ranch-style house. She had dark, reflective skin, constantly glowing alongside sleepy, heavy-lidded eyes and full red lips. Her most defining feature was her elegant, slender hands, which she put to work as a seamstress for fashion designer Todd Oldham. I remember sitting quietly in her garage as she worked among racks of garments in plastic bags. The only sounds were the needle and thread meeting the fabrics and the machine's humming motor, a steady music of labor. Grandpa Charlie was also constantly at work, spending his nights on the highways as a cross-country truck driver.

Despite Grandpa's absence, Grandma's house was filled with family. I played hide-and-seek and tag with a gaggle of cousins, all a few years apart from one another. Each of Dad's four siblings had one or two kids, except for my perpetually single Uncle Bernard, who was Dad's shadow and even lived with my parents for a bit when they were in Long Beach.

There were too many Mocks in Dallas for me to ever feel alone. Even when the sound of questions regarding my identity began ringing louder in my head, I rarely had room to reflect because the sound of family was overwhelming. Grandma's metal pots and pans clacking; Dad and Uncle Bernard and Uncle Ricky's cheers for the Cowboys; Auntie Linda Gail's mouth-smacking gossip and Auntie Joyce's soothing *mhmm*s; my cousins' yelps from the backyard; Sadie, the family's slate-gray pit bull, barking at the applause from the house as her chain collar rubbed against the metal back gate; the white-noise gurgling of the crawfish pond outside Grandma's property line.

Grandma Shellie prepped dinner before Sunday service, and her house filled up with people and good food afterward. Dad scoffed at church and rarely attended. He said church was two hours too long and all arrogance, and that he didn't need a minister serving as his medium to God; he could speak to God whenever he wanted. He apparently spoke to him every day, with a can of beer in one hand and a Newport in the other. It was one of the many things Grandma and Dad disagreed on, including suffering and hard work being the prerequisite of living a good life, as Grandma often said.

"Mama, don't tell my babies that," Dad once rebutted Grandma. "That ain't true."

"Babies, that's why your daddy ain't got shit," she said, serving Chad and me unfiltered truth about the ways of life.

I was enamored by my grandmother and lurked around her kitchen, where the Mock women—Grandma, Auntie Linda Gail, and Auntie Joyce—gathered. I eavesdropped on them discussing grown folks' business, about the way Ms. Cindy, Auntie Linda Gail's neighbor, had been asking after Dad. It was all the more scandalous because she had just split from the father of one of her three sons, and Dad quickly filled the vacancy, secretly staying nights at Cindy's.

"Now, he ain't got no business to be sneakin' at his age," Grandma said from the stove, where she stirred two pots of gumbo. (She always made one without shrimp because Uncle Ricky and I were allergic to shellfish.)

Auntie Joyce, whom we lovingly called Wee Wee (her childhood nickname), nodded and *mhmm*ed in agreement, her eyes looking through the glass cup, where she was measuring vegetable oil for a chocolate box cake.

"Well, that ain't nothing," Auntie Linda Gail clucked as she tore her long, curved acrylic nails through stems of collard greens she was washing over the sink. "When I asked Cindy about it, she had the nerve to tell me that it was none of my business. I 'bout bopped her on her head."

I had to do everything in my power not to laugh with them. I silently soaked them up like a biscuit to honey butter. Then Auntie Wee Wee, with her large eyes and tall, slender frame and sweet smile, winked at me and said, "Come help me out, baby." Making the chocolate cake gave me entry to graduate from eavesdropping to being one of the girls. Auntie Wee Wee whipped the batter with a wooden spoon as I greased the pan with a stick of butter. She beat the mix for a couple of minutes before pouring the brown gooey sweetness into the round cake pan. I placed it in the oven and watched it bake under the light's glow while licking the bowl quietly as they continued talking.

This is womanhood, I thought, watching the women in Dad's life cook and cackle in the kitchen. Auntie Linda Gail had two sons and paid her bills with the help of welfare but stayed fly in the projects by doing hair out of her kitchen. She rocked an asymmetrical haircut, with a long, honey-blond weave bang that sat prettily over her left eye. She had more style than any woman I have seen in my entire life, the epitome of ghetto fabulous before there was such a thing. Auntie Wee Wee, on the other hand, chose an effortless approach to beauty. She wore small silver hoop earrings and black shoulder-length hair that she tied back in a ponytail. Her large eyes were usually rimmed with a stroke of black liner, and her lips were perpetually painted plum.

My grandmother and my two aunts were an exhibition in resilience and resourcefulness and black womanhood. They rarely talked about the unfairness of the world with the words that I use now with my social justice friends, words like *intersectionality* and *equality*, *oppression*, and *discrimination*. They didn't discuss those things because they were too busy living it, navigating it, surviving it.

Witnessing these women, albeit in the bits and pieces and slices that I was lucky to observe, contributed greatly to my womanhood. Collectively, they made the demure secretary I had said I wanted to be in the second grade look like a caricature. They elevated my possibilities of being someone more powerful. They were pleasure-seeking, resourceful, sexy, rhythmic, nurturing, fly, happy, stylish, rambunctious, gossipy, feeling, hurt, unapologetic women. They were the kind of women I wanted to be.

With my hands properly sticky and my cake in the oven, I walked into the living room and began to chant, "Wait till you taste my cake! Wait till you taste my cake! You're gonna love my cake. Wait till you taste my cake!" Legend says I punctuated this freestyle rap with the Cabbage Patch dance. I adamantly deny ever doing the Cabbage Patch.

Twenty minutes later, the smell of something burning cut the air. I heard the oven slam and Grandma grunt, "Sheeeiiit!" I ran into the kitchen and saw my charred cake in Grandma's oven-mitted hands. She had set the oven on broil rather than bake.

Dad, who seemed to have ignored my cooking (partly because the Cowboys were on, partly because he didn't want to berate me for baking), came into the kitchen. He saw the burnt cake and my head bowed and—like anyone with impeccable comedic timing and an insatiable appetite to be the center of attention—sang, "Wait till you taste my cake . . . You're gonna love my cake . . . Wait till you taste my cake." He mocked my rap by improvising the Cabbage Patch. My cousins soon joined in. They were the chorus that created the "Wait Till You Taste My Cake" family legend.

I was sensitive and easily wounded in the presence of Grandma and my aunts. I tearfully ran into the guest bedroom, the one where we stayed during our first few months in Dallas, while Dad cleaned himself up. I sank my face in the nearly flat pillows and cursed him. Seeing him do that song and dance of my own creation made me reflect on myself. I had seen my eerie similarities with my father. He was proud and selfish and wanted to be the center of attention. I was also those things, half formed. I yearned to be seen and appreciated but had done nothing notable. Being chosen to help with the cake had made me feel special, and I wanted everyone to see that I mattered. The chaos came to a halt when Aunty Wee Wee spoke.

"Toosie," Aunty Wee Wee said, using Dad's nickname (he was Grandpa Charlie's namesake, the second Charlie in the Mock family, hence Two C, or Toosie). "Leave him be."

When she came in the room, Aunty Wee Wee said we could buy another cake and do it right this time. She offered the kind of coddling I craved. She let me be soft and never forced me to be anything other than who I was. My aunts and grandmother were the iridescent cellophane I needed, another layer of protection and care that complemented Dad's shiny foil—the kind of protection that often cut.

A few Sundays later, we left Grandma's house and began spending our nights at Cindy's, which was across the hall from Auntie Linda Gail's. Cindy was rail-thin but no one could stop her from flaunting her size-zero frame and stick legs in cutoff shorts and miniskirts. Her boys were just as frail, with matching buckteeth. Two of them regularly peed the bed, even though they were around our age. What disturbed me wasn't that they peed the bed but the fact that their family grew accustomed to the urine smell. I remember getting my head smacked for pointing the stench out to Dad our first night there. Fortunately, Chad and I couldn't sleep in the crowded urine room, so we gladly shared the plastic-covered living room sofa, sleeping foot to head during our time there.

I settled into fourth grade in Dallas at the first of many uninspiring schools there. We were enrolled and transferred according to Dad's love life. Cindy was the first in a long line of girlfriends we shacked up with in Dallas. Dad went after women with children, single moms who felt lucky to call Toosie theirs, even though he had no job, was raising two kids, and was rarely faithful.

After Cindy came Teeny, Diamond, Sandra, and finally Denise, who became Dad's longest live-in girlfriend in Dallas. Denise loved to party and drink beer just as much as Dad, which I believe sustained their relationship. Denise had the freedom to be a good-time girl because her children were way past puberty. Anthony, Denise's eldest, didn't live in the two-bedroom apartment we shared with Makayla, sixteen, and Kevin, fourteen, with whom Chad and I shared a room. Makayla slept in the living room, the hall closet being her only private area in the apartment.

Makayla was the first young woman who made an imprint on me. Her vibrant, fabulous presence, her endless string of cute outfits, and her bouncy press-and-curl impressed me. She had a petite figure with a pop of booty. She was just as brown as I was, with lips that looked permanently puckered and soft features that needed only a wad of mascara and some lip gloss. Makayla knew she was cute and boasted about her "I Got It Going On-ness." She was sweet on me, letting me hang around with her in the living room as she talked on the phone and got ready for the mall.

I watched in awe when she treated boys as if they were entertainment, toys she returned to their shelf when she grew tired of them. When Makayla was over a guy, my job was to get rid of him for her over the phone. I'd lie that she wasn't home, but one day when she actually wasn't home, I stretched the lie a bit further, creating an imaginary friend who proudly took Makayla's sloppy seconds. If Makayla didn't want these guys, I wanted to have fun with them.

"Makayla told me you were calling," I said to a guy named Alan.

"Who is this?"

"Keisha," I said as effortlessly as breathing.

I liked any girl name that ended in a prolonged *ahhh*: Makayla, Alicia, Aaliyah, Keisha. It sounded elegant and unique. In my sketches of Keisha, she was cute, curly, and flirty, the kind of girl Makayla would hang out with at the mall. In the guise of my alter ego, I daydreamed out loud about my life as a girl. I told Alan stories about my girlfriends at school, about trying out for the dance squad, about buying a new outfit at the mall, about the guys who asked for my number in the food court. I let myself inhabit the life of the teenage girl I yearned to be. Talking on the phone was my first bit of storytelling, and Keisha was my heroine.

I spoke to Alan and maybe three other guys over those months, rotating calls and conversations. Alan was my only steady, the guy I'd talk to at least once a day. He had been to our apartment complex before to hang with Makayla. She told me she didn't like him because he gave her a weird vibe. "Like he wanted to kiss me or hold my hand, but instead of doing it, he would just stare at my lips or my hand while I talked," she said. "Creepy."

I found his lack of courage sweet, but I knew nothing about dating. I was only eleven. Alan and Keisha were a good match, though. He was the only guy who didn't get antsy about meeting up. It was as if he were more comfortable talking on the phone than in person. After a few weeks of talking every day, I began looking forward to the bell ringing at school at three P.M. so I could run home and chat with Alan. We'd talk for half-hour intervals. Everyone assumed that I was talking to my best friend, Veronica, a chunky girl with oily shoulder-length hair that stuck to her head like a helmet. She always wore one piece of clothing that was purple. That's why jerks at school called her Barney in the hallways. We bonded over the snickers, though, and Veronica was the only one who knew I had a phone boyfriend and engaged with Keisha.

With her friendship, Keisha felt more and more real to me. So real that I agreed to meet Alan at the playground across the street from Veronica's apartment, the same spot where I would meet her in the mornings to catch the school bus. In Veronica's room, I swapped my Cowboys starter jacket for one of her purple sweaters and plum barrettes. Being a girl was simple in my preadolescent mind, just a change of clothes and accessories.

My heart was beating fast as we approached the playground together, Veronica's round figure shielding me from Alan's view. He sat on the top of a park bench, his long legs hanging over the tabletop; stretching to a height that would make him six feet tall. As we got closer, I saw peach fuzz over his full lips and dark brown eyes under a baseball cap. He smiled as Veronica and I walked side by side past him. He was taller, cuter, and manlier than I had expected. Seeing him sitting on that bench, I realized I was in over my head.

I didn't approach Alan because I was scared he'd find out the truth and Keisha would be dismissed as a fraud. She was no longer imaginary to me; she was the most authentic thing about me. I don't know if Alan knew that the girl with the plum barrette and purple sweater pretending to be fourteen, pretending she was woman enough, was Keisha. I avoided his calls by deepening my voice when I answered the phone. I said Keisha wasn't there, like I had done for Makayla just months before. Alan eventually stopped calling, and I became bored of being a girl on the phone.

"Ooohhh, I couldn't stand your little ass," Dad recently admitted with a chuckle while we spoke on the phone. I could almost see him shrugging as he laughed about it.

In my late twenties, I began having these raw, revelatory conversations with my father, the kind a person can have only when they accept the faults, flaws, and fierceness of the people who happened to wrong them when trying to do right. Dad never used a filter in his conversations with me, regardless of my age. He never dumbed down his message or softened his language. "You know your dad," he'd say after what some would take as a controversial statement, such as admitting that he couldn't stand me.

In my half-remembered, wounded memories, my private soap operas involving Dad, I was the victim: the helpless child who had to follow him wherever his heart and dick said we were going; the one who had to hide who I was and listen to lectures on why I shouldn't play so much with girls; the one who was forced to play "Smear the Queer" with Chad and his roughhousing pals.

"Aww, baby, you almost made it all the way. Remember?" Dad said, taking us back to that courtyard with the patchwork of grass and brown dirt.

I see myself at eleven, all limp wrists and swaying hips, running around with my cousin Mechelle, Auntie Wee Wee's only child, as Chad, all dirt and scraped knees, sprinted with the boys at Auntie Linda Gail's. The tangy taste of Now and Laters in supersize pickles and chili-topped bags of Fritos filled those Saturdays, the same ones Auntie Linda Gail, Uncle Bernard, and Dad enjoyed with weed and beer. They were an inseparable trio who loved to party and shit-talk. A sober Auntie Wee Wee was there, too, high on the company of her siblings.

Chad was the Queer in Smear the Queer, a childhood game of tag in which whoever carried the object (in this case the football) was "it" and would need to be tackled. "Sheeit, that's my boy!" Dad, with a bottle of Colt 45 in his hand, cheered from the stairwell overlooking the courtyard.

I watched from the sidelines, half interested in the game as Mechelle showed off the sassy moves and anthems she'd learned at cheer practice. Chad was quick, but he couldn't outrun his crowd of pursuers, who tackled him in the "safe zone." I watched him stand up, brush the dirt off his shirt, and walk away with such humble swagger.

The next thing I knew, Dad was beside me, pulling me by the T-shirt and throwing me into the crowd with Chad and his friends. I could smell the beer on his breath even though he didn't say a word to me. "You didn't want to play," he later reflected. "But I didn't know any better."

Chad handed me the football because, as the new kid, I was being initiated as the Queer. "Do you even know how to play?" one of the boys said, laughing.

"He does!" Chad defended before whispering to me, "Okay, you're it, so you get a five-second head start. Make sure you run as fast as you can to the safe zone. You get there, you can't be tackled. If you can't make it there, throw the ball to me, and I'll take the tackle."

I placed the ball securely under my arm and ran as fast as I could. When the five seconds were up, ten dingy and ashy boys were on my tail. I heard Chad screaming, "Go! Go! Go!" and Mechelle's clapping and cheering. Then, just as I was approaching the safe zone, the collar of my T-shirt squeezed tightly around my neck and a pair of hands wrapped around my waist. My knees hit the gravel first, stinging, as my mouth tasted grit. I was on the ground with three boys screaming, "Yeah! We got him!"

"Are you okay?" Chad said, offering his hand to lift me up.

I nodded, taking his hand and then walking into Auntie Linda Gail's apartment. The smell of burned hair and weed enveloped me. I heard Dad's applause behind me. "Man, you almost made it," he said, satisfied.

My knees stung badly and I wanted to wash my mouth out. I could feel bits of dirt between my teeth. "You okay, baby?" Auntie Wee Wee asked as I entered the bathroom.

I nodded, avoiding eye contact with her. I knew if I looked at her, she would say something sweet, something that I needed to hear, something that would allow me to let those tears drop from my stinging eyes. This would only upset Dad, whom I was acutely aware had a complex about my sensitivity. It would squash his sense of pride and accomplishment. Dad proved to his drinking buddies and our family that his son could take a hit like any good ole boy. All I had to do to assuage his insecurities about my femininity was to hurt myself.

My femininity was heavily policed because it was seen as inferior to masculinity. My father, though he didn't have the words, couldn't understand why I would *choose* to be feminine when masculinity was privileged. What I had to negotiate at a young age was embracing who I was while rejecting whom others thought I should be.

"I knew you were different. But I just didn't know no different," Dad said during one of our conversations. "We butted heads, but I knew Janet. Damn, I knew my baby was different. I could see it in you all the time, and your dad didn't understand. I didn't want to see it. But you just like me, the only one of my kids that's just like me."

Like my father, I grew confident in my choice to be true to myself, despite what anyone thought, despite the fear of what was to come. I knew that if I chose to make myself happy, to live in the pursuit of me and my dreams, that I would be free. That was how my father lived. Sure, he brought pain to people—my mother, my brother, all of my half siblings—but at the end of the day, he took responsibility for his own happiness.

"Your dad is a selfish bastard," he once told me. "I always do me every day. And if you like it, then we cool, and if you don't, see ya."

I can't remember if Dad told me this when I was six or twenty-six or both.

"Hey, remember the time you burnt that cake?" he asked, chanting the song through the phone. "Ooohh, you were so mad at me, man."

Chapter *Six*

"You got pretty hair," Jamie said, staring at my wet curls with red-tinted eyes. "Can I touch it?"

I ducked underwater in response, swiftly swimming away from his compliment as my hair did its own floating, ethereal choreography in the blue that surrounded me. I swam with my hair loosely tied, my shirt on, and my eyes wide open, never wanting to miss a moment or someone's foot kicking my way. I sought refuge underwater because I didn't know how to receive a compliment from a boy I liked. Down below, I touched the bottom of the eight-foot-deep pool, hoping to find comfort in the clear blue vision of the water.

It was spring break 1994, and "Whatta Man" was the only song I was determined to memorize before I had to return to school at the close of the week. The Dallas sun had made me three shades darker, and my week at Auntie Wee Wee's apartment had introduced me to Jamie, my latest crush. He lived in the building adjacent to Auntie Wee Wee and Mechelle. Jamie was a year older than I was, with a nearly shaved head of dark brown fuzz and matching thick eyebrows. His skin was smooth and all the more golden from the sun.

Swimming to the edge of the pool, I unwound my purple scrunchie and let my drenched curls drop over my shoulders. Wet and full, my hair glistened while soaking up the heat. Jamie placed his golden hands against my black hair. My heart raced as I sat shin-deep in water. Though kids were splashing around us and screaming "Marco! Polo!" I felt as if Jamie and I were all alone, the hot cement under our butts. His eyes twinkled under the reflective light of the moving water. I wanted to kiss him and ask him to be my boyfriend, but I knew that would be taking it too far.

"The food's ready," Mechelle called from just outside the gate. "We gotta go."

She had stopped swimming on day three of our break, weary of dodging the splashes from the pool. "They too wild," she complained during her final swim, adamant not to get her fresh just-permed edges wet. I told Jamie I'd be back outside after dinner as I pulled my hair back with both palms, tying it with my scrunchie. My tank top and shorts stuck to my skin as I walked over to Mechelle, who pursed her lips at me.

"Pinkie-swear you won't tell your mom," I told her as we made our way up the stairs to her apartment. It was probably the fourth time I'd made her promise not to blow my cover. She finally relaxed her pursed lips, smacking them in defeat as her pinkie met mine. I knew she thought the Keisha game had gone on too long, but I also knew she'd keep my secret because I was her favorite cousin, and she was mine.

Keisha was more real to me than I was to myself. There was no doubt when I was in the moment as Keisha. She was fully me, the me I knew myself to be in those quiet instances when all I had to do was merely be. But I was certain the falsity of Keisha, no matter how real

she felt to me, would result in a whipping or something worse. The boundaries of gender, I was taught, were unmovable, like the glistening white rocks that surrounded Grandma's crawfish ponds. Keisha proved, though, that self-determination—proclaiming who you were to others—wielded the power to lift those rocks toward a more honest place.

Mechelle and Auntie Wee Wee's apartment was the only quiet place I remember in Dallas. It wasn't filled with gossip or cluttered by the noise of children running around. My aunt, willowy and sweet, created this home for mother and daughter. There were bursts of purple and green throughout their apartment, resembling a ripe eggplant at a farmer's market.

I admit that I was envious of Mechelle's life, which probably fueled my snap decision to introduce myself as Keisha to her friends. I didn't consult Mechelle. She followed my lead. I longed to wear her barrettes, to shake her pom-poms, to bask in a boy's attention, to call Auntie Wee Wee Mom. Mechelle had a room of her own, a sacred space that I wouldn't have well until adulthood. Her room was occupied by Barbies, a Lite-Brite, an Etch A Sketch, coloring books to fit any mood, and videotapes of *Free Willy*, *Aladdin*, and my favorite, *Beauty and the Beast*. I wore that tape out to the point where the ballroom scene played through a layer of permanent static. I see Belle clearly now, spinning on that dance floor in her golden gown as everyone looked on. I yearned to grow to be as beautifully bookish as Belle.

The usual vanilla scent of the apartment was dominated by a fishy odor. It was pungent and alluring to me, the kind of aroma that hit notes of a home I longed for. Auntie Wee Wee crumbled Ritz crackers between her hands, topping her tuna casserole, which she made because it was my favorite. Tuna reminded me of Mom; I could see her reading a book, just like Belle, and spreading tuna over crackers, white crumbs collecting on her lap. Like Mom, Auntie Wee Wee

had a calm presence, one that made me feel safe to be just as I was. She acknowledged my tenderness in big and small ways without reprimand or rehabilitation. I'll never forget the time she took me to Kmart and bought me a sleeping bag for my sleepovers. In the aisle, she asked me to pick out the one I wanted. Skipping my eyes over the burgundy, the blue, and the green bags, I pointed at a lavender sleeping bag that called loudly after me. It *had* to be mine. My aunt didn't bat a mascaraed lash as we carried it to the checkout.

Full of tuna and fresh out of the shower, I went back outside alone to the playground, just as the sun was retiring for the day. I found Jamie, at one with the gray-blue sky, swinging, the soles of his Jordan-clad feet parallel to the gravel I stood on. The little follicles on my forearms rose as I joined him up there. My hair flirted with the wind, and in the air with Jamie, I felt like the only girl in the world. Soon we settled down, lazily swaying from side to side in our adjacent swings. He leaned in toward me and fingered a ringlet with his right hand. Soon my coarse curls struggled to make their way between his golden fingers. It was the first time someone had admired me. My hair, the only mark of my girlhood, was being touched in a way I had never been before.

Sunday soon came, marking the end of my springtime retreat. Keisha would remain here as I returned to life as Charles. I was mourning her end as I gathered my stuff in Mechelle's room. Dad sat in the living room watching TV with Auntie Wee Wee, waiting to take me home. Then I heard an unexpected sound: Jamie's voice. "Are Keisha and Mechelle here?" he asked from the front door.

"Hold on, baby," Auntie Wee Wee said. "Mechelle?" she called toward the back.

I hadn't planned on saying good-bye; I thought we'd just pick up the relationship over the phone. Mechelle looked at me and clucked her tongue as she crossed the threshold of her bedroom.

"Hey. Where's your cousin?" Jamie asked Mechelle.

"Let's go outside," she said, hurrying out of the house.

"Uh-uh, little girl. Don't you leave this house. You got company," Auntie said.

"Where's Keisha?" Jamie asked again.

Mechelle just shrugged.

"Who's Keisha?" Auntie asked, pressing Mechelle for answers.

Mechelle was only in the fourth grade and had probably never lied to her mom. She didn't know what to say, so she began crying. That was when Dad shifted his gaze from the TV to the door. My heart beating rapidly and my fingers interlocked and twisted, I walked out of Mechelle's room. My hair was tied in a ponytail, low at the back of my neck, as Jamie smiled.

"Hey, Keisha," he said, making Dad stand from the couch.

I didn't get to say good-bye to Jamie and explain to him who I was. I didn't have the words as an eleven-year-old to explain who I was to anyone beyond myself. All I knew was that Keisha was real to me, and under the glare of my father, I feared for her survival. Dad wrote Keisha off as some bad joke I was playing, one that had gone on way too long, one that he ensured I wouldn't play again. He talked nonstop on our way to Denise's house, his words packing the car.

"You're not gay, are you?" he finally pleaded, defeated after his fifteen-minute diatribe. Dad's face was glowing red, reflecting in the stoplight hovering before us. His voice was sweet as he asked the question, one he was sure I had the answer to. He hoped that my answer would assuage his concerns about me, his sissy boy, the one he gave his name to—the first of his children he held in his arms—as he said, "I saw you come out of your mother, man. I was there!"

I didn't know if *gay* was the right fit for me. The label hovered over me for years like the red glare settling over my father's face. I'd been called *gay* and *sissy* and *faggot* ever since I stepped foot on playgrounds in my earliest youth. My father's thoughts filled the car: *My son is an effeminate boy pretending to be a girl in front of other boys, so he must be gay, right?* Uncertainty rode shotgun in our conversation.

As a tween, I was living in the murkiness of sexuality and gender. I knew I was viewed as a boy. I knew I liked boys. I knew I felt like a girl. Like many young trans people, I hadn't learned terms like *trans*, *transgender*, or *transsexual*—definitions that would have offered me clarity about my gender identity. For example, a trans girl who is assigned male at birth and attracted to boys may call herself gay for a short time—a transitional identity on her road to self-discovery. In actuality, though, since her gender identity is that of a girl, and she is attracted to boys, then her sexual orientation mirrors that of a heterosexual girl, not a gay man.

Regardless, gay was foreign enough to my father—a proud black man raised in a Southern Baptist home—that I can't imagine proclaiming that I was trans would've put him at ease. For many parents, having a gay or lesbian child is a lot less daunting than having a trans child, especially in a culture where gay and lesbian people are increasingly becoming more accepted, whereas transgender people, especially trans women, are still stigmatized.

I didn't have answers for myself or my father, so I cried. I was hurt and afraid. By the time we got home to Denise's, Dad was talked out, and he wearily whispered to me, "Get in the bathroom."

I had pulled the vinyl polka-dot shower curtain back and begun taking off my shirt to prepare for my shower when Dad opened the door. He had a stool in one hand and his clippers in the other. I didn't see this coming, and cried harder in protest. Dad didn't say a word as he plugged his clippers into the outlet by the sink. I kept my eyes closed and opened them only when containing my tears stung. With the sound of each buzz, my curls fell against my bare shoulders and back before finding their way to the floor. When the buzzing stopped, the black-and-white-tiled floor was covered in tendrils and tears. The mirror reflected a hard truth: *You are a boy. Stop pretending.*

By the New Year, when every television was tuned to the proceedings of the O.J. Simpson trial, my curls had returned thicker and wilder. They were no longer silky, choosing to grow up rather than down and demanding more room. The only thing to tame them was Blue Magic grease, which I lathered on my hair after every shower, waking up with an oil-stained pillowcase and consistent dreams of Mom.

Though her phone calls and birthday cards halted after my eighth birthday, I held tight to the day that she'd rescue us. I extended blind optimism to Mom. I expected the best from her because my image of her, despite her actions, was untarnished. Instead of facing the reality of rejection, I made excuses for her: Mom was busy; she had a career; she just needed a little time to build a new life that would include me one day. My optimism won out in 1995 when Auntie Wee Wee's phone rang as the news commentators discussed the latest from the courtroom. "Baby, it's for you," she said with the widest smile.

"Hello?" I said into the receiver.

"Charles? It's Mom."

When I heard her voice, the opportunity for better emerged, and I immediately forgave her years-long absence because she was a dream come true. I can't remember what we talked about, but I remember the feeling that things would be better, that Chad and I would have the life we deserved. Auntie Wee Wee had gotten ahold of Mom through Grandma Pearl, who was listed by the operators in Honolulu. Our aunt didn't tell us about her search because she said she didn't want to get our hopes up. I realize now that she didn't trust Mom to follow through and call back; many on Dad's side of the family didn't understand how a woman could leave her children.

Abandoning us broke some golden rule in the motherhood guide, an invisible set of laws that they all silently abided by.

Over a series of conversations, I learned that Cori was eighteen and had two little girls. I learned that our baby brother, Jeffrey, was in kindergarten and couldn't wait to meet us. Most important, I learned that Mom wanted us back, something she and Dad would debate for months. Dad later told me that he fought hard to keep us but knew that Mom would give us the stability that we needed.

Dad didn't drink during the weeks leading up to our flight to Honolulu in May 1995. He didn't say much as he drove Chad and me to Dallas/Fort Worth International Airport, where they had two Continental tickets with our names on them.

The sun was shining through the windows of the gate, where we stood looking in awe at the plane that would take us to Mom. My anticipation of my reunion with her didn't allow me to think about how this move affected Dad or Chad. This moment was what I had dreamed of since the day Mom sent me to Oakland so I could have a proper male influence. I felt I had done my time and my move was long overdue. I thought Dad had taken his turn, done his part, and now it was Mom's shift. I didn't give my father much credit and didn't take his heartbreak into account.

As we were readying to board, Dad squatted down in front of us. He looked unblinkingly into our eyes; his were teary and sullen. "Y'all gotta take care of each other, man," he said. "And never forget that if you have no one, I mean no one in this world, that you feel loves you, remember that your dad will always love you."

He wrapped his arms around us, cradling us in his grasp. I kissed his ear and held on to him in a way I never had before, because I knew that this time, when I let go, I would run into the arms of my mother. My father bid farewell to us with a kiss as we followed the lady in the blue uniform and sensible pumps down the Jetway. Unknowingly, I would evolve beyond the boy he had raised and greet him nearly a decade later, in 2004, in that same airport, as my own woman, his daughter, at age twenty-one.

Dad would dance toward me with his golden grin, his contagious zest for life, and his new wife, Auntie Wee Wee, and Auntie Linda Gail and Uncle Bernard in tow—a welcome party designed to ease all apprehension.

"I told you I was bringing *everybody* to see *my* baby," he told me in my ear as he hugged me. "You *my* baby—no matter what."

Part
Two

All my life I had been looking for something, and everywhere I turned someone tried to tell me what it was. I accepted their answers too, though they were often in contradiction and even self-contradictory. I was naïve. I was looking for myself and asking everyone except myself questions which I, and only I, could answer. It took me a long time and much painful boomeranging of my expectations to achieve a realization everyone else appears to have been born with: that I am nobody but myself.

—RALPH ELLISON, *THE INVISIBLE MAN*

Chapter *Seven*

M y head rested in my mother's lap. She laid a hand on my hair, frizzy from the humidity of Hawaii. It had been more than five years since she had sent me away, since I had felt her. Now I was finally home. She smelled of plumeria blossoms in the sunshine. Her soft, steady breathing matched the lightness of her touch. My warm face rested on her bare olive-skinned thighs. She wore black high-waist denim Bongo shorts, the ones with large red-and-white letters blazoned on the back label, the kind I noticed all the girls wearing in Honolulu in 1995. Her hair was wavy except for her straight blown-out bangs, and lifted at the roots a bit, strategically covering her large ears, handed down from Papa, who was out on the lanai drinking beer with my uncles.

We lounged in the living room at Grandma's that first day in Ka'ahumanu Housing, where I had spent my early grade-school years on Oahu. Like Grandma Shellie's house, Grandma Pearl's was packed with family, elated to welcome Chad and me back. Mom and I sat on a twin daybed covered in a soft aloha-print quilt, perched above Chad and Jeff, who sat in reluctant brotherhood on the wicker love seat. They were feeling each other out. It would take a couple of months for them to find their groove, both battling for the role of baby in our family.

Mom was no longer a dream. She and Hawaii were real, beyond anything my twelve-year-old mind could imagine.

What's difficult about being from Hawaii is that everyone has a postcard view of your home. Hawaii lives vividly in people's minds, like the orange and purple hues of the bird-of-paradise flower. It's a fantasy place of sunshine and rainbows, of high surf and golden boys with golden hair, of pigs on a spit and hula dancers' swaying hips, of Braddah Iz's "Somewhere Over the Rainbow" and the North Shore, of hapa goddesses with coconut bras and Don Ho's ukulele.

Like the chalky, sweet taste of poi, Hawaii can be appreciated only from the locals' perspective. It's a special place, a melted and cooled lava rock in the middle of the Pacific Ocean, the anchor of Polynesia, once ruled by kings and queens before religious, military, and tourist occupation, a place where the people, those from the land and others, adopted and migrated, harvested sugarcane for little profit and created their own collective language (pidgin) and food (mixed plates) that became their portal to home, belonging, and fellowship.

Ages before Hawaii's sugar boom, voyagers from Tahiti left their home to see what was beyond the horizon. Navigating the seas in handcrafted canoes with the mere guidance of the stars, they arrived in Hawaii and created new lives. Centuries later, I landed in 1995, and it was here, on the island of Oahu, that I would mirror my ancestors on my own voyage, one guided through a system of whispers, to reveal the person I was meant to be. I will forever be indebted to Hawaii for being the home I needed. There is no me without Hawaii.

Our first home was on Owawa Street in Kalihi, where the sound of our neighbor's finicky rooster woke me every morning. With his full black tail and flaming reddish-gold feather mane, he'd call out to the world, his cock-a-doodle-doo met with the collective cackling of neighboring cocks. Their chorus shook our block awake, making it impossible to sleep past seven A.M. in our home, a shabby mustard-colored house that Mom rented from an elderly Filipino couple who lived on the ground floor.

I woke every day with red, itchy eyes and a runny nose, unknowingly allergic to the fragrant plants that surrounded us. Our neighborhood was not rural or rustic. It was urban, a heavily trafficked Likelike Highway away from Kamehameha Shopping Center on School Street, where I'd get formula or diapers for Cori at Long's Drugs, the place where I would later get busted for slipping clear nail polish and a bottle of remover in my pants in the eighth grade.

Many of the roosters on Owawa Street and other Filipino neighborhoods like ours were in training, living in makeshift wood and steel pens expertly hidden in backyards. The rooster behind our house had long since retired his spiked boxing mittens. He was cranky and omnipresent, clucking near us as we played or fought. He was there when I punched his owner in the face after hearing him call Chad and Jeff "niggers" while shooting hoops in his driveway. I was fiercely protective of my brothers in the seventh grade, adopting a persona that aligned with my goal to be the perfect son for Mom.

Many of our neighbors' houses were two-story McMansions, and there were always a few under construction. They were palatial pads, symbols of success for first-generation emigrants from the Philippines holding tight to the American dream. The blocks were overrun with columns and balconies and etchings in marble and gurgling fountains where mongooses would splash around and large driveways that could hold a hundred-plus people on first-birthday or graduation celebrations.

Still, Kalihi was all potholes and *pansit*s, plumerias and *paifalas*.

Walking up and down Gulick Avenue, I'd smell gardenias, lychees, and mango trees, and then I'd pass a house with pungent fish being fried by nanas at dinnertime. Our house wasn't as impressive as our neighbors', but it was packed as if it were just as spacious. Cori and her boyfriend—the one she ran away with at thirteen, returning pregnant with Britney a year later—lived in the room in the back. They had their own entrance and a sliding rattan door that separated it from the living room. I can still hear baby Rissa, Cori's second daughter, crying from her room while lying in mine. Rissa was the first baby I'd ever held and watched grow to become a young woman.

Chad, Jeff, and I shared the bedroom near Cori's, with a queen-size bed and a six-drawer chest that we split evenly, packed with polo shirts and denim shorts that Mom bought for us from JCPenney long before I started picking out my own clothes. Chad and I slept at the head of the bed, sharing a long body pillow, with Jeff in between us, his dirty feet occasionally kicking our faces. We had two jalousie windows framed by translucent white curtains that blew as the trade winds burst our way. I often looked through those jalousies as I ironed Mom's work outfits, a chore I took pride in completing every week. We got into a routine where she'd lay the silk shirts and print jersey dresses and polyester skirt suits she'd want for the week on the ironing board, which I always kept unfolded, and I'd display the freshly starched garments on her bed.

Mom's room had wood paneling that gave off a stagnant, just-opened-for-the-season cabin-like smell, which was apt, as she spent most of her nights at her boyfriend's house in Hawaii Kai, fifteen miles away on the eastern end of the island. This was a rude awakening to me. In my twelve-year-old brain, I thought that if I ironed her clothes, cut my hair, kissed a girl, threw a football, and made honor roll, then she'd come home more often.

Cori, barely twenty, was our stand-in mother, babysitter, and ringleader. With her teased bangs and ponytail (her hairstyle resembled that of a groomed shih tzu), my big sister was loving and loud, attentive and demanding. Despite the years of distance, the closeness I felt to Cori never faded; she was in all of the childhood photos from when Mom, Chad, Dad, and I were a family.

Cheraine was raised by Grandma Pearl and spent most of her time in Kaneohe, which was connected to Kalihi by the Likelike Highway. She was seventeen, independent, and guarded. She created a life of her own on the windward side of the island with her boyfriend's family, coming to town only if there was a birthday party or some other family gathering at Grandma Pearl's.

Chad, Jeff, Cori, the girls, and I would sit around as Cori's boyfriend smoked weed, and we'd watch every talk show that aired in the mid-nineties. *The Ricki Lake Show*, *The Jenny Jones Show*, *Sally Jessy Raphael*, and *The Montel Williams Show* were Cori's favorites. When I got home from school, *Ricki* would be on, and I'd giggle watching three-year-old Britney chanting, "Go Ricki, go Ricki, go Ricki!" bouncing her chunky legs in front of the TV as if she were singing the *Barney* "I Love You" song. The only time I had control over the TV was in the mornings, when Chad, Jeff, and I would watch *Sailor Moon*. We also watched *Poetic Justice*, *What's Love Got to Do with It*, and especially *Friday*, with Ice Cube and Chris Tucker, on repeat; everyone in the house rewatched the movie as if it were the very first time, gamely repeating lines ("You ain't got to lie, Craig. You ain't got to lie." "Puff, puff, give.").

When Cori was bored with the TV, she'd make Chad and Jeff wrestle, using their irritation with each other as fuel for entertainment. "You can lick him or what?" Cori would ask Jeff.

"Yeah, I not scared of him!" Jeff would say, all bones and bronze and bravado, though he was half a foot shorter than Chad. Jeff had Mom's sharp features and her crooked front teeth; one sported a green cavity right in the center. No other six-year-old could be as cute with a decaying grille.

"You all mouth, Jeff," Cori would cackle from the couch, her feet tucked under her butt. "You tink you so bad, ah?"

Chad would just shake his head. It was hard to get a rise out of him: I'd never seen him get aggressive over anything that didn't involve a ball and a goal. But there was something about the combativeness between them that got a rise out of Chad. No one could get him as pissed as Jeff. They were like that well into adulthood.

Jeff would sit next to Chad at this point, nudging him to fight. "Chad, you should just crack him already," Cori would instigate.

"Nah, I don't want to hurt him," Chad would say under his breath.

Then, boom, Jeff would smack Chad right in the face and they'd be on the floor wrestling, with Chad obviously dominating Jeff and Jeff fighting dirty, going for blood. All you'd hear would be Cori's cackles, high-pitched and piercing, as she stood up in her short denim overalls.

Like everyone else on the islands, we ate every meal with sticky steamed white rice, which we took turns cooking. I learned from Cori that you measured the water by placing your index finger on top of the uncooked rice and filling the pot with water until it touched the first line on your finger. She made us crispy Spam and Vienna sausages for breakfast, and pork chops, chicken long rice, and ahi poke for dinner, and bought us Jack in the Box burgers when we craved them. She was the best sister you could ask for, always wanting us around. Even when Mom decided to spend a Saturday or Sunday night at home with us, Cori was still the woman of the house. Though neither will admit it, Mom's longest-lasting, most functional relationship is the one she has with Cori.

When I think back on Owawa Street, my favorite memories are the sound of Cori's laugh and those viewings of *Friday* and the lazy afternoons when I'd lie in the family room, the oscillating fan humming on the floor and Rissa, just a baby then, lying on my flat chest. Her whimpering little breaths tickled my chin, and the newness of her existence overshadowed the newness I felt for Mom. My dreams of her yielded to a reality that proved I had gained much more than a mother.

Saturday mornings were a treat. Mom would pick Chad, Jeff, and me up at eleven in her silver Honda, and we'd drive to McDonald's, Burger King, or the Original Pancake House, where we'd get Portuguese sausage and eggs over rice drenched in soy sauce. Mom wasn't a big talker, but three kids craving a single parent's attention easily shattered silence. We'd argue over who got to ride shotgun, what movie we'd see at the Restaurant Row matinee, who'd hold the popcorn, and which two would flank Mom in the dark.

After breakfast and a matinee (I can recall the twisted nightmares I had after watching the gritty thriller *Se7en* one afternoon), we'd shop for bargains at JCPenney or Ross. Mom loved a good deal and was one of those people who could browse sale racks for hours; this was a pastime I inherited. I glowed as her assistant, perusing racks and showing her shirts or dresses I thought she'd like for their price. She'd let me hold what she found as Chad and Jeff made up games while finding a seat by the dressing rooms.

As we drove home in the late afternoon with new clothes, I'd be filled with angst. I would cross my fingers, hoping that she'd turn off the engine when we arrived in our driveway. The parked car meant we'd see her in the morning and she'd drive us to school, a rare treat. If she left the ignition running, we wouldn't see her until midweek, when she'd come home to give us Manapua Truck money and grab the change of clothes I left on her always-made bed.

What stays with me about that first year in Hawaii is that Mom did everything "right" despite her absence. She enrolled Jeff in his school's A-Plus after-school program and Chad in Little League and basketball at the recreation center. She ensured that we had new clothes and ordered us stacks of school photos that we'd sign and give to Grandma and Papa and all our aunts and uncles. One of my brightest memories at the beginning of our life together was visiting the library with Mom, where she helped the three of us complete our library card applications. Though Chad and Jeff weren't into reading, I spent a lot of my free time in the stacks at the Kalihi-Palama library, just a few blocks from our house. I remember the exhilaration I felt in using that glossy red card and checking out all the *Goosebumps* serials I wanted, reading *The Giver* and *To Kill a Mockingbird*, and sneaking *Waiting to Exhale* into my bedroom. Mom got pleasure from seeing that I'd inherited her love of books.

Books were majestic to me—precious, even. I wanted shelves of them in my house when I grew up, just like Mom's. Now I see her stacks of books, like our movie dates, as an escape. Even when she was home, she'd lie in bed reading, indulging in other people's journeys and imaginings. Mom once told me she wanted to study English and be a writer when she was younger. She was a promising student near the top of her class (her shyness kept her from asserting herself), but her childhood was cut short, and so were her dreams, when she found out she was pregnant at sixteen by the troublemaker from the special ed classes—the one boy who asked her out.

I couldn't imagine what it would be like to be five months pregnant, scared, and only sixteen; to walk up to your mother as she cleaned the dishes from dinner and tell her, your heart beating, that you were having a baby with a boy whom you knew was unworthy of you, the daughter your parents thought would do "big things." Mom said she thought Grandma would yell at her, call her a dumb-ass, and kick her out. She imagined the worst, so she was surprised when Grandma told her, "We need to go doctor, yeah. Make sure you're healthy." Mom said that loving reaction from Grandma was pivotal, a moment she looked back on with love decades later when her first-born daughter, pregnant at just fifteen, reached out to her. I believe Mom used that same moment with me when I reached out to her in my own moment of revelation at our kitchen table.

Grandma Pearl grew up on the windward side of Oahu, where the island curves before it meets the oft-photographed North Shore. She was the baby girl in a family of thirteen kids. She eventually moved to town and married Papa Arthur, a rambunctious, resourceful, big-eared boy who had grown up with an absent, party-girl mother in downtown Honolulu. In May 1959, they had my mother, Elizabeth, who grew up in public housing with her five younger siblings. Mom said the eldest three had a different experience with my grandparents than the younger ones, citing Papa's youthful bravado and taste for alcohol as the main reasons for those turbulent years. Papa, a former marine turned unionized city employee who drove a street sweeper along the curbs of Honolulu, worked hard and played hard.

Papa could be jovial one moment and brooding the next. You just never knew what you were going to get. Mom would tell us, "Stay out of Papa's way." Beyond his mood swings, he had a raunchy sense of humor. He relentlessly tried to get Grandma (or, as he lovingly called her, "The Hawaiian") into bed. He used to stick his right index finger into a hole he created with his other hand and wink at me, trying to get Grandma's attention. He was inappropriate but happy and horny, and Grandma would just roll her eyes, telling him, "Shut up, baboose!" He rarely called Jeff by his name, instead referring to him as "Chimp," which pissed Mom off.

"That motherfucker was so racist. How offensive is that?" Mom said to me in reflection. I could feel the rage she'd held in all those years. She had a strained relationship with Papa, one that would mirror itself in her messy lineup of love interests, including my father, whose blackness definitely widened the wedge between her and her father.

Though we came from our native Hawaiian mother, Chad and I were perceived and therefore raised as black, which widely cast us as outsiders, nonlocals—and being seen as local in Hawaii was currency. When we first returned to Oahu, we spoke with a Texas twang that also got us teased. Chad has strong emotions surrounding those first few months; he was traumatized by his apparent blackness, which was a nonevent in Dallas and Oakland, where we were among many black kids. In Hawaii, we were some of the few mixed black kids around. And both our parents taught us that because the world would perceive us as black, we were black.

That didn't erase the unease I felt when the kids in the housing complex took notice of our darkness and kinky hair. Skin color wasn't necessarily the target as much as our blackness was the target for teasing. I say this because the kids who teased us were as brown as us, but we were black. There was a racial order that existed even in this group of tweens. They teased that Chad and I were *popolo*, Hawaiian slang for black people. *Popolo* are shiny berries that grow in clusters in the islands and are so black that they shine purple on branches. Hearing *popolo* on that playground didn't sound as regal as its namesake berries. It sounded dirty, like something that stuck on our bodies, like the red dirt of the playground. I craved belonging, especially to be reflected in my mother and her family, local-bred Hawaiian people, and spent my earlier years trying to separate from my blackness. I've since learned that I can be both black and native Hawaiian despite others' perceptions and their assertion that I must choose one over the other.

Ethnicity is a common part of conversations in Hawaii. Two questions locals ask are: "What high school you went?" and "What you?" Your high school places you on the island, shedding light on your character and where you are from. "What you?" refers to your people, whom you come from, what random mixture has made you.

Jeff, whose father was also black, was perceived as Hawaiian, taking after Mom's side, looking like those bronze-skinned local boys who surfed and threw shaka signs at Sandy Beach. Jeff later told me that he didn't even know he was black until he was about eight because he didn't look it and barely knew his father beyond the two-hundred-dollar monthly checks Mom received throughout his childhood.

Quickly, Chad and I assimilated as best as we could, speaking pidgin like the local kids on the playground, though Mom couldn't stand the sound of it. Pidgin is the language of the islands, not to be confused with the Hawaiian language of the indigenous people. Mom rejected pidgin as "broken English," but it was hard to dismiss because it was the tongue of the people, created by the people. The sugar plantation laborers who were brought to the islands in the nineteenth century from China, Portugal, Japan, and the Philippines slowly created a common language out of their varying tongues, a hodgepodge of Hawaiian, Japanese, Portuguese, English, and Cantonese. It was a tool of resistance that allowed the plantation workers to communicate without the mediation of the English-speaking haole (a Hawaiian term for someone who is foreign, particularly white, and not of the islands) plantation owners.

Looking back on my return to Hawaii makes me think about what family has come to mean to me. In Hawaii, family showed itself in the way that my siblings and I never dared to call one another "half" anything. We were fully brothers and sisters. Family appeared in the pile of rubber slippers and sandals that crowded the entrance to everyone's home; in the kisses we gave when we greeted one another and said good-bye; in the graceful choreography of Grandma hanging the laundry on the clothesline; in the inclusiveness of calling anyone older *auntie* or *uncle* whether or not they were relatives; in the sound of Papa and Uncle Junior and Uncle Toma's empty beer cans bouncing against the grass; in the way all the folks in Ka'ahumanu Housing remembered Chad and me despite all those years away.

No one knew where I'd been, knew about Keisha, or had heard Dad's incessant complaints about my femininity. There was freedom in a clean slate, in new beginnings, in being able to leave the past behind and start anew. I vowed silently to be the good son I thought Mom wanted. I would leave my swishiness behind, I would play catch with Chad and the boys in the park, I would pretend to be into girls, I would keep my hair short, I would do well in school. If I did these things, then Mom would never send me away again, I told myself. I could stay with her right here forever.

On the road toward self-revelation, we make little compromises in an effort to appease those we love, those who are invested in us, those who have dreams for us. Those people tend to be our parents. I didn't want to be without my mother. I wanted her to be happy, and I believed I could make her happy if I were the kid she'd always wanted, the one who stopped all the girlie stuff that had angered my father for years. Mom never asked me to butch up; I just did it, and the world reacted differently. I noticed a shift in how other kids treated me. The teasing that I had endured in Oakland and Dallas stopped. The name-calling that I had grown desensitized to came to a halt. There was no longer a target on my back, and for once, it felt good to be invisible, even if I was masked by untruth.

Hiding myself for that brief period allowed me to operate under a guise of normality that made me feel temporarily secure. For many trans people, the pretending can last months, years, even decades; no two people have the same journey, yet a common fear threads us: *Being who I really am will lead to rejection.* Concealing who you are warps your sense of self and heightens feelings of hopelessness about ever being able to be your true self. A defeatist feeling loomed over me, telling me that no one would ever understand and accept me. I began believing that people, including my family and friends, would be disgusted by me, and these new belief systems anchored in the shame that I internalized from the world around me led to further isolation. It's no surprise that trans people are more likely to struggle with depression, suicidal thoughts and actions, substance abuse, and a wide range of self-harming behaviors that make it that much more difficult to live healthy, thriving lives.

Thankfully, suicidal thoughts were not part of my journey, though feelings of isolation and hopelessness followed me. In rare moments of self-reflection, when I faced no one but myself, I dropped the mask. I didn't have the words to define what I saw or who I was, but I recognized *me* and often chose to dismiss her with the one question that pushed me to put the mask back on: *Who will ever love you if you tell the truth?*

Chapter *Eight*

Wendi's first words to me were "Mary! You *mahu*?"

I was sitting on a park bench as Jeff ran around with his friends on the lawn that separated my school from his. Wendi was passing by with her volleyball in hand, her backpack bouncing on her butt, and her drive-by inquiry in the air. Though there was definitely a question mark floating around, her direct yet playful approach made me internalize her words as a statement. *If she's asking—even kiddingly—then I must be suspect*, I thought.

Everyone took notice of Wendi. She was hard to miss, prancing around Kalakaua Intermediate School in super-short soccer shorts, with her green mop of hair vibrantly declaring her presence. Subtlety was not—and still isn't—her thing. Her irritated red skin, peppered with acne, glistened with sweat as she played volleyball on campus. I'd never been this close to her, and her scrutinizing stare was intimidating.

Jeff, whom I picked up every day after school while Chad was at basketball or baseball practice, wasn't paying attention, but I remember feeling self-conscious. I was afraid that if I got close to Wendi or someone saw me interacting with her, I would be called *mahu*—a word that I equated to *sissy*. In my playground experience with the term, it was an epithet, thrown at any boy who was perceived to be *too* feminine. Until Wendi crossed paths with me, I was under the impression that I was doing a good job at being butch enough that such words wouldn't be thrown my way.

I was afraid that Wendi had seen me, but beneath that fear of being visible was a sense of belonging that thrilled me. I recognize now that her stopping to ask, "You *mahu*?" (though I would later learn she didn't identify as such) was her attempt at finding others like her—a connection I wasn't ready to make. I gave her a scrunched, crumpled expression resembling adamant denial, which made her roll her eyes and prance away.

At the time, *mahu* was limited by our Western interpretation, mostly used as a pejorative. What I later learned in my Hawaiian studies classes in college was that *mahu* defined a group of people who embodied the diversity of gender beyond the dictates of our Western binary system. *Mahu* were often assigned male at birth but took on feminine gender roles in Kanaka Maoli (indigenous Hawaiian) culture, which celebrated *mahu* as spiritual healers, cultural bearers and breeders, caretakers, and expert hula dancers and instructors (or *Kumu*s in Hawaiian). In the Western understanding and evolution of *mahu*, it translates to being transgender in its loosest understanding: to cross social boundaries of gender and/or sex. Like that of Hawaii's neighboring Polynesian islands, *mahu* is similar to the *mahu vahine* in Tahiti, *faʻafafine* in Samoa, and *fakaleiti* in Tonga, which comes from the Tongan word *faka* (meaning "to have the way of") and *leiti* (meaning "lady"). Historically, Polynesian cultures carved an "other" category in gender, uplifting the diversity, span, and spectrum in human expression.

To be *mahu* was to occupy a space between the poles of male and female in precolonial Hawaii, where it translated to "hermaphrodite," used to refer to feminine boys or masculine girls. But as puritanical missionaries from the West influenced Hawaiian culture in the nineteenth century, their Christian, homophobic, and gender binary systems pushed *mahu* from the center of culture to the margins. *Mahu* became a slur, one used to describe male-to-female transgender people and feminine men who were gay or perceived as gay due to their gender expression. Despite *mahu's* modern evolution, it was one of the unique benefits of growing up in a diverse place like Hawaii, specifically Oahu (which translates to "the gathering place"), where multiculturalism was the norm. It was empowering to come of age in a place that recognized that diversity existed not only in ethnicities but also in gender. There was a level of tolerance regarding gender nonconformity that made it safer for people like Wendi and me to exist as we explored and expressed our identities.

The first person I met who took pride in being *mahu* was my hula instructor at school. Kumu Kaua'i was one of those *mahu* who reclaimed her place in society—specifically, being celebrated in the world of hula, where the presence and talent of *mahu* was valuable. Some trans women, who actively engaged in restoring native Hawaiian culture, reclaimed *mahu* at that time, choosing to call themselves *mahuwahine* (*wahine* is Hawaiian for "woman"), just as some people in marginalized communities reclaimed formerly derogatory words like *dyke, fag, nigger, queer,* and *tranny*. It was theirs to claim, use, and uplift. Kumu didn't call herself a woman or gay despite her femininity and preference for *she* and *her* as pronouns. She simply identified as *mahu* and had no qualms about the vessel she was given and nor any desire to change it.

Kumu had long, bushy black hair that waved all the way to her behind, which she draped in bright floral-print *pareo*s or *lavalava*

103

(wraparound skirts). I marveled at the unique ways she wrapped her *pareo*s around her neck, letting the lush fabric flow over her rotund belly to her long, thick legs. Her skin was the color of coconut husks (a combination of her Hawaiian-Filipino-Chinese ancestry), her nose was broad, and her eyes were framed by thin high-arched brows that curved fiercely, mirroring the sway of her hips when she showed us how to *'ami* and *'uwehe.*

"Soft hands," she would gently instruct our small *hula halau* (Hawaiian for "dance troupe"). "You must always offer the gods *soft*, graceful hands. Don't stomp the land like you're mad! Be gentle and gracious. This dance is our offering to the gods, thanking them for everything."

Kumu bewildered me initially because I had been raised within the strict confines of male and female. This was a far cry from football Sundays with Dad in the projects. I was shaken by the dissonance of bright floral dresses and long hair on the form of a male-bodied person, someone who expressed her femininity proudly and visibly. Adding to that was the regular presence of Kumu's "husband," a tall, masculine man who appeared Samoan in stature and looks. He would pick up Kumu at the end of our practices, affectionately kissing her and helping her load the truck with the hula instruments—the *ipu* (a drum gourd) and *'ili'ili* (set of smooth black stones)—that she brought for us to dance with. I now realize that my fascination with Kumu wasn't that she puzzled me; I was in awe. She resonated with me at age twelve as I yearned to explore and reveal who I was. With time, I accepted Kumu's own determination of gender and learned to evolve past my ironic need to confine her to the two boxes I had been raised to live within. Kumu Kaua'i, like *mahuwahine* who came before, staked a given righteous place in Hawaii by uplifting, breeding, and spreading many aspects of native Hawaiian culture, specifically through hula. Kumu taught me, this mixed plate of a kid, how to mirror the movements of my ancestors and give thanks for the island culture that respected various other identities.

Wendi similarly captivated me because she refused to be jailed by anyone's categories or expectations. There was no confining this girl. I noticed her everywhere after our brief exchange, during which she recognized something in me that I thought I had expertly hidden behind buzz cuts and polo shirts. I took note of her slamming her volleyball at recess, whipping her flamboyant bob around campus, carrying her black flute case as she sashayed to band practice. What still stuns me about Wendi is that no one tolerated her. She was not something to be tolerated. She was accepted as fact, just as one would accept the plumpness of the lunch ladies or the way Auntie Peggy, the counselors' secretary, would grab your palm as you waited for a meeting and read you your future (I recall her telling me, "You're going to get married in white!"). Wendi's changing hues, her originality, her audacity to be fully herself, was embraced and probably even more respected at an age when the rest of us were struggling and striving to fit in.

I refuse to pretend, though, that her uniqueness didn't make her a target. Wendi was called *faggot* at recess and asked when she was going to get her sex change. She used such ignorance as ammunition, threatening to kiss the boys who sought to humiliate her. I wasn't as daring as Wendi, and looking at her I was frightened by what I saw: myself. I told no one about her calling me *mahu* at the swings and avoided her as her long legs in her rolled-up shorts and knee-high socks glided past me in the halls.

Instead, I became all the more unwavering in my commitment to being the good son that year. I didn't put up a fight when it came to haircuts at the beauty school that offered barber discounts. I earned awards for my academic performance in class, was bumped into advanced courses, and even worked as an editor for the yearbook and the quarterly newspaper. My teachers praised and encouraged me, and in the spring of 1996, I was inducted into the National Junior Honor Society. I was the only boy from our class to be inducted. I loved the distinction of *only*, though the boy part I could've done without.

At our induction ceremony, Mom, Chad, Jeff, Cori, and the girls sat in the audience as I received my certificate and posed for pictures with Mr. Higa, my counselor and our NJHS faculty adviser, and the rest of the girls, who surrounded me in white dresses. I wore a white button-down shirt with black slacks and my knockoff Timberland boots. This was around the time when I began parting my shorn curls at the side, resembling what I imagined was a Halle Berry–esque hairdo, a haircut that Cori loved to tease: "You look like Gumby!" All teasing was aside that day as I beamed in our school library with its gray carpet and rows of books and encyclopedias and Hawaiian quilts hanging on the wall. My family sat in the brown metal foldout chairs, listening to our rendition of Celine Dion's "Because You Loved Me."

That same year, I had my first and only girlfriend for a couple of weeks. We met in Mr. Wong's social studies class, where she sat behind me, wearing gray contact lenses that made her sharp eyes look catlike and a short haircut that complemented her petite frame. Like the majority of kids in Kalihi, she was Filipino. I adored her. We spoke on the phone regularly as friends, and then all of a sudden I was her "boyfriend," something instigated and encouraged by our peers, since we hung out so much. I reluctantly went along with it, carrying the title for those two weeks because she made me appear normal. I didn't want to stick out like Wendi, who would enter my every day during the second half of seventh grade, when we had band class together.

I played tuba, she the flute and piccolo. I was envious of her compact, feminine instrument. We both were first chair of our sections, she swaying noticeably to her own sound. Early in the spring semester, Wendi sat near me one day as the room emptied and I wiped the saliva out of my mouthpiece. Her closeness made me nervous, just like the first time she asked whether I was *mahu*, because I worried others would think we were friends. I knew I could be called out by association, but something about that day made me not care.

"I'm going to the gym to play volleyball," she said. "Like come?"

It was another invitation to connect; she was subtle this time. I think she knew it would take baby steps for me to be as out there as she was, and I knew that denying her would mean denying myself. I nodded discreetly, and volleyball became the foundation of our relationship. On the hot cement courts behind our school, Wendi taught me to bump, set, and spike, which was a feat, because I was about four inches shorter than she was at the time. I approached the ball with confidence and sass despite my height, and I even hit the ball with my head snapping at the exact moment my open palm hit the ball, just like Wendi. It was a flamboyant habit that my high school coach would later drill me to unlearn.

Wendi and I grew inseparable through middle school, a bond that would link us for the rest of our lives. Through association, my classmates learned that I was like Wendi—who hadn't yet adopted any labels to describe her shifting self. I was fortunate to meet someone just like me at such a young age. It was empowering to see myself reflected in her, and I rapidly shifted in her presence. I began dressing like her, shopping at Savers, the thrift store at Dillingham Plaza, scoring soccer shorts and vintage T-shirts. Wendi shopped with a stapler and staple remover to swap price tags according to the day's color-coded half-off specials. If blue tags were half off, we'd shop for what we wanted, then hunt for garments with blue tags, removing them with the staple remover and restapling the tags to our garments.

"Sickening, yeah?" Wendi would snap as we giddily skipped out of the thrift store, swinging our white plastic bags filled with donated clothes for just under twenty dollars.

We became a regular sight on Gulick Avenue, prancing up and down that main road in Kalihi from her two-bedroom apartment, where she lived with her grandparents, to my house on Owawa Street. What strikes me now is that no one in my family raised an eyebrow when Wendi came to our house. Mom didn't pull me aside and have a talk with me about my friend. Cori never teased me or Wendi. Chad and Jeff were nothing but cordial, gamely sleeping in the living room so Wendi and I could have the room all to ourselves. Wendi quickly became a regular, welcomed presence in my house. A part of me believes that I brought her around at a time when I was reluctant to vocalize who I was. Her presence allowed me to show another layer of my identity to my family. Their nonchalance helped rebut my fears of rejection.

My baby brother, Jeff, who was only seven at the time, later confessed that he was "confused" by Wendi's flamboyance and even more "confused" by my evolution. "You were always different," he later told me, citing that when he heard he had two older brothers, he thought Mom had misspoken because he'd seen a boy and a girl with wild curly hair get off the plane.

"You were never like Chad and me," he said. "You never wanted to do the things that we liked to do." Jeff even recalled an incident (that I don't remember) when I was picking him up from school. A group of boys at the recreation center asked him how he felt about his brother becoming his sister. Jeff's memory strikes me because I think my growing confidence and self-assuredness under the light of my friendship with Wendi blocked memories of the verbal brutality thrown our way.

As I look back, what impresses me about my family is their openness. They patiently let me lead the way and kept any confusion or worry to themselves during a fragile period in my self-discovery. I recognize this as one of the biggest gifts they gave me. On some level, I knew they were afraid for me, afraid that I would be teased and taunted. Instead of trying to change me, they gave me love, letting me know that I was accepted. I could stop pretending and drop the mask. My family fortified my self-esteem, which I counted on as I embarked on openly expressing my rapidly evolving self.

Reflecting on this pivotal time in my life, I think of the hundreds of thousands of LGBTQ (lesbian, gay, bisexual, transgender, queer or questioning) youth who are flung from intolerant homes, from families who reject them when they reveal themselves. Of the estimated 1.6 million homeless and runaway American youth, as many as 40 percent are LGBTQ, according to a 2006 report by the Task Force and the National Coalition for the Homeless. A similar study by the Williams Institute cited family rejection as the leading cause of the disproportionate number of homeless LGBT youth. These young people are kicked out of their homes or are left with no choice but to leave because they can't be themselves. That's something both Wendi and I fortunately never faced.

With an air of acceptance at home, it was fairly easy to approach my mother and declare my truth. Sitting at our kitchen table, I told Mom, with no extensive planning or thought, "I'm gay." I was thirteen years old and didn't know how to fully explain who I was, conflating gender identity and sexuality. What I remember about that brief exchange was Mom's warmth. She smiled at me, letting me know that it was okay. I felt loved and heard and, more important, not othered. From her lack of reaction—her brows didn't furrow, her brown irises didn't shift from side to side—I felt as if I had announced that I had on blue today, a simple fact that we were both aware of. Mom later told me that she remembers feeling afraid for me because she sensed that there was more I wanted to say but didn't know how to. "My love for you never diminished, but a part of me was scared that people would hurt you, and that is what I had a hard time with," she told me recently.

A part of me was scared, too. I couldn't acknowledge the gender stuff because I didn't have a full understanding of it. Saying "I think I am a girl" would have been absurd for many reasons, including my fear that it would be a lot for my mother to handle. I didn't know that trans people existed; I had no idea that it was possible for thirteen-year-old me to become my own woman. That was a fantasy.

But no matter how incomplete my revelation to my mother was, I felt freer and began openly expressing my femininity under the grooming of my best friend. On a throw pillow in Wendi's lap, I rested my head as she tweezed my eyebrows on her grandmother's plastic-covered couch. I held an ice cube to my swollen eye, trying to numb the stinging pain.

"You wanna look good, right?" she asked as I flinched from her tweezers. "Now I gotta make these even."

As she studied the curve of my brows, I felt them getting thinner with each sting. Wendi claimed she knew what she was doing, and I didn't doubt her skills because she excelled at everything, from volleyball and flute to beauty, her latest obsession. Wendi was unwaveringly authoritative; she'd read something in a magazine or a Kevyn Aucoin book, and suddenly, she was an expert. I accepted her as nothing less. I also didn't doubt her because I trusted her. The tweezing was my first experience of intimacy with another person, and it foreshadowed our current professional roles, with Wendi serving as my makeup artist for photo shoots and TV appearances.

Wendi's bedroom was sponge-painted purple, black, and white, and her grandparents gave her the freedom to be who she was, despite neighbors who referred to her as *bakla* (Tagalog for "sissy," "gay," or "fag"). She had a bunch of male underwear catalogs that she stacked atop her white dresser. She didn't hide anything.

We'd stay up late talking about everything and nothing, the only way two people eager to know each other can. I have never been as open as I was in those first few months of my discovering friendship with Wendi. I had butterflies about having found someone like me with whom I didn't have to explain anything. I was fearless about sharing myself with her. Wendi was the first person I told about Dad's crack addiction, about the disappointment of my mother's absence and her preference for men over me, about the times Derek had made me blow him. She in turn told me things she had never told anyone.

Wendi (I've known her only as Wendi; given names and "before" photos are irrelevant in our friendship) grew up in Kaneohe with her mother, who, like her father, struggled with meth addiction. I remember her giggling at her younger self when she told me she lost her virginity at eleven to a playmate a few years older than she was. "Girl, I was such an itchy queen!" she told me in reflection, adding that she'd been attracted to boys for as long as she could remember. There was never a point in her life when she pretended to be anything other than who she was. "That's a waste of time," she said. "And, girl, you were not fooling anybody, trying to be butch. I clocked you right away."

For as long as I've known Wendi, she's been unapologetic about who she is. I can see her clearly at six years old, snatching her cousin's pink one-piece bathing suit and proclaiming, "I'm a girl! I'm ovah!" Wendi told me she remembers older *mahu* who frequented her family's flower shop. "They were tall, with long hair, and wore *pareos*," she said. "But, girl, you could clock them right away. I didn't want to look like that!" When she learned that her mother was having an affair with a neighbor, cheating on her stepfather, whom she adored, Wendi said it was easy for her—at only eleven—to make the decision to run away, taking the bus across town to her paternal grandparents' home in Kalihi, where she sought refuge and stability. "I knew that I wanted to transform without interruptions," she laughed. "And grandparents are always easy." Her Filipino grandparents took her in with no complaints about her femininity or the girls' world that she had created for herself.

It was in Wendi's room that I heard about hormones. She mentioned them as if discussing milk, something you had to drink in order to grow. She told me the older girls she knew ("These fierce, unclockable bitches!") went to a doctor in Waikiki who prescribed hormones for girls as young as sixteen. "I'm going to get my shots down when I turn sixteen," Wendi, who was fourteen at the time, said with excitement. "Trust."

I knew about hormones and puberty and safe sex from the handouts Coach Richardson gave us in health and physical education class. On Tuesdays and Thursdays, he'd lecture us about how we were raging with hormones, changing the shape and feel of our bodies. I felt nothing, barely five-two and a little chunky in the face and thighs; puberty hadn't really touched me. But I noticed the suppleness of the girls in class, the ones who seemed to be towering over many of us in height and shape. They began to separate from the pack swimming way behind in the puberty kiddie pool.

"Your grandparents are going to let you do that?" I asked Wendi, stunned.

"They don't know what *that* is and can barely speak English," she said matter-of-factly. "My aunt's gonna take me."

I trusted that she would do exactly as she said she would, and I admired her unstoppable determination. Wendi's friendship gave me the audacity to be noticed. One morning after one of our beauty experiments, I walked into student council homeroom with arched brows that framed my almond-shaped eyes, which were sparkling with a brush of silver eye shadow that Wendi said no one would really notice because it was "natural-looking." The girls in class, the ones who wore the white SODA platform wedge sneakers I so coveted, said, "I like your makeup." I remember tucking my short curls behind my ears, beaming under the gaze my new look warranted.

One early evening after playing volleyball, Wendi and I visited a group of her friends in a reserved room at the recreation center. They were rehearsing for a show they did at Fusions, a gay club on Kuhio Avenue in Waikiki. Most of them were drag queens, but a select few were trans women who performed as showgirls. Society often blurs the lines between drag queens and trans women. This is highly problematic, because many people believe that, like drag queens, trans women go home, take off their wigs and chest plates, and walk around as men. Trans womanhood is not a performance or costume. As Wendi likes to joke, "A drag queen is part-time for showtime, and a trans woman is all the time!"

The lines continue to be blurred due to the umbrella term *transgender,* which bundles together diverse people (transsexual, intersex, genderqueer, drag performers, crossdressers, and gender-nonconforming folks) living with gender variance. Unfortunately, the data on the transgender population is scarce. The U.S. Census Bureau doesn't ask about gender identity, how trans people self-identify varies, and many (if asked) may not disclose that they're trans. The National Center for Transgender Equality has estimated that nearly 1 percent of the U.S. population is transgender, while the Williams Institute has stated that 0.3 percent of adults in the United States (nearly seven hundred thousand) identify as transgender, with the majority having taken steps to medically transition. This number does not take into account the number of transgender children or individuals who have expressed an incongruity between their assigned sex and gender identity or gender expression.

Despite the misconceptions, I understood the distinction between a drag queen and a trans woman because I came of age in the
mid-nineties, and drag queens were in vogue. There was the 1995 release of *To Wong Foo, Thanks for Everything! Julie Newmar.* I hated that
movie because Wendi would tease that Noxeema Jackson—Wesley
Snipes's drag character—was my "Queen Mother." Drag queens were
on Cori's favorite talk shows, *Sally* and *Jerry Springer*, and then there
was RuPaul, "Supermodel of the World." It was a time when a brown,
blond, and glamorous drag queen was a household name, beaming
on MAC Cosmetics billboards at the mall in shiny red latex.

Like RuPaul, the queens at the rec center staked their claim on a
smaller scale in Hawaii, part of the fabric of Oahu's diverse trans community. Toni Braxton's "Unbreak My Heart" was blasting from a boom
box, and they were huddled together, about ten of them, discussing
their choreography. I watched, seated on the cold tile floor with my
backpack and volleyball at my side. They soon reconfigured, gathering in a circle of arms as one woman knelt at the center, hidden by
the fort of mostly rotund queens. With the tape rewound, each queen
walked clockwise, slowly descending into a kneeling position as the
lady in the center rose, lip-synching Toni's lyrics.

The lady had long, full wavy hair that served as a backdrop to
her curvy body. She gracefully moved her head to the lyrics, basking
in the glow from the yellow-tinted lightbulb directly above her. Her
deep-set brown eyes, magnified by a pair of full false lashes, looked
straight ahead, stoic, almost numb, mirroring the turmoil of an unbearable heartbreak. She was a diva among a moving mass of chorus
queens who appeared blurred; only she was in focus.

"Tracy's ovah, yeah," Wendi whispered at me, snapping her finger.
"You can't even clock her!"

I want to be her, I thought, half nodding to Wendi, speechless and
captivated. I was excited and afraid of my silent revelations. Though

she didn't look it, I knew Tracy had been born like us. I knew she had wondered at night about how she was going to change. I knew she had climbed the insurmountable summit of trans womanhood. Unlike the queens she was performing with, Tracy was a woman of her own creation, and I was moved and on the verge of so many emotions that I was fragile when they stopped the tape and Wendi approached the group.

Lani, who wore a pair of knee-length denim shorts and a stretched white tank top with black bra straps visible on her shoulders, kissed Wendi on the cheek. I stood behind Wendi, looking at Lani's winged black eyeliner, which she had whipped all the way to a sharp point where it nearly intersected with her penciled-in brows. The other girls gathered around her when Wendi turned around to introduce me. They were the first trans women I had met outside of Wendi.

I extended my hand to Lani, and she pulled me to her fleshy chest and gave me a kiss on the cheek, which left a red lip print on my face. My heart was racing because they were staring at me. Tracy was standing off to the side, uninterested, brushing her hair. I could hear her raking through her mane, strands snapping with each stroke of her brush.

"Mary, she's fish, yeah," Lani said with a chuckle, holding me at arm's length by the biceps. The girls around her nodded. Then, looking directly into my eyes, she added, "You're going to be pretty, girl. Trust!"

I tried my best to smile, aware that she was giving me a compliment—blessing me, even. To Lani, my fishiness was something to boast about. To be called fish by these women meant that I was embodying the kind of femininity that could allow me access, safety, opportunity, and maybe happiness. To be fish meant I could "pass" as any other girl, specifically a cis woman, mirroring the concept of "realness," which was a major theme in *Paris Is Burning,* the 1990 documentary about New York City's ballroom community, comprising gay men, drag queens, and trans women of color. Ball legend Dorian Corey, who serves as the sage of the film, offering some of the most astute social commentary on the lived experiences of low-income LGBT people of color, describes "realness" for trans women (known in ball culture as femme queens) as being "undetectable" to the "untrained" or "trained." Simply, "realness" is the ability to be seen as heteronormative, to assimilate, to not be read as other or deviate from the norm. "Realness" means you are extraordinary in your embodiment of what society deems normative.

"When they can walk out of that ballroom into the sunlight and onto the subway and get home and still have all their clothes and no blood running off their bodies," Corey says in the film, "those are the femme *realness* queens."

Corey defines "realness" for trans women not just in the context of the ballroom but outside of the ballroom. Unlike Pepper LaBeija, a drag legend who said undergoing genital reconstruction surgery (GRS) was "taking it a little too far" in the film, a trans woman or femme queen embodies "realness" and femininity beyond performance by existing in the daylight, where she's juxtaposed with society's norms, expectations, and ideals of cis womanhood.

To embody "realness," rather than performing and competing "realness," enables trans women to enter spaces with a lower risk of being rebutted or questioned, policed or attacked. "Realness" is a pathway to survival, and the heaviness of these truths were a lot for a thirteen-year-old to carry, especially one still trying to figure out who she was. I was also unable to accept that I was perceived as beautiful because, to me, I was not. No matter how many people told me I was fish, I didn't see myself that way. My eyes stung, betraying me, and immediately I felt embarrassed by my visible vulnerability.

"Oh, hon, no worry," Tracy said, her brows furrowed in concern. "She never mean nothing by it."

"Sorry, babes," Lani said, pursing her lips emphatically. "I meant it as a compliment."

As Wendi and I walked out of the room, I could hear Toni Braxton singing, and I imagined Tracy rising from the sea of queens.

"How come you cried, Mary?" Wendi said, confused by my emotion. It was the first time I had cried in front of her. I'd learn with time that expressing vulnerability or sentiment made Wendi defensive, uncomfortable. In all the years of our friendship, I've never seen her break down or her eyes well up with emotion.

"They were all staring at me, like they expected something from me, you know?" I said. "It just made me uncomfortable."

"Mary! Life is uncomfortable," Wendi said, rolling her eyes as she remained focused on the dark streets ahead of us. "You have to get used to it or you're going to live your life trying to make people comfortable. I don't care what people say about me because they don't have to live as me. You gotta own who you are and keep it moving."

I pushed myself to stay in step with Wendi's long-legged stride. She didn't have a stroll in her. I reluctantly let her words soak into my skin, like the tears that watered the conversation. We remained in silence for the rest of our walk home. When we reached Gulick Avenue, she leaned in and her cheek met mine. Then she spread her arms around me and squeezed. She turned around swiftly and crossed the street at King and Gulick. I stood on that corner for about thirty seconds, watching her backpack bounce on her behind as she headed home.

With Wendi at my side, I felt I could be bold, unapologetic, free. To be so young and aiming to discover and assert myself alongside a best friend who mirrored me in her own identity instilled possibility in me. I could be me because I was not alone. The friendship I had with Wendi, though, is not the typical experience for most trans youth. Many are often the only trans person in a school or community, and most likely, when seeking support, they are the only trans person in LGBTQ spaces. To make matters worse, these support spaces often only address sexual orientation rather than a young person's gender identity, despite the all-encompassing acronym. Though trans youth seek community with cis gay, lesbian, bisexual, or queer teens, they may have to educate their cis peers about what it means to be trans.

When support and education for trans youth are absent, feelings of isolation and hopelessness can worsen. Coupled with families who might be intolerant and ill equipped to support a child, young trans people must deal with identity and body issues alone and in secret. The rise of social media and online resources has lessened the deafening isolation for trans people. If they have online access, trans people can find support and resources on YouTube, Tumblr, Twitter, and various other platforms where trans folks of all ages are broadcasting their lives, journeys, and even social and medical transitions. Still, the fact remains that local trans-inclusive support and positive media reflections of trans people are rare outside of major cities like Los Angeles, New York, Portland, San Francisco, and Seattle.

Recently, the media (from the *New Yorker* and the *New York Times* to ABC's *20/20* and *Nightline*) has focused its lens on trans youth. The typical portrait involves young people grappling with social transition at relatively young ages, as early as four, declaring that they're transgender and aiming to be welcomed in their communities and schools as their affirmed gender. As they reach puberty, these youth—with the support and resources of their welcoming families—undergo medical intervention under the expertise of an endocrinologist who may prescribe hormone-blocking medications that suppress puberty before graduating to cross-sex hormones and planning to undergo other gender affirmation surgeries.

To be frank, these stories are best-case scenarios, situations I hope become the norm for every young trans person in our society. But race and class are not usually discussed in these positive media portraits, which go as far as erasing the presence of trans youth from low-income communities and/or communities of color. Not all trans people come of age in supportive middle- and upper-middle-class homes, where parents have resources and access to knowledgeable and affordable health care that can cover expensive hormone-blocking medications and necessary surgeries. These best-case scenarios are not the reality for most trans people, regardless of age.

Certainly, this was not the reality for Wendi and me or the girls and women we would soon cross paths with in Honolulu.

Chapter *Nine*

C hin down, Mary. Hide that Adam's," Wendi said from behind her Kodak disposable camera. She wasn't reading; she was aiming to capture me at my best.

I smiled into the little round plastic lens, trying to keep my balance in her black platform heels. They were chunky and heavy and a size too small. I had grown a few inches over the summer, topping off at five-six at age fourteen, the same height as Wendi, with a size-ten foot, or, as Wendi would call it, "supermodel, supercanoe size."

Wearing her black wig, which she had cut into a sharp, angular Vidal Sassoon bob, and her black-and-white chevron-print halter pantsuit, I was *feeling* myself, and Wendi was cheering me on. She painted my face in bronzes and browns and tweezed the ends of my brows so she could have a wider shadow palette to work with. She didn't ask, she just did it. To this day, my brows are struggling to grow back in full.

"Arch your back and stick your butt out," Wendi said. I did as she instructed. "Yaaaasss, bitch! Stay just like that."

I glowed under her focus and creative direction. She consistently made me feel good about myself; it was the kind of relationship I now know to be rare, in which the other person wants to see you at your best. Wendi has always wanted me to shine beside her, not behind her.

Wendi was more comfortable behind the lens, behind the brush, behind the curling iron, even though she was one of the prettiest girls I knew. Wendi's black eyes were held in wide-set slanted lids that flanked her flat, wide nose. She called it "too Filipino for my taste" because she didn't have what she called an "elegant bridge," something she would later attain with the help of a plastic surgeon. She often wore her jet-black bra-strap-length hair in a ponytail to stay cool in the humidity, and she effortlessly maintained a yellowish-brown glow that most people can achieve only with a spray tan.

After using every click available, we booked it to Long's Drugs at Kam Shopping Center and dropped off the camera at the one-hour photo. We grabbed gravy fries at Kenny's and browsed Everblue Casuals to kill time. When we picked up the double prints, Wendi praised, "Oooh, bitch! You're serving it."

I sat, incredulous, with the photos. I loved my makeup, my hair, and my smile. But other features I hadn't taken note of before came into focus: shapely arms and shoulders that had developed from volleyball; a bubble butt that looked like Auntie Linda Gail's; a small, sharp Adam's apple playing peekaboo under my chin. There was no denying that my body was changing. Seeing the things I disliked made it hard to see the good. The photos became an image-shattering moment that birthed insecurity in me about my growing body. Most teenagers grapple with body image, but to be a pubescent trans girl with few resources to change what you don't like only magnifies the features that begin negating a mental self-image. It probably didn't help that the beauty standards I held myself to were rigid and impractical. Like most teen girls (whether they're trans or cis), I had a vision board of my ideal, pulled mostly from the pop-culture images that MTV fed me. I wanted Halle Berry's or Tyra Banks's breasts, Britney Spears's midsection, Beyoncé's curvy silhouette and long hair, and I prayed that I wouldn't grow any taller so I didn't tower over the petite Asian girls who were the barometer of beauty in the islands.

Holding myself to this impossible beauty standard led me to pick myself apart critically. The incessant comparing and measuring of my body and physical attributes against this ideal occupied my mind, and the chasm between my physical reality and the elusive ideal led to personal discontent. I was chasing an ideal that was separate from my personal appearance, and my preoccupation with this pursuit amplified the tick-tock of a clock alerting me daily that it would take only a couple of years for me to become a man, something I wanted to avoid at all costs. Though Wendi always said hormones were "not a miracle drug," I knew that starting them would mean the beginning of my *real* life.

"Promise not to show anyone, okay?" I said to Wendi, who nodded while studying the photos.

We were nearing the end of eighth grade, and I was frequently frustrated that I dressed basically the same as I did in seventh grade, while my best friend seemed to blossom under the blind eyes of her grandparents. Her hair was long, her jeans tight, her T-shirts snug. She'd come to school in the baby tees that all the girls were wearing with the platform sneakers I so envied.

Though my uniform wasn't quite as girlie as I wished, it leaned in bits and pieces toward my own femininity. I didn't have the independence Wendi had when it came to buying clothes. Everything I had I had to ask Mom to buy. When we went to Ala Moana, I'd ask her to get me Keroppi notebooks and pens at Sanrio Surprises. I'd try on jeans a size smaller in the dressing room and not show her, and she'd trust that they fit. But I always lost the hair battle. I remember the three haircuts I got in the eighth grade that absolutely broke my heart. When my "Halle Berry meets Gumby" hairstyle grew too bushy for Mom's taste, she would force me to sit in the barber's chair next to my brothers. With each haircut, I was reminded that I was nothing but a boy pretending to be something I was not. Mom couldn't handle tears, especially ones she created, so she did what she did best: ignored them.

It was a balancing act to express my femininity in a world that is hostile toward it and frames femininity as artifice and fake, in opposition to masculinity, which often represents "realness." I straddled the line of gender as well as I could and made concessions and compromises. I clutched tightly to my green Keroppi folders and my size-too-small jeans and my arched brows and, when I could grow my hair long enough, my side part. These elements, though small and insignificant to passersby, made up my girlhood, and I fought hard to ensure that they were seen.

My most prized possession was my lanyard of Lip Smackers. Mom bought my first one at Long's; it was green apple flavored. She thought nothing of buying me lip balm, and I remember snatching it out of the plastic shopping bag at checkout, afraid she'd realize what it was and return it. I tore it out of the confines of the paper package, which read, "All the flavor of being a girl." I balled the package in my fist, hiding it from her view. In the car, I draped the black lanyard around my neck with a single green plastic balm dangling. I proudly dangled my girlhood in all its fruitiness. It cost only $2.99.

As I was transitioning, our family was about to experience yet another change. I met Rick on that rare day when I came straight home from school because I didn't play volleyball, have band practice, or hang at Wendi's. I saw Mom lying on her bed with a bronze-skinned man who had a prominent underbite and brows in focused judgment. Mom hopped out of bed, and he followed her to me, just outside her room. "This is Rick," she said, looking to the man behind her, who stood about five-ten, with wide shoulders that made Mom look smaller than she was.

I said hi, and he said hi back. That was the extent of our interaction. He wasn't a talkative man. Going straight to Cori's, I asked if she knew who that was. Cori knew everything, the original *Gossip Girl.*

"Heeelloooo, dummy, that's my dad," she said, looking at me as if I was supposed to know that the man with the furrowed brow was her father.

"Why is he here?" I said.

"They're back together," she said nonchalantly, as if a twenty-year reunion with your high school sweetheart who gave you two adult children was not a head-scratching moment. I blamed Cori's desensitized delivery on the fact that she watched way too much *Maury* and *Jerry.*

"I'm confused," I said, wondering how it all had happened.

"Well, that wouldn't be da first time, Mary," she joked. Cori went on to explain that they had rekindled their romance after seeing each other at his mother's funeral. Cori claimed to have seen sparks flying, predicting their reunion. "Next thing you know, she grabbed all her stuff from Hawaii Kai, dumped her boyfriend, and now they can't get enough of each other," she said.

Rick soon moved in with us. He didn't have anything of his own because he had been in and out of jail since he was a teenager, arrested for everything from drug possession to petty theft. He was a crystal meth addict and a repeat offender who seemed at ease with having spent most of his life in prison, succumbing to the fact that he didn't know how to make it on the "outside." Mom had a bottomless capacity to forget and embrace, and I assumed that history bound them. The nostalgic fairy tale of rediscovering your first love was irresistible to my mother, and Rick knew this, feeding her illusion that maybe, just maybe, the man she first fell in love with at sixteen, the one who changed the trajectory of her life, was The One she was supposed to be with. This was their second chance.

Rick was no Prince Charming, though. He butted heads with nearly everyone in those first few months on Owawa Street. Chad and Jeff weren't too keen on having a sudden live-in Dad, and I wasn't about to be governed by another man; I had just escaped a home ruled by masculinity. I wasn't sacrificing the new set of rules I had so expertly worked to my own advantage.

"The little queen seems to be able to come in and out as he pleases," Rick said to Mom one night in the living room. I overheard them from my room. Not one to avoid confrontation, I walked out of my room and rolled my eyes at him.

"You get one problem?" he asked, walking toward me shirtless, his broad shoulders towering over me, blocking my view of Mom.

"It's okay," Mom said through a shaky smile, unnerved by the tension.

"Why is he always here?" I asked, assuming Mom was on my side.

"What'd you say, faggot?" Rick erupted in anger, waking the house and scaring the shit out of me. I hadn't been yelled at like that in my entire life. Jeff and Chad peered from the crack in our bedroom door, and Cori rushed out of her room. I looked to Mom to defend me. She said nothing, grabbing Rick by the arm as tears blurred my vision. They went into her room as *faggot* lingered in the air and my siblings looked on. It became clear to me that when I was six, she had sent me away for a man. It became clear to me that she hadn't spent time with us that whole first year back in Hawaii because she preferred being at her then boyfriend's house. And it became clear to me that she had chosen this convict over me. It was difficult to face the reality of my mother, someone I had seen as my heroine, the one who would save me. In fact, Mom had done nothing to deserve this dream-girl role in my childhood imaginings.

A few months later, I heard a crash in Cori's room and deep groans. Cori screamed, "Stop it!" Her daughters were crying. Her boyfriend and her father were tangled on the ground. That fistfight pushed Cori to finally move out on her own, choosing Kuhio Park Terrace, a large public housing complex down the street. Mom could no longer afford our three-bedroom house without Cori's share of the rent, so the rest of us relocated to Salt Lake, a nearby suburb. Despite its material upgrade, our new two-bedroom apartment felt lifeless without Cori and the girls. It was quiet, compact, and sterile.

Salt Lake's demographics reflected middle-class Honolulu, its residents mostly Japanese and Korean, compared to Kalihi's mix of Filipinos and Samoans. There were no rooster wakeup calls or shopping carts rattling down the sidewalks. Still, I saw my beloved Kalihi daily, commuting to Kalakaua on the bus with Chad and Jeff to finish eighth grade. In the fall, I would enroll at Salt Lake's Moanalua High School, which was considered stronger academically than Farrington, the school Wendi and the rest of my friends would attend.

"You transferring to Moanalua next year, yeah?" Mr. Higa, my school counselor and National Junior Honor Society adviser, asked over the buffet at Pizza Hut during our final volunteer outing as NJHS-ers. "You excited? They got one good marching band, I hear."

"I guess," I said as Mr. Higa took in my Lip Smackers necklaces and snug jeans and tee. "But I don't know anyone there."

"Ahhh, you gone make new friends. No worry." He winked. "People like you."

I shrugged, blocking my smile with my pepperoni slice. "I'm just scared I won't meet anyone like me," I confessed, trusting Mr. Higa, who always welcomed me into his office even when I didn't have an appointment or anything to say.

"Eh, we all different, you know. What matters is you one good person, and people will see that," he said, wiping his greasy fingers on the napkin across his lap. "You're gonna find your place there, like you did when you moved here from the mainland."

I nodded again, knowing that Mr. Higa wasn't being all after-school-special on me. That wasn't his style. I thought about the blue poster in his office with the cheery white starry letters: "The decisions you make will dictate the life you will lead." He was being as honest as he could be. That short exchange was just what I needed as I began studying the horizon of who I would become. I was able to reveal who I was to myself and others because I was surrounded by people who allowed me to explore despite not having the answers themselves.

"Like give me one?" Mr. Higa winked again, looking at my lip balms.

I rolled my eyes and laughed, delighted that he saw me.

Chapter *Ten*

Moanalua High School sat haughtily atop a sloping hillside, looking down at the rest of Honolulu, painted gray with accent squares of blue. Its mascot was the *menehune*, mythical Hawaiian dwarves. I felt there was an advantage in calling myself a Moanalua Menehune. To say you went to Farrington was to say you were from Kalihi, which meant you were rough around the edges, tough because you had to run away from Samoan bullies asking you for "dollah" on a daily basis. To say you went to Moanalua was to say you were solidly middle-class, with test scores as high as the school's altitude and on your way to college, a summit no one in my family had climbed.

I was eager to move up in the world and gladly sloughed Kalihi from my résumé during my time at Moanalua, where I basked in extracurriculars and the focus of teachers who'd kneel beside me and praise me for my essays. It was in English class, through *I Know Why the Caged Bird Sings* and *The Color Purple*, where I met a young Maya

Angelou and her brother Bailey, and Celie and Nettie. I had never read stories about people who looked like me, about girls who had been touched and told to be quiet about it. I was deeply struck by Maya Angelou's self-inflicted muteness brought on by guilt and abuse. And though I am unable to carry a child like Celie, I, too, was pregnant with trauma and fear. Celie's audacity to write to God to give her life meaning continues to influence me.

When the 2:40 bell rang, I would sprint to either volleyball or band practice. I was the starting setter on the junior varsity boys' volleyball team. I wore the shortest shorts and my growing curls in a topknot, accessorized with a brown tortoise headband. I loved volleyball, a sport I excelled at. Though I hadn't publicly proclaimed that I was a girl, I did consider playing with boys, and in effect being categorized as a boy, one of the many compromises I made during my girlhood.

At the time, I wasn't aware of athletic trailblazers like Renée Richards, a professional tennis player who was banned from playing in the 1976 U.S. Open because she was a transsexual woman. After disputing the ruling, the New York Supreme Court ruled in her favor, and the landmark decision gave her access to play tennis with other professional women athletes. Today trans athletes are helping change the game, pushing the International Olympic Committee (IOC) and the National College Athletics Association (NCAA) to create regulations that are making the sports world, which is segregated by sex, more inclusive of trans athletes.

In my experience, the only thing that mattered on a court was that you were skilled. I played setter and outside hitter, taking charge of our team's offense. I blossomed in this position of leadership, which earned me a level of respect despite my visible difference. In Hawaii, volleyball was an LGBT-friendly sport, one where even the fiercest queens and flamboyant gay boys dominated. Expressing femininity on the court didn't underscore or negate my skill as a player. During

my first year on the team, I was just happy to be starting as a freshman, but during my sophomore year, as I embarked on transitioning, the dissonance between my gender identity and my team sport
heightened. Despite those conflicting feelings, I was co-captain of our
team as a sophomore, and I ended the year with the Best Offensive
Player award before quitting volleyball because the sex segregation
that forced me to play on the boy's team was unsettling, publicly negating my identity.

I soon became known at Moanalua as the bell-bottom and baby-
tee-wearing boy-girl freshman who'd tweeze your brows for five dollars. I found refuge among the girls, most of whom were also volleyball
players. They took me under their wing and complimented me on the
photos I took with Wendi, which I finally had the courage to display
in a transparent slip on the school binder I clutched to my flat chest.
It was a gesture, reminding myself that I was a girl. "Oohhh, you look
good!" one of the senior girls said to me one day during lunch, passing
my binder around. "I wouldn't even know you were boy."

I took their words as nourishment, the kind of affirmation I needed
to grow the courage to transition. Their words fed me more than the
lineup from the cafeteria's make-your-own-nachos station. I don't believe a single student truly understood me, but I think I projected a
high level of self-confidence that made most of my classmates leave
me alone. It was something I learned from Wendi: Fake it until you
make it. I was no wallflower, but I also wasn't encroaching on anyone
else's life. I didn't believe in asking for acceptance or permission to be
myself; I took what I felt I deserved. That self-assuredness prepared
me for the monumental summer to come.

Living in Salt Lake, I grew comfortable taking the city bus thirty
minutes to Wendi's with my weekend bag packed. Separate schools
couldn't break our sisterhood, though if I suggested that Wendi jump
on the bus to meet me at the mall, she'd roll her eyes and say, "Girl, do

I look like I would have a bus pass?" Thus the birth of pooching rides anywhere we needed to go, whether it was Ala Moana or Waikiki or town, where the older girls hung out. I have no idea where the term *pooching* originated. It feels like an innate phrase, but it definitely predated us. Pooching basically meant to hustle rides, money, or anything from guys. It began innocently to get rides from Dillingham Boulevard, near Wendi's apartment, to Ala Moana, where we hung with the salesgirls at the MAC counter. The first time I ever pooched with Wendi—I'm sure she did it long before I joined her— we pranced on a corner a few blocks from her apartment. I was in my usual uniform of bell-bottoms and platform sneakers paired with a T-shirt while Wendi flaunted her long, skinny legs in tight spandex pants and a sparkly top that plunged low on her padded chest. I watched her flag down cars with her wrists flailing in the air. A silver Mustang slowed, turning on a side street near us and signaling us with his lights.

"Come on, girl. Let's book it," Wendi said as I followed her apprehensively.

Everything was an adventure with her, and I was along for the ride. The man was in his forties, with blond hair that matched the brightness of his car. He wore an aloha shirt and khaki pants, the uniform for professional men in the islands. From where I stood, peering over Wendi's shoulder into the car, I saw that he had kind blue eyes, which eased my fears.

"Like give us ride to Ala Moana?" Wendi asked, pointing him to Oahu's biggest shopping center. He nodded.

Wendi opened the door with familiarity, pushing the seat forward so I could jump in the back. I watched her as she talked about the weather, asking him what he did for a living, and where he lived. He seemed unconcerned with our age and treated us as the girls we failingly presented ourselves as. Danger never entered my mind; I never thought about how easily he could've driven us past the mall to a place of his choosing. Nothing that dramatic ever happened during any of our pooching antics. Riding in cars with strange men soon became habit.

The ladies at the MAC counter in Liberty House, Hawaii's version of Macy's, always made us feel welcome as teens experimenting with our look. The saleswomen, with their all-black ensembles and smoky eyelids, were as open and affirming as the sight of RuPaul's spread legs in the Viva Glam lipstick ads. We spent entire Saturday and Sunday afternoons getting our makeup done by the girls, who would tolerate us because we let them go *in* on our faces, painting dramatic, clownish looks. Wendi would spend her allowance from her grandmother on new products for her growing artist's kit. I didn't have an after-school job or an allowance, so I giddily got C7, Amber Lights, and Prrr applied to my mug for free.

It was during these afternoons that I witnessed Wendi discover her passion. She never spoke about how school was going; I knew she was fidgety to get somewhere. But when we were filling out those paper face charts, I watched her become still and focused, as attentive as she was when she studied her Kevyn Aucoin and Sam Fine books. It was a gift to watch my best friend take those steps toward becoming the person she was meant to be. It pushed me to begin asking myself questions about who I wanted to be and how I would get there.

With MAC on our faces and strappy sandals on our feet, we took our style outside of Wendi's room that summer—the same summer Wendi concocted one of her best creations: hip pads. We walked into Savers, the same thrift store where we'd bought our soccer shorts in middle school, wielding a pair of scissors. Going into the dressing room with a bunch of bold-shouldered blazers, we cut the shoulder pads out of the jackets and threw them in our backpacks. Back at

Wendi's, we sewed the pads together, creating half-moons that we stuck into our underwear to pad our hips. Since she had a flat ass, Wendi would double the pads and put some on her butt as well, while I used mine to fill out the sides of my hips.

We'd flaunt our faux-hourglass figures at night in Waikiki, prancing up and down Kalakaua Avenue and stopping outside Fusions, where all the older girls, the queens, and the gay guys partied. We'd gallivant outside, cackling at each other and flirting with military guys and tourists. I also remember the sex workers imported from the mainland in their clear pumps and pleather skirts. There was this one black woman who had the longest legs I have ever seen in my life. She galloped along the sidewalk in a black leather dress and a shiny black ponytail to match the luster of her outfit. Wendi and I nicknamed her Tyra because we thought she resembled Tyra Banks. I watched her closely when she did her rounds on Kuhio Avenue. I stood slack-jawed when she whipped her ponytail purposefully in the face of a short Japanese tourist to get his attention. Her choreography was undeniable as she invited him to make a proposal for the night, her long legs ready to wrap around his slender shoulders. In my denim capris and leopard-print halter top, I yearned to be that sexy and powerful.

Wendi was sixteen that summer, a year older than I was, though we were in the same grade. As she had mapped out in the eighth grade, she was beginning hormone replacement therapy. Her grandmother, who I'm confident was unclear about what Wendi was asking permission for, outsourced the task to Wendi's aunt, who took her to Dr. R.'s office in Waikiki, the go-to place for transsexuals on Oahu. Wendi told me that she and her aunt had a short consultation with the esteemed endocrinologist, who assured her aunt that the medicine was safe and well tested. They left his office with a prescription for Premarin, a conjugated estrogen from the urine of pregnant horses. I remember the excitement I felt when I met Wendi at Long's Drugs to get her first script filled. She paid thirty dollars for a month's supply of pills, the copay from her grandmother's insurance plan. I silently brainstormed how I would convince Mom to let me follow Wendi's lead.

"Do you feel different?" I asked Wendi as we lay in her bed after she took the first pill.

"Mary, didn't I tell you it's not a miracle drug?" she said, slightly exasperated. I figured she was just moody from her first dose. "Why?" she said after a brief silence. "You like take one?"

I nodded, and she handed me one as if it were a Tic-Tac. I ran to her bathroom sink, staring at the maroon tablet in my hand. Despite Wendi's assertion that they were not magic, I believed they were. This little oval pill would reveal to everyone who I truly was. I bent over the sink and tossed the two and a half milligrams of Premarin into my mouth, forcing it down with a sip of water from the faucet.

"Mary, you feelin' fish now, huh?" Wendi laughed. "We gotta get you more, girl."

When she graduated to Estradiol injections weeks later, Wendi passed her Premarin bottles to me. She claimed she didn't like the pills because they bloated her, but I knew part of her didn't want to go on the journey alone. When I think of this time with Wendi, I'm reminded of the line from Toni Morrison's *Sula*: "Nobody was minding us, so we minded ourselves." I was her sister, and she didn't want to leave me behind. We needed each other to create who we were supposed to be. I gave her thirty dollars to cover the copay, which I had saved in my underwear drawer from weeks of lunch money and handouts from Papa. I had enough money to cover about three months of medication.

This underground railroad of resources guided me during the years of uncertainty, giving me an agency that empowered me to take my life, my body, and my being into my own hands. Wendi and I were low-income trans girls of color. We didn't have many resources, but what we were blessed with was being at the right place at the right time. Hawaii's community of trans women was vast and knowledgeable. There was a deep legacy of trans womanhood passed on to us by older women who had been exactly where we were. And this provided us with stability despite what some view as a dramatic shift in our adolescence.

We were also under the examination of a sensitive endocrinologist who gave transsexual patients the medicine they needed with minimal barriers. Dr. R. believed in self-determination and diversity in gender and bodies, which is not the norm in the medical establishment. In order for trans people to gain access to hormone replacement therapy and gender affirming surgeries, these procedures must be deemed "medically necessary" from the standpoint of mental health professionals, according to the World Professional Association for Transgender Health's Standards of Care (SOC) guidelines. Though the series of steps the SOC recommends is not legally mandated, they are held as the standard to which transsexual patients have been treated, viewed, and covered financially by the medical establishment.

According to these recommendations, in order for a transsexual to undergo treatments or surgeries, they must be pathologized, diagnosed with "gender dysphoria" (previously "gender identity disorder"), as described in the American Psychological Association's bible, *Diagnostic and Statistical Manual of Mental Disorders* (*DSM*). These diagnoses stigmatize transsexual patients as mentally unwell and unfit. The diagnosis does help those with health insurance, decreasing out-of-pocket costs for medically necessary hormone treatments and surgeries, which are usually excluded from most insurance plans that often categorize gender affirming surgeries as "cosmetic" rather than medically necessary. It's a tough compromise. Regardless, it's expensive to see a therapist without adequate health coverage. The medical barriers lead many transsexuals to self-medicate with little to no medical supervision, which is dangerous and can be fatal.

Not all trans people followed these guidelines. Frankly, Wendi and I didn't even know they existed. We were able to operate outside the system because we had a physician who championed body autonomy and the idea that we should make our own decisions about our bodies.

Everyone deserves access to quality health care, yet access is challenging for trans people who live in rural areas or cities without trans-inclusive clinics. Even those with insurance must take their health care into their own hands, often tasked with educating their physicians about recommendations for treatments because most doctors are unfamiliar with transsexual patients. Many low-income young trans women self-medicate in spite of the risks. I've heard stories of girls who buy vials of injectable estrogen from other trans women with prescriptions or young trans women who share P.O. boxes so they can receive hormones from online pharmacies without a prescription or a parent's approval. Like these young women, I created a system that worked for me without my mother's knowledge, piggybacking on Wendi's access to Dr. R. and health insurance.

After a few months on Premarin, I noticed bloating from increased water retention. My appetite was insatiable, leading to weight gain in my thighs and butt, which settled to a shapely size seven in juniors' jeans. My skin, which was never affected by facial hair, began breaking out with heavy acne across my forehead, a direct effect of my hormone levels. There were desirable effects, too, like the suppleness of my skin, which was unnaturally smooth, like a puppy's hairless belly. Breasts were my favorite feature. I remember being struck by the sensitivity of my areolas, which swelled within weeks, prompting the

137

budding of my breasts. If they rubbed too hard against my shirt, my nipples throbbed. Despite the pain, I flaunted my fleshy chest during our weekend nights out in a push-up bra filled out with a pair of silicone cutlets.

My breast growth was extraordinary compared to Wendi's; she was basically as flat as she was before she started hormones. She didn't gain any weight at all, her long legs thin as ever, though she did experience a change in her complexion. Her skin, which was always covered with acne, was now clear, and the shape of her face became less angular and subtly filled out, giving her an overall softer appearance. Despite her gradual shift, she never had to hide her changes like I did. The breasts that I flaunted in my friends' company had to be concealed at home under layers so I could keep my pill popping under wraps.

The hormones also made me more emotional. I found myself snapping at Chad and Jeff for blasting The Rock and Stone Cold Steve Austin on TV. I also was more prone to isolation, vegging out in my room, listening to Janet Jackson's *The Velvet Rope* on loop while reading heavy heroine novels like *Madame Bovary, Anna Karenina, A Room with a View*, and *The Age of Innocence*. My thoughts in bed and in the shower darkened around this time. As long as I could remember, I'd felt discomfort with my genitals, and this only escalated with the emotional changes brought on by puberty. I had a foreboding impatience to be rid of it. My tuck was a temporary solution to make it nonexistent for a few hours.

In the bathroom, I was forced to engage with my penis. It had to be cleaned and it wanted to be touched. The pleasure I'd give myself filled me with a combination of release and revulsion. I felt guilty for achieving gratification from a part that separated me from my personal vision of myself, and I felt despair because I didn't have the means to change it. Premarin stimulated that sense of discord and angst, one that cradled me as I cried myself to sleep at night, hoping that some genie would magically appear and all my troubles would be solved.

No one came, though, and I struggled in secret, wielding nothing but despair and fierce determination.

Part

Three

Nobody's going to save you.
No one's going to cut you down,
cut the thorns around you.
No one's going to storm
the castle walls nor
kiss awake your birth,
climb down your hair,
nor mount you
on the white steed.
There is no one who
will feed the yearning.
Face it. You will have
to do, do it yourself.

—GLORIA ANZALDÚA, "LETTING GO"

Chapter *Eleven*

G ood morning, Class of 2001!" I shouted from center stage in
our school's cafeteria. "I'm Janet, your class treasurer, and I just
want to thank you for your votes and your support!"

More than three hundred sophomores applauded as I unwrapped
my blue-polished nails from the microphone. The riotous reception
signaled my successful reintroduction, and the sight of my fellow
elected leaders standing with me at our back-to-school assembly em-
boldened me. The majority of the people in that cafeteria were aware
that they had elected Charles to office the previous semester, but I
had known Janet would reign.

I was obsessed with *The Velvet Rope* for a year straight, letting
Janet Jackson's confessional lyrics lull me to sleep and comfort me
when I felt lost. I felt that the album was the vehicle onto which Janet
finally expressed her full self, her anger and pain, her fluid sexuality
and passion. I loved her fiery red curls and her equally vibrant smile,
features that the older girls said I had in common with the singer. I
was deeply flattered when they nicknamed me Baby Janet, a name

that stuck and that I took as my own. There's power in naming yourself, in proclaiming to the world that this is who you are. Wielding this power is often a difficult step for many trans people, because it's also a very visible one.

To announce your gender in name, dress, and pronouns in your school, place of work, neighborhood, and state is a public process, one in which trans people must literally petition authorities to approve name and gender marker changes on identification cards and public records. Becoming comfortable with your identity is step one; the next step is revealing that identity to those around you. As with medically transitioning, there are economic and legislative barriers that make it difficult for low-income trans people to make the public changes that align their lived and documented gender.

To legally change my name at fifteen would have required me to appeal to my mother to petition for my name change, pay the three-hundred-dollar-plus filing fees, and plead with my father in Dallas to cosign on something he had absolutely no knowledge of. So I postponed the legal process until I was eighteen and wielded the power of self-determination, announcing to my peers and my family that I would only answer to Janet and *she* and *her* pronouns.

Though I kept the fact that I was taking hormones a secret over the summer before my sophomore year, I was not hiding my dress, makeup, and longer hair from my family. Mom allowed me to spend my back-to-school clothing allowance on skirts, dresses, tight denim jeans, and tops. As long as I brought home good grades, I was in the clear. This was our informal, unspoken agreement. The only conversation we had was about my name and pronouns during that summer.

It had been nearly three years since I had sat down with my mother in our house in Kalihi and discussed my sexuality. I was now asking my family to embrace me as Janet. I realized even then that it would take them time to adapt. They slipped from time to time when it came to my name and pronouns, and I forgave those early slips because they were part of our collective growing pains. What mattered to me was that they loved me enough to go on the journey with me and willingly adapt their lives to mine. Though the changes were about me, I couldn't deny they were also about my family, who reacted positively and grew accustomed at their own pace.

Jeff, who was nine at the time, adapted the easiest, accepting my gender identity as something natural with little concern, the way children do when we present change as positive. Cheraine and Cori, who were busy with their growing families, shrugged at my announcement, claiming that they'd always known. Cori was the proudest of all my siblings to have another sister, lovingly calling me *tita* (pidgin for "sister"). Chad was the only one I felt a bit self-conscious discussing the gender stuff with. I avoided him, opting to seek refuge in my relationship with Wendi rather than open up to him about what I was going through. I felt accountable to him and our siblinghood because we had spent our entire lives together. Our diverging paths sent us into our respective womanhood and manhood. Though Chad embraced me without rebuttal (he was the most careful with my name and pronouns), I knew he needed time to figure out who he was, come to grips with who I was, and mourn the loss of the big brother he thought he'd always wanted.

My mother, who was preoccupied with bills and Rick, defaulted to her signature hands-off approach with my social transition, which I took into my own hands. She was and has always been the kind of mother who recognized her children as their own beings rather than an extension of her. Her outlook benefited me because it allowed me to set the tone for who I would become with minimal consultation. I purposefully remained silent with Mom about taking hormones. I was immature enough to believe that I could do it all on my own; I didn't give her the opportunity to be an advocate for me at school and beyond. It wasn't that I was afraid of my mother freaking out; I just didn't have the skills to communicate my growing needs, and there was a part of me that was unsure she would be able to meet those needs. Expecting things from other people always led to heartache, I believed at the time, and I didn't want to be disappointed, so I chose to go it alone for a while longer.

After that class assembly, I continued to improvise, creating the space I needed for myself in school within a cocoon of supportive friends, teachers, and teammates. Instead of embarking on a series of conversations with Moanalua's staff, I let my denim capris, my brown tribal-pattern choker, my crown of curls, and my growing bust do the talking. It hasn't been until recently that I have been able to appreciate the brave girl standing on that stage, walking in those hallways, sitting in class, who made herself seen, heard, and known.

My presence as a fifteen-year-old trans girl must've been radical to many, but to me it was truth, and my truth led me to form a womanhood all my own. What I failed to realize was that the people outside my home, specifically the school's staff, weren't equipped with the resources and experience to help a student like me. Some of them were unwilling to seek that knowledge and chose to view my presence as problematic. I admit that my approach may have appeared abrasive to some, but I was unapologetic about who I was and never felt the need to plead for belonging in school. Though my entitlement aided my survival, it also created problems.

Social transition is the process by which a trans person begins openly living as their true gender. Trans youth who openly express their gender identity at home are usually aided by parents, who speak with teachers, administrators, and other parents about their identity, pronouns, and name. Open, clear communication helps detail the student's and the family's journey, educate people about what it means to be trans, and set a precedent of support for the young person. GLSEN (Gay, Lesbian & Straight Education Network), a national organization that advocates for all students regardless of gender identity and sexual orientation, offers a model policy resource for schools to help foster safe, affirmative environments that will meet the needs of trans students.

Ideally, administrators clearly communicate to teachers the importance of assisting the student by using the preferred name and pronouns and ensuring that other students do so as well. A teacher sets the tone in the classroom by ensuring that misuse of names and pronouns is not tolerated and that harassment and name-calling will be grounds for discipline. Though most of my teachers were on board with role modeling in the classroom, I can still feel the sting of my chemistry teacher purposefully calling out "Charles" every morning during role call, to the giggles of my peers. To add insult to injury, she repeatedly misgendered me, deliberately referring to me as "he" and "him" and refusing to reprimand bullies who interrupted class by shouting, "I can see your balls!" or "How big are your tits now?" Instead of taking a leadership role and proclaiming that intolerance would not be tolerated, she chose to turn a blind eye to insults, going as far as blaming me for putting a target on my own back for dressing the way I did. She viewed my femininity as extra, as something that was forced and unnatural.

Femininity in general is seen as frivolous. People often say feminine people are doing "the most," meaning that to don a dress, heels, lipstick, and big hair is artifice, fake, and a distraction. But I knew even as a teenager that my femininity was more than just adornments; they were extensions of *me*, enabling me to express myself and my identity. My body, my clothes, and my makeup are on purpose, just as I am on purpose.

My teacher's judgments fostered an environment that became increasingly uncomfortable for me daily. If I hadn't valued my education and hadn't been accepted at home, skipping class or dropping out of school to avoid the harassment would have been an appealing choice. It's no wonder nearly one-third of LGBTQ students are driven out of school—a dropout rate nearly three times the national average, according to Lambda Legal.

Administrators can also navigate gender-segregated activities, sports, restrooms, and locker rooms based on the circumstances of the student and the school facilities, with the intent of maximizing safety, comfort, and social integration. Some students may be comfortable using restrooms, locker rooms, and changing facilities that correspond with gender identity (for example, I freely used the girls' restroom), while others may prefer a single-user and/or gender-neutral restroom or changing room (for example, I used my teacher's locked classroom to change for physical education). While some students and parents may express discomfort with sharing such gender-separated facilities with a trans student, school staff must work diligently to address concerns through education that fosters understanding and empathy and creates a safe campus for all students, regardless of bodily differences.

It's important to note confidentiality and discretion, as some students (with the guidance of their parents) may choose to attend a school where no one knows that they're trans. Others may not be open at home for reasons such as safety concerns, lack of acceptance, or potential rejection. For these students, school may be a safer environment to express themselves truly, and school staff should remain open and supportive as they help navigate social transition. Disclosing to a parent that a child is trans carries risks for the student, such as being forced to leave home. Let the student lead the way, be willing and open to educate yourself and others, and set the tone in the classroom about how a trans student should be treated.

Unfortunately, I was going at it all alone, with little guidance from my mother and a lack of leadership and sensitivity from school administrators who chose to view me as a nuisance. I remember Vice Principal Johnson, a forty-something white woman from the South, tapping me on the shoulder during lunch to follow her to her office. She was a regular sight at lunchtime, hard to miss, standing five-ten, her bright blond pixie cut reflecting the high-noon sun.

"Do you know why I called you in here today?" she asked as I sat in the metal chair near her desk. I shook my head, having never been summoned to the administrators' building, a place I associated with delinquents and truant students. "We have a 'standard rules of conduct and dress code' policy," she said. "Have you read it?"

"I haven't, miss," I said, cradling my right hand nervously in my left palm.

"If you did read it, you'd see that your dress is inappropriate," she said. "Young men don't wear skirts," she said, narrowing her green eyes on my denim skirt with rhinestones lining the pockets.

I had to exert everything in my limited power from reacting to the shade she was throwing at me. "I'm going through some changes," I said, aiming to explain myself to her. "I'm sure it's just a misunderstanding, because I'm not a boy."

"Really?" she said quizzically.

"I see myself as a girl, and I know the way I dress isn't bothering anyone," I said. "I'm an honor student, class treasurer, and captain of the volleyball team."

"I'm glad you're doing well," she said, cutting me off. "We need more good students. But I've spoken with your teachers, and from my understanding, the way you're dressing has caused disruptions in class."

"Yes, I'm teased frequently," I argued, "with some teachers choosing not to defend me."

"Consider this a warning," she said after a short pause during which she took in the hint of cleavage from my white V-neck sweater. "We have dress codes to avoid the disruptions you've encountered in class. Do you understand?"

After a few weeks of wearing bell-bottoms and denim shorts, I chose to wear a skirt, but this time self-consciousness crept in. I was no longer as carefree. To wear a skirt, to be proud and unapologetically feminine, was a badge of honor for me initially, but it had transformed into another thing I was forced to hide. I should have been allowed to wear whatever I wanted as long as it was within the dress code for all girls. I often successfully dodged VP Johnson in the halls, but there were a number of times when she sent me home to change.

Home was no refuge, as I incredulously watched Mom picking up lint, on all fours, from our carpet. She was totally zoned out on the floor, holding her findings in her palm while using her free hand as the picker. I was suspicious that Mom was smoking meth with Rick. When I brought it up with Chad, he adamantly denied it, helping to assuage my anxieties. "She wouldn't do that," he said. I could see he was offended by my accusations that Mom could be like Rick.

Putting aside Mom's alleged drug use, her volatile relationship set the tone in our house. Rick was normally calm and quiet, unengaged, but out of nowhere he'd explode. He and Mom usually yelled from behind their bedroom walls, something we adapted and grew accustomed to. We'd turn up the television when they fought, trying our best to ignore Rick's roars and Mom's whimpers. We grew accustomed to their screaming matches, which usually ended with the two of them leaving the house together, giving us money for dinner.

Mom followed Rick everywhere, even if it meant missing work. I would wake in the mornings to grab Raisin Bran, and she'd be on the couch in denim shorts and a T-shirt with her bag at her side, ready for one of his "adventures." He was a thief and would pull stunts regularly to stay afloat, selling or pawning goods for money or drugs. He worked as a security guard for a hot second and eventually was fired after he spent off-the-clock hours stealing from the offices and homes he was supposed to surveillance. Mom told me she went on a bunch of these stunts with him, including the time he stole our first computer. I wasn't apologetic about having a stolen computer, just happy to have one, gleefully chatting on AOL Instant Messenger.

Shit got real one night when we were grabbing dinner at L&L near the airport. On our way home, Mom began whining that she wanted to go somewhere with Rick. This pathetic sound was one I had grown accustomed to hearing. Usually, it would end with Rick going along with her begging, but this time he wasn't having it.

"Why you wanna come with me for?" Rick asked.

"I just want to be with you," Mom said.

They were quiet until we pulled in the parking lot of our apartment. Mom passed the food to Chad, putting her and Rick's plates in a separate bag, which she placed on her lap in the front seat.

"Elizabeth, get out of the car," Rick said, obviously fed up.

"I'm not going anywhere," Mom said, unmovable.

"I'm only going to say it one more time: Get out of the fucking car, Elizabeth!" he roared.

Mom didn't move. Chad, Jeff, and I stood by the elevator watching Rick open the driver's door, lean over, and scream, "Get the fuck out!"

"This is my car," she said. "Get your own car if you want to leave."

"Get the fuck out of here," he shouted as his right hand smacked her in the back of the head, rocking the car. My heart was beating fast.

My eyes followed Rick as he slammed his door, stomped to my mother's side, and dragged her out of the car with a fistful of her brown hair in his hand. Gravy from her hamburger steak plate was all over her shorts as she sat in her own food.

I watched my mother pick herself up from the oil-stained cement. She stood up, grabbed the styrofoam plates, and threw them at Rick. Defeated, he returned to the driver's side, and they drove off together.

It was this "I have nothing to lose" climate, this understanding that the bottom couldn't be far away and that I didn't have stability anyway, that gave me the courage to open up to my mother about the fact that I had been taking Wendi's hormones behind her back. It was just after dinner. I was damp from my shower, bare-faced, wearing pom-pom shorts and a tank top covering the full A-cups that I was proud of. I was helping Mom load the dishwasher as I detailed that I had been taking medicine for the past six months that would help me become a girl, that my mind was made up, that I had a plan, and that I needed her help. "I never ask you for anything," I said, "but I need you to take me to Wendi's doctor in Waikiki, who specializes in this medicine, and sign off on my treatments."

Mom looked at me with a knowing glare, as if she had known years before—maybe back when I mistakenly told her I was gay, maybe way back when she was sixteen and told her mother in their kitchen she was pregnant with Cori—that we would be right here, with me telling her that I needed her help. I felt she was finally looking at the daughter she had overlooked this entire time.

"Whatever you need, Janet," Mom said without argument, returning to the dishes in the sink. My mother knew the train had left the station and that she had a choice: to jump aboard or let it reach its destination without her. Thankfully, she chose to ride it out with me. That didn't mean my mother didn't have her reservations. She later told me she worried about what others thought and said, about the second-guessing of family and friends who told her she shouldn't encourage me in this way, that she was doing the wrong thing by letting me dress like a girl. I'm not a parent, so I can only imagine the guilt, judgment, and pressure my mother must've silently endured those years as she let me steer the way toward my future.

A few Saturdays later, Mom drove Wendi and me to Dr. R.'s for my first physician-monitored hormone appointment. The three of us sat in the waiting room as Wendi (whose skittish presence had become constant in the office over the years) signed herself in. I had accompanied Wendi a number of times to Dr. R.'s office—I was a familiar sight to him—but this was the first time I had signed myself in for an appointment. He called Wendi first, spending about twenty minutes taking her weight and blood pressure and injecting her with estrogen. After she returned, Dr. R. called my mother and me into his office. "Hi, Mrs. Mock," he said, extending his hand to Mom while shooting a knowing glance my way. "So I hear Janet is ready to take the next step."

My mother smiled apprehensively from her seat across from the doctor, taking in his gray hair, blue smock, thick glasses, and perpetually chapped lips. I was sure his empathetic and direct approach would ease any reservations Mom had. I watched her closely as she took in the bulletin board covered with photos of past and present patients, including a snapshot of Tracy onstage at Venus and Wendi's freshman yearbook photo.

"Great, and are you both clear about the regimen?"

"I know the next step is shots, since I've been taking Premarin for the past six months," I explained excitedly, knowing that Dr. R. had experience with patients who self-medicated.

"You are right: The next step does include weekly doses of Estradiol Valerate, which is the estrogen I prefer for my patients. I find that injections reduce the strain that oral medicine has on the liver," he said. "It's twenty dollars for a twenty-milligram shot of Estradiol, which I pair with the supplemental vitamin B12. We will start Janet off with half a dose, monitor that for three months, and then graduate her to the full dose."

During our consultation, Dr. R. detailed the potential side effects, including mood swings, altered hunger patterns, slower metabolism, weight gain, water retention, increased risk of blood clots and breast cancer, and of course infertility. I was a child, so having children was never on my mind; I can only echo Morrison's character Sula: "I don't want to make someone else. I want to make myself." Dr. R. assured my mother that I was in good hands and that he had been treating transsexual patients for nearly thirty years in Hawaii.

"Most important, your daughter will remain healthy and will be pleased to finally appear as she feels," he said. "She will also be able to live in the world as a young woman, an attractive one at that, something that isn't easily achieved or possible for most of my patients."

It was vital to me to be seen as the girl I was, and Dr. R. was the first person to vocalize that possibility as a reality. Becoming my own woman was no longer the unrealistic fantasy of a thirteen-year-old. His statements about my appearance validated my dreams, easing Mom's anxieties about my prospects and the effects of the irreversible steps. The fact that I fit our society's narrow standard of female appearance also eased my mother's worries about my future and the harsh discrimination and harassment that often comes with being read as trans.

Though I am unapologetic about the way I look—an amalgamation of my parents' features and early access to medication that halted the effects of testosterone—my appearance has granted me an advantage in life. I have been able to navigate this world mostly unchecked, seen as my true self without being clocked or spooked, as the girls would say colloquially. When I was younger, I remember taking pride in people's well-meaning remarks: "You're so lucky that no one would ever know!" or "You don't even look like a guy!" or "Wow! You're prettier than most 'natural' women!" They were all backhanded compliments, acknowledging my beauty while also invalidating my identity as a woman. To this day, I'm told in subtle and obvious ways that I am not "real," meaning that I am not, nor will I ever be, a cis woman; therefore, I am fake.

These thoughts surrounding identity, gender, bodies, and how we view, judge, and objectify all women brings me to the subject of "passing," a term based on an assumption that trans people are passing as something that we are not. It's rooted in the idea that we are not really who we say we are, that we are holding a secret, that we are living false lives. Examples of people "passing" in media, whether through race (*Imitation of Life* and Nella Larsen's novel *Passing*), class (*Catch Me if You Can* and the reality show *Joe Millionaire*), or gender (*Boys Don't Cry* and *The Crying Game*), are often portrayed as leading a life of tragic duplicity and as deceivers who will be punished harshly by society when their true identity is uncovered. This is no different for trans people who "pass" as their gender or, more accurately, are assumed to be cis or blend in as cis, as if that is the standard or norm. This pervasive thinking frames trans people as illegitimate and unnatural. If a trans woman who knows herself and operates in the world as a woman is seen, perceived, treated, and viewed as a woman, isn't she just being herself? She isn't *passing*; she is merely *being*.

With the consultation behind us, my mother sat in the waiting room with Wendi as I embarked on my first hormone shot. Dr. R. fitted his rubber gloves on as I sat on the white-paper-lined exam table. Grabbing a syringe, he stuck his needle into a brown vial of Estradiol Valerate, then filled it with a translucent oil that had a slight golden color. He stuck the same needle into a brown vial of vitamin B12, which added red to the syringe. He wiped an area of my right butt cheek with an alcohol swab and quickly stuck me with the needle.

"Thank you, Doctor," I said as I handed him the ten-dollar fee for the half-dose shot. Dr. R operated on a cash-and-check basis and billed Mom's insurance only for the quarterly blood tests that monitored my hormone levels and liver and kidney functions.

I blossomed under Dr. R.'s care, and the potential he saw in me slowly became a visible reality. As my body began evolving, the world treated me differently, and I learned firsthand that society privileges physical beauty. Being beautiful is a personal and a social experience, one that has an effect on how you're treated in addition to how you feel about yourself. I was still the same person (and knew how it felt not to be perceived as desirable or good-looking), yet suddenly people were kinder, enamored by my apparent beauty.

This desirability put me in sharp focus of the male gaze. Being subjected to catcalls, whistles, and unsolicited phone numbers became a norm, and during my nights out in Waikiki with Wendi and her gaggle of trans gal pals, I quietly based my self-worth on the number of times I made a guy's head turn. Objectification and sexism masked as desirability were a bittersweet part of my dream fulfilled.

At the same time, I began looking in judgment at the girls Wendi and I hung out with. We were in varying phases of our development as trans girls. Some of us were considered "passable," while others were not. I glared at those whose shoulders spanned broadly, who were over five-ten, who twisted their hips as they walked, who laughed a bit too loudly or deeply. My body and appearance had been policed my entire life, so I began policing other girls. As a teen, I wanted badly to pass. Due to this investment in keeping appearances, I grew self-conscious when I hung out in large packs of trans girls because the risk of being read as trans heightened. So I began stealthily separating myself from the group.

As they gallivanted on the Waikiki Strip, I would stroll a few yards behind, distancing myself. The first time I got hit on by a guy, I was walking slowly with my friends on Kalakaua Avenue in a black cotton corset and light pink pants. His name was Adrian, and he was mocha-skinned, with model good looks. He was a marine stationed in Kaneohe and spoke with a slow Southern drawl, a reflection of his Alabama roots. He was tipsy and twenty-one, with striking white teeth and an unflinching stare that made me feel like I was the only girl in the world. I remember lying about my age (I said I was eighteen, two years older) and about my friends, claiming that I knew only one of the girls, the most petite of our group. Adrian and I exchanged numbers quickly so I could catch up with the girls, who kept walking up Kalakaua Avenue.

I was on cloud nine, really feeling myself. It was the first time that a guy I was attracted to had approached me with equal desire. When I caught up with the girls, a few were quick to call me out for "acting fish."

"That bitch thinks she's too fish for us," one of the girls said loudly enough that I could hear. I chose to ignore it, hoping that it would just go away and Wendi would deflate the situation with a joke, the way she usually did.

"She thinks just because she's pretty that she's better than us," another girl said, prompting the first girl to turn around and approach me.

"Just because you look good doesn't make you better than anybody. Trust!"

I vividly remember the sting of the bitter truth, echoing the concept of beauty as currency and the hierarchy it creates: If she's *prettier* than I am, then she is more valuable, and thus has access to *having it all*. Instead of fighting back, I chose to be silently defensive, denying my actions as misunderstood and refuting their claims under the guise of jealousy. It was one of the last times I chose to hang out so-cially with a large group of girls. Isolation made me feel safer, though the irony of separating from the pack, of separating myself from my trans sisters in an effort to be welcomed into larger society (into the gaze of a guy), is glaring to me now.

I personally know many women who choose to leave behind their pasts—their family and friends, anyone who knows they're trans—in an effort to blend in as cis. The trans community calls this "living stealth." For many, it is an act of survival. Many choose not to lead with the fact that they are trans, in order to avoid the stigma, preju-dice, discrimination, and safety concerns that come with being vis-ibly trans. At twenty-two, I would choose to leave family and friends behind to live my life openly as a young woman in New York City. But as a teenager on a small island where it seemed I couldn't escape my past, I banked on my looks, which allowed me to live visibly without people harassing me or gawking at me. Usually, when I attracted at-tention, it was in the form of a lustful gaze from guys like Adrian, whose interest in me further validated my womanhood.

For our first date, Adrian picked me up in his red Jetta, and we ate at the Spaghetti Factory at Ward Warehouse, the same place where my family gathered every year for Grandma Pearl's birthday. Honestly, I was paranoid, fearful that I'd see someone from school who'd call out "Charles!" in front of Adrian, whom I assumed didn't know I was trans. Periodically, I'd look around to see if anyone I knew was in the restaurant. But as dinner progressed, my nerves subsided, and I fell into the groove of a girl on a date with a guy. We talked about our siblings, about where we grew up, and about Adrian's fear of having to one day use the infantry skills he had learned as a new marine.

Just as I began enjoying his presence over dinner in the dimly lit restaurant, he kissed me softly and a bit off target, on the left side of my mouth. The entire date, I reasoned that we hadn't been physical, so not telling him was fine. Things changed after that kiss. I was anxious about how and when I'd tell him: over the phone? Outside the car? In a letter?

When he dropped me off that night, I told him I needed to talk to him. He turned the key in the ignition, silencing his engine. I could see the whites of his eyes, so bright, as he looked at me intently.

"I don't know what you'll think of this, but I just wanted to let you know," I started, "that I'm a virgin and committed to not having sex until I find the right person."

Adrian just smiled, kissing me on my forehead and saying he wasn't in a rush. I went home thinking that statement would get me a few more innocent dates. Lying in bed that night, I felt giddy, though I knew that telling Adrian I was trans would most likely lead to the courtship's end. The next time we got together at his friend's apartment to watch a football game, I kept my business to myself. I held court with Adrian on a love seat, where his muscular arms were draped over my shoulders as he whispered jokes and random sentiments to me. "You are the prettiest girl in Hawaii," he said. "Do you realize that?"

I felt close to Adrian despite knowing nothing about him. I was a sixteen-year-old virgin, and I knew that disclosure was imminent. The moment I decided to tell him was the moment when I stopped being a girl and became a woman. Carelessness was not an option for a girl like me. I had a responsibility to own who I was, despite the stigma that existed about being trans.

As we pulled up in front of my apartment building, Adrian asked, "When can I see you again?"

I smiled, aware that this would be the last time he would look at me with the glow that comes from the newness of infatuation.

"That's sweet, but I'm not like other girls, you know?" I began.

"I like that about you," he said cheekily. I could tell by his playful expression that he had no idea about my past, about my present, about the girl he had been wooing for the past two weeks.

"I'm being serious. I'm not like other girls," I stammered. "I was born with the wrong parts and am waiting to have surgery to change that." I was vague on purpose; having to say that I'd been born a boy and was years and thousands of dollars away from having any kind of surgery was a reality I couldn't own up to yet.

He pulled away instantly. His face turned from the sweet, soft-eyed expression I had admired to one that was coarse, suited not for a girl but for men preparing for battle. I was afraid I had made a tragic mistake, telling him in his car with no one around.

"I can't believe this," he said, not so much to me but to himself. "Why didn't you tell me earlier?"

Because you'd look at me the way you're looking at me now, like some creature from a faraway land, void of human feeling, I wanted to say. I could hear his disgust in his tone, see it in his expression. I was no longer an attractive woman he was eager to see again; he perceived me as something artificial. To Adrian, I was this inauthentic woman trying to deceive him, possibly with the intention to get him into bed. In our patriarchal culture that values masculinity over femininity, my disclosure shook Adrian, challenging his heteronormative and cis-normative ideals.

"Sorry," I said, apologizing for who I was, ashamed of who I was, too young to know the right thing to have done. "I just didn't know how to tell you."

"I'm not like that. I'm not gay," he said, shaking his head. "This is just too much."

Heartbroken, I opened the car door, crying over how this would be the first of a long line of romantic rejections, how no man would ever love me because I was a different kind of girl, how unlucky I was. Now, over a decade later, I look at how lucky I was to walk out of

Adrian's car, to cry in my bed, to wake up the next day. I now know that the world can be a brutal place for a girl with a penis.

Many cis people assume that trans women, whether we "pass" as cis or not, are pretending to be someone we are not, and often expect us to disclose that we are trans to all we meet. Disclosure should be an individual personal choice based on circumstances such as safety, access, and resources. Discussions around disclosure often get heated when we discuss trans women and their romantic relationships with heterosexual cis men. When disclosure occurs for a trans woman, whether by choice or by another person, she is often accused of deception because, as the widely accepted misconception goes, trans women are not "real" women (meaning cis women); therefore, the behavior (whether rejection, verbal abuse, or severe violence) is warranted. The violence that trans women face at the hands of heterosexual cis men can go unchecked and uncharted because society blames trans women for the brutality they face. Similar to arguments around rape, the argument goes that "she brought it upon herself." This pervasive idea that trans women deserve violence needs to be abolished. It's a socially sanctioned practice of blaming the victim. We must begin blaming our culture, which stigmatizes, demeans, and strips trans women of their humanity.

Months later, I spotted Adrian walking toward me on the Waikiki Strip while hanging with a few girlfriends. I was immediately anxious and considered ducking into a store to avoid crossing paths. His jovial smile when he saw me threw me, and the hug and kiss he gave me surprised me. He was just as tipsy as when we first met, and he immediately asked to speak to me privately, leading me away from my friends to a bench in front of an ABC Store on Kalakaua Avenue.

"You know, I still feel bad about the way I reacted," he said. "I just never had that happen to me. It's the kind of shit you see in a movie, not in real life."

I was too young and eager for his attention to be offended by the comparison of my life as fiction, so I thanked him and hugged him. We chatted for a bit before kissing again. This time I felt freer because I was just me without the obligation to tell him anything more about me. We soon headed across the street to Waikiki Beach, where we made out heavily as the dark sea rumbled in front of us. Weeks later, I lost my virginity to Adrian in his barracks in Kaneohe, and he was sweet to me despite the awkwardness I felt with my body, covering my genitals with my hands as he slid inside me.

"It's okay," he said, kissing me sweetly and pulling my arms above my head. "You're beautiful, do you know that?"

It was fun and sweet, and we had sex a few more times, usually late at night, when I was bored and he was tipsy. I felt beautiful when he was inside me, looking at my face as I gave him pleasure, but it was always bittersweet. I could make him feel good with a body that I had yet to recognize as good.

Chapter *Twelve*

Mom and I stood on the balcony overlooking the parking lot, watching a burly man hook her silver Honda to his tow truck. I expected her to run downstairs and plead for her car, but she just rolled her eyes as it rolled away.

"Fucking idiot," Mom sputtered, unapologetic about her raw language, one of the bad habits she had adopted during her nearly three-year relationship with Rick, who hadn't been to the apartment in days. Though Rick's absence irked the hell out of my mother, she was used to it. He had landed himself back in jail a few times during part deux of their relationship so often that I can't even recall when he was in or out. I just enjoyed his absences, whether they lasted weeks or months.

I rarely crossed paths with Rick, but my brothers spent time with him daily as he shuttled them to and from school in Kalihi. Chad, fifteen, was a freshman at Farrington, where he was a receiver on the JV football team and saw Wendi regularly in the hallways. Jeff, ten, scoffed at any kind of activity that required him to be away from the Disney Channel. I can see him clearly, lying on his stomach in front of our television with his dirty feet up in the air, glued to the antics of *Lizzie McGuire*, Shia LaBeouf in *Even Stevens*, or *That's So Raven*.

Our apartment was still in Rick's absence. I felt safest when it was just the four of us, quietly watching TV together without the interruptions of his pacing. He had been to dark places and brought a foreboding shadow into our home and his relationship with Mom. His drug-fueled presence was hard to miss. It was apparent in his eyes rejecting any spark of light, in the way his bottom lip jutted in and out unconsciously, and in the way Mom's attention narrowed on his needs, wants, and desires. Her focus on Rick dug her deeper into a self-imposed isolation that distanced us from our grandparents, aunts, and uncles.

Papa was vocal about his intolerance of Rick, whom he still saw as the teen delinquent who knocked up his firstborn child, and in return, Rick was vocal about his dislike of Papa. My mother, feeling judged by most of her family, who suspected she was on drugs, slowly dodged family gatherings at my grandparents' home. We had been away from our grandparents' apartment for more than a year, a time period that coincided with my most transformative years. Though I missed my family, their absence eased my worries about being accountable to even more people in my life.

The only person we saw with regularity was Grandma Pearl, who remained Mom's nonjudgmental ally. Their closeness was apparent in the way they whispered to each other on the phone. I remember Mom discreetly reaching out to Grandma with frequency in desperation as her economic instability worsened, always pleading, "Please don't tell Dad." My mother has said on many occasions in reflection that she would not have been able to stay afloat if it weren't for Grandma, who stepped in when she needed her most, from raising

Cheraine and babysitting each of us to the cash handouts she offered without expectations of repayment.

"Take care of your mom, yeah," Grandma told me after breakfast at the Original Pancake House around the corner from her apartment. There was a note of defeat in her voice that shook me. She knew that she had done all she could for my mother, and she knew it wasn't enough to pull her from Rick's grasp.

Weeks later, Rick returned to the apartment, and an epic screaming match ensued about the car's repossession, about the missed rent payments, about the fact that he wasn't holding up his end of the bills. We had grown used to their fights, but nothing prepared us for the plan Rick returned with.

"We're moving," Mom announced one Saturday morning, giving each of us one big blue storage bin to pack our things in. "Anything that you don't need now, we'll box up and leave at Cori's."

Plainly, Mom wasn't earning enough to renew our lease in Salt Lake. She couldn't commit to the monthly rent, knowing full well that Rick's share would be spent on drugs. With the help of a long-time friend whose pity led him to give Mom his beat-up Volvo wagon, we took temporary residence at a motel near the airport. Our room at the Pacific Marina Inn had two twin beds—one for Jeff and me, the other for Mom and Rick—and a cot where Chad slept without complaint. Mom and Rick scrounged up money every week to cover the room. Chad and Jeff initially found the motel exciting, splashing around in the pool and running to Byron's, a favorite local diner, for a bite when they got antsy. It was an adventure, something new and thrilling and fleeting.

The motel was filled with transient sounds, from the clacks of well-worn heels signaling the comings and goings of sex workers, to the planes distantly buzzing at the airport, to the jingling of the charms on Mom's purse as she returned home late at night with Rick tweaking at her side. I thought our living situation, like these sounds, would be temporary. I knew that they wouldn't be able to sustain this chaos for much longer, yet I didn't see a solution in sight. There was nothing I could do to lift my brothers out of this place, and loyally, I felt my place was beside my mother, whom I didn't want to leave with Rick.

I remember the fear that woke me the night Mom returned to the room at three A.M. with her hand wrapped in a bandage after getting stabbed by Rick. Apparently, Rick, coming down from a high, had confronted a driver who cut him off on Nimitz Highway, the road leading to the motel. When the guy approached the Volvo at a stoplight, Rick reached for his Swiss army knife and jumped out of the car. Mom followed Rick, trying to calm him down. As Rick aimed the knife at the guy, Mom reached for the blade.

"She thinks she's Wonder Woman," Rick told us, shaking his head, obviously amused.

"Fucking asshole was about to stab the guy," Mom said, thinking it made sense to grab a knife to save her man from getting arrested.

They were beyond dysfunctional. I watched them cuddle closely in the twin bed, Rick kissing her forehead as she rested her head on his bare chest. I had no frame of reference for this kind of love; my mother's dangerous attraction puzzled me.

Rick was blatantly not good for Mom from the start of their courtship at Farrington High School, where they met in her junior year. Mom liked his sweet, brooding nature. She felt he was misunderstood, and she became his first ally. Mom had been looking for an escape from the verbally abusive and volatile environment Papa created at home, and Rick became that escape for her. Mom welcomed Cori in November 1976, just six months before graduation. Rick was soon sentenced to juvenile detention and then prison, the setting of most of his adulthood. Mom recently told me that she married Rick while he was in jail after Cheraine was born in 1979. I couldn't conceal the shock on my face. It was difficult imagining my mother, with two babies at her side, marrying Rick in a men's prison.

Decades later, my mother led herself back to this man, with whom she created another desperate situation, with three children sleeping in a motel room on the cusp of homelessness. When their evening antics could no longer fund the room, we packed our blue storage bins in the Volvo and crashed at Rick's friend's home in Kalihi. His name was Nicky, and he stole, pawned, and smoked with Rick. I slept on the couch in Nicky's living room (on nights when I didn't crash at Wendi's), while my brothers slept on a bunk bed in the backyard toolshed.

I was unable to express my heartbreak over the dismal state of our family. I didn't have the words to describe the layers of despair I was experiencing. I can't speak for my brothers, but I do know that while I worried about them, I couldn't bear the responsibility of their fears. The load I was carrying was too burdensome. I separated from them, from Mom, from the entire situation, because I needed to care for myself. The money my mother had promised me to cover my weekly shots was inconsistent. Worrying about and funding my transition was not her priority, and as a result I improvised, going every other week to Dr. R.'s or skipping treatments altogether.

I was ashamed to define our situation. Speaking about our experiences with poverty and homelessness would have made it too real for me. I was living it, surviving it, and had no strength to spare to define it. It was also difficult to acknowledge the stark reality of my mother's diminishing appearance. She was scarily thin. The bags under her eyes grew darker. Her complexion was rough with blemishes, belonging to a woman a decade older than her forty years. And her teeth were ravaged by her pipe smoking. She no longer smiled. None of us had anything to smile about.

Any confidence I had about my mother being sober, or at least reasonable, was shredded. She was strung out, desperate, pathetic. It took her a decade to admit her drug use. She told me she smoked meth with Rick because she wanted to be around him, to fit into his druggie world, to numb herself from the dark truth she was living. "For me, it was an escape from reality," she explained. "I knew the relationship was not healthy, but drugs allowed me to not care or feel the pain."

The woman I had dreamed about as a child, the woman with the perfume, long, dark hair, and shelves of books, did not exist. Mom was no longer my dream girl. I had to become that dream.

My vulnerability, resentment, and desperation to survive were the backdrop of my first nights at Merchant Street in downtown Honolulu. The first thing I remember about Merchant's, as we called it, is a red tube-top dress. A woman, standing at six feet in flat sandals, had the hem of her spandex dress resting above her hips as she squatted on the steps of the Alexander & Baldwin Building. Her new vagina was exposed in the dark as boys in a white Lexus screamed, "I like sample!"

She stood up, pulled her dress down to the middle of her lengthy thighs, and descended the steps. She was gorgeous and knew it, the kind of woman who could find her reflection in the dark. Approaching the car, she leaned into the window, dropped her top, and unzipped the passenger's pants. With his penis in her hand, she yelled in a forcefully deep voice, "Honey, nothing here is free!" The girls who were watching, including Wendi and me, hooted as the car sped away.

Shayna towered over Merchant Street. Statuesque, slender, with *ehu* blond beachy hair that mirrored the waves at Waimea Bay and a body just as curvy, she profited from her beauty. She was one of a dozen girls who made coins on the block, hustling nightly in downtown Honolulu, the historical stroll for the trans women of Hawaii.

Dating back to the 1960s, when the legendary Glades Show Lounge touted in lights on its billboard "Where Boys Will Be Girls," downtown Honolulu's red-light district has been an attraction for seamen and soldiers, tourists and admirers, looking for a woman with something extra.

"Look at you, Mary!" Shayna shouted to Wendi, who kissed her and introduced me. "Sickening, yeah?"

Shayna was examining me from my toes (I had on strappy black heels from Slipper Warehouse's clearance sale) and my hips (blue capris stuffed with my homemade pads) to my face and chest (covered in my favorite leopard-print halter). That was where she paused. "Girl, you already got your chi-chis done?" Shayna asked.

"They're hormone breasts," Wendi said like a hype man at a hip-hop show, punctuating all the things that were sure to make Shayna gag.

"I like see," Shayna said, reaching her hand into my bra. There were no personal boundaries when it came to the women on Merchant's. "Maaarry, they're big. So fleshy," she said, scanning my figure. "And that's all your body?"

"Yes, girl," Wendi said, smacking her padded hips, which caused a deep, dull sound.

"Girl, whatchu got in there?" Shayna asked her. "Sofa cushions?"

We all laughed. No one could ignore a good read.

"It's soooo slow tonight," Shayna said with a pouty face. Talking about the traffic on Merchant's was small talk, like discussing the weather. "All these young *kanes* like have for free, but I gotta make coins."

"Those guys were really cute, though," I said.

"It's always the cute *kanes* who no like pay, girl!" Shayna said, rolling her eyes. "My freebie days are over."

Shayna used to come to town from Kaneohe to hang out until she got serious about getting "her change." She was nineteen when she began saving, and by twenty-one she had her own car, apartment, vagina, breasts, and hips filled with medical-grade silicone from a doctor in Tijuana who pumped most of the girls. She had also done mysterious things to her nose, forehead, and cheekbones that no one was able to pinpoint. I admired her work ethic, her determination to execute a plan. To me, transitioning was different for everyone, but one thing was a constant: It wasn't about becoming some better version of yourself or a knockoff of some unattainable woman; it was about revealing who you'd always been.

"Where you guys came from?" Shayna asked.

"Oh, we was just cruising," Wendi said. "Then we pooched a ride from my place."

"What? You like work, Wendi? I get more clients who like *laka* than pussy anyway," Shayna said, pointing out that because we hadn't had bottom surgery we could make more money on Merchant's.

I looked at Wendi with sharp eyes, wondering what she'd say next. She just shook her head.

"Mmmm-hmmm," Shayna hummed skeptically.

Merchant Street was our sanctuary. Every Friday and Saturday night, swarms of girls dressed in their evening best congregated on a street named after commercial dealing and trade. Some girls came to work, others to hang. I came to Merchant's curiously and naively, thinking that merely hanging there would have no effect on me. It was my chance to meet all the legends I had heard about from Wendi: Rebecca was the most successful self-made woman on the block, with a house of her own in Kapolei and double-bagged breast implants to match her plus-sized stature; Heather was one of the fishiest girls on the island with a Barbie body that she stealthily flaunted at a famous strip club in Waikiki; Angela was the only other Hawaiian-black girl I knew of, with long, wavy copper-toned hair, a silicone-free derriere that would make Sir Mix-a-Lot scream, and zero desire to have "the surgery," like the majority of girls I knew.

The women owned the entire block, from Merchant and Bishop to Queen and Bethel. The streets were dimly lit by the buzzing streetlamps and anchored by the Fort Street Mall, a walkway that connected all of downtown Honolulu. The street garnered a national profile after being featured in the 2005 HBO documentary *Downtown Girls: The Hookers of Honolulu*, directed by Brent Owens, who narrated the film in a deep baritone that matched the film's seedy, sensational, sleazy tone. One of the women featured explained the appeal of survival sex work simply: "It was the money and [the men] thinking that I am a woman."

I could see the appeal of profits and the appeal of men, no matter their horny, objectifying, fetishistic intentions, validating the women we knew ourselves to be. Many women used their bodies for profit, but mine wasn't for sale, I haughtily told myself. There was no way *I* could do that. It didn't fit the image I had of myself as an honor student, a class representative, as someone who wanted to do bigger, better things. What I failed to see through my youthful lens was the complexity of these women's roles as surviving outlaws. They came to Merchant Street and took control of their bodies—bodies that were radical in their mere existence in this misogynistic, transphobic, elitist world—because their bodies, their wits, their collective legacy of survival, were tools to care for themselves when their families, our government, and our medical establishment turned their backs.

The varied, often conflicting portraits these women presented shaped my developing composition of womanhood. When I am asked how I define womanhood, I often quote feminist author Simone de Beauvoir: "One is not born, but rather becomes, a woman." I've always been struck by her use of *becomes*. Becoming is the action that births our womanhood, rather than the passive act of being *born* (an act none of us has a choice in). This short, powerful statement assured me that I have the freedom, in spite of *and* because of my birth, body, race, gender expectations, and economic resources, to define myself for myself and for others.

Self-definition has been a responsibility I've wholeheartedly taken on as mine. It's never a duty one should outsource. Of this responsibility, writer and poet Audre Lorde said, "If I didn't define myself for myself, I would be crunched into other people's fantasies for me and eaten alive." Self-definition and self-determination is about the many varied decisions that we make to compose and journey toward ourselves, about the audacity and strength to proclaim, create, and evolve into who we know ourselves to be. It's okay if your personal definition is in a constant state of flux as you navigate the world.

My mother contributed to my sense of womanhood: She taught me tenacity, she taught me that I am my own person, she taught me that I had to do for myself. Admittedly, she didn't know how to raise a girl like me, but the women on Merchant Street did, because they *were* me. In the presence of the mothers and sisters who walked the path before and alongside me on those streets in downtown Honolulu, I uncovered statements that guided me on my path toward womanhood: We are more than our bodies; we all have different relationships to our bodies; our bodies are ours to do what we want with. I stood in awe as these women fought for their womanhood. They taught me, from car to car and date after date, to take ownership of my life and my body.

What I initially chose to do with my body was wield it to gain the affection I craved. Standing on those streets, slightly hidden by the awnings of local businesses and lit by unmoving lamps, I wished for someone to reach out and cradle me, to tell me I was beautiful and worthy and better than the world I had come from. I wanted a man to tell me that there was no money in the world that could buy me. I wanted him to take care of me in the ways that my parents had failed to. When my wishes weren't granted, I chased affection in the cars of cute guys. I believed that these boys looking to get their rocks off would make me worthy, someone better than who I actually was: an incomplete girl-child.

Adolescence is that passageway linking childhood and adulthood, a period in a person's life when you're figuring out who you are in a body taking form, and how that stacks up to the images you've seen and internalized. When I think of my adolescence, I think about the Britney Spears song "I'm Not a Girl, Not Yet a Woman" (please bear with me here). It explains a sense of discovery, in which you're seeking definition while experimenting and changing and asserting who you are in relationship to your peers, your culture, and your and others' expectations. It's that chasm between your reality and your dream.

Coupled with my issues about my body and the instability of my home life, riding in cars with boys became a way to find relief. Wendi and I hung out, drank beer, and fooled around with a string of guys. We'd make out and blow them high atop Mount Tantalus, and if we were feeling a postcoital connection, we'd grab a late-night bite at Zippy's. We'd go to Wendi's at the end of the night on a high, giggling about what the other had done, who had the cuter guy, plotting our next adventure. I felt so adult and so powerful.

Being sexually available was how I validated myself in a world that told me daily that who I was would never be "real" or compare to the "real" thing. Being promiscuous helped me establish a sense of control over the pain and turmoil I was dealing with at home and with myself, my body, and my identity. If I couldn't radically change our homelessness, my mother's addictions, and my own body, then at least I could let a boy look at me with desire.

Growing up, I learned that no one would want me as I was, that sex was secret and shameful. I didn't have the tools to refuse the advances and gaze of men. I saw how my father went from woman to woman with little regard or apology. I witnessed my mother modeling severe neediness with men, as if the only way to have worth was to have a man by your side. I learned from them to never be alone; that I needed a man to make me worthy. My sense of self was partly shaped by how men viewed me. The craving I had in my belly to feel special and desired was insatiable. No man's warm body would be able to assuage my appetite. That bottomless craving was a portal that made it easier for me to break the silent commitment I had made to myself the first time I judged the other girls on Merchant Street.

A silver sports car stopped in front of Shayna, who leaned her lengthy body into the passenger window. After chatting and laughing familiarly with the driver, who was shielded by the darkness of the street, Shayna turned around and signaled me over with a flick of her head. I mouthed "Me?" with a surprised look. She nodded. That walk to the silver car was one of those pivotal moments we all experience when we're presented with an opportunity that reveals our character. The sign in Mr. Higa's office from middle school flashed in my mind: "The decisions you make dictate the life that you will lead."

Shayna introduced the driver as Max. He had a gentle face and blue eyes that sparkled in the glow of his dashboard. I told him my name was Skye, the street name I'd chosen because it sounded ethereal.

"Me and Max go waaaay back," Shayna said.

"Yes, we're old friends," Max said with a deep chuckle. "Actually, I'm the old one," he added with a wink.

"Nah, you still look good, babe!" Shayna said sweetly.

This friendly banter was performance. She pretended to be invested in what he had to say, and he knew the conversation was vital to getting what he wanted. I knew, hovering in Max's window, that he wanted me, just like he had Shayna. He was Shayna's first regular when she was my age, pooching rides from Kaneohe to town. She vouched that he was a good date and would take care of me.

"I've never done this," I whispered to Shayna, removing myself from the car window.

"Girl, I've seen you go with the young *kanes*, romancing them for free," she said. "It's the same thing, except this time you're getting something out of it. You gotta be smart, girl."

"What does he want?" I asked.

"A hand job," she said. "Charge him forty-five dollars. He's got *kala*."

It didn't take much debate to convince me to open the door and enter into premature adulthood, because somewhere within I knew I had been groomed to do it. I had been isolated as a child, raised by absent parents, sexually abused, trained to pleasure men over myself, led to feel a sense of detachment from my body, and haunted by a reality of economic powerlessness. I sometimes wonder in reflection how my life would've turned out if there had been a woman out there that night who told me I didn't *have* to do this, that the money wasn't worth it, that there were *other* ways to get the money I needed, that not *all* girls did this. In all honestly, I see my sixteen-year-old self rolling her eyes and jumping in the car because she knew it was inevitable.

Max's house sat in the shadows of Diamond Head, just a few houses away from *The Real World: Hawaii* residence. His bedroom was toward the back, large, dark and cold. He flicked a switch, which cast a dim light around his king-size bed and highlighted the crow's-feet that didn't go away after he rested his smile. He was at least fifty. Though I told him I was eighteen, I knew he knew I was not, and that was why I was there.

Max signaled for me to take a seat on his bed as he freshened up in his adjacent bathroom. I could hear the water splashing in the sink, and I didn't know what to do with my hands. I sat on his bed and looked around his room, which had framed surf photographs and a long and short board mounted on the wall. His nightstand had a picture of a young, kinda hot blond guy who I later learned was his college-age son.

Max returned wearing white boxer briefs, his bare chest covered in blond hair and freckles. He was muscular, in shape from early mornings spent surfing the neighboring beaches of Waikiki. He knelt in front of me and rubbed my legs, which hung from the foot of his bed, exposed in a short denim skirt. His touch felt forced, like the banter between him and Shayna on Merchant's. Usually, when I was getting it on with guys, I was attracted to them. That sense of desire was one-way with Max, who pulled down my skirt and panties and lifted me to the head of his bed. I pulled the bag of condoms from my purse, prompting Max to shake his head.

"Just a hand job," he said as he reached for a bottle of baby powder, which he handed to me. I had never jerked someone off with powder, but he was paying, so I didn't really study it. Resting on my knees, wearing nothing but my black push-up bra, I poured half a handful of baby powder into my palm. I rubbed them together and stroked him slowly, alternating my hands. Clumps of powder settled on my palms. As he was climaxing, Max announced in a demanding voice, "Flex your arms. Make a big strong muscle for me, baby."

Random, I thought as I balled up my left fist and flexed my bicep. Max screamed, "Oh, baby," ejaculated, and whimpered. It took about eight minutes. When I was dressed and he was cleaned up, he handed me two twenties, a five-dollar bill, and a handful of Claritin.

"It's for your sniffles," he said, touching my cheek. "You must have allergies."

With a diagnosis and enough money to pay for a month of hormones, I felt unstoppable when Max dropped me back to Wendi on the streets. I told her how he wanted me to flex and how grimy it had felt with the baby powder rubbing against his raw flesh.

"Girl, haole men are always so freaky," she said. "Did he want to touch your *laka*?"

"No, he just wanted me to keep flexing," I said.

"Yes, show him that She-Ra, girl!"

That night I had discovered that my body was worth money, and as long as I had a body, I would never be poor. I felt with Max's money I could do more, be more, and so I craved more. Freebies with cute boys would no longer fly, not after getting paid to do much less. Sex was no longer something to do for fun; it was something to trade for the things I needed.

Max became my first and only regular for a long while. I saw him about twice a month for the same old chalky hand job. A whiff of baby powder still transports me back to Max's bedroom, those random nights and late afternoons when I got my hands dirty for his pleasure and my profit. I learned to use my beauty as currency to get the things I needed. I no longer had to rely on Mom for the medicine. I became my sole provider of my hormones, my clothes, my makeup, and my hair appointments.

My experience with sex work is not that of the trafficked young girl or the fierce sex-positive woman who proudly chooses sex work as her occupation. My experience mirrors that of the vulnerable girl with few resources who was groomed from childhood, who was told that this was the only way, who wasn't comfortable enough in her body to truly gain any kind of pleasure from it, who rented pieces of herself: mouth, ass, hands, breasts, penis. I knew, even at sixteen, that I did what I had to because no one was going to do it for me.

Chapter *Thirteen*

Near the end of my sophomore year, Rick was arrested. Mom was by his side in Nicky's shack as police officers cuffed him. I expected her to fight for him, to stand by his side as he sought bail and release, but she surprised me with her lack of engagement. She actually seemed relieved when she learned that his drug-fueled antics garnered him a two-year prison sentence. In that time, Mom slowly picked up the pieces.

We sought temporary shelter with Cori, now a mom of three, having welcomed her third daughter, Alexis, who resembled Snow White, with pale skin, big dark eyes, and jet-black hair. Unfortunately, Cori, the big sister who'd spent her life raising babies, struggled as a single mother in her mid-twenties, following a similar path as Mom, full of babies and unworthy men. In retrospect, it's easy to see the pattern, and that recognition has helped my family to heal and forgive.

At the time, I was unforgiving to my mother despite her improvements after Rick's arrest. I looked at her with a seething skepticism as she climbed her way out of the hole she had dug us into. After a year of unemployment and six months without a home, Mom landed a job with the Department of Transportation, which enabled her to rent a two-bedroom apartment at Richard Lane, a blue apartment building just a block away from Cori's. She was providing us with a long-forgotten stability. This didn't impress me, because she had already failed me. Mom had lost my trust, just like my father had the day he put that pipe to his mouth. The only difference was that I never dreamed of my father. I had no expectations of him, and maybe it was unfair, because the ones I had of her were unattainable. She couldn't live up to the image I had created.

I side-eyed her as she attended all of Chad's basketball and football games and shuttled my brothers to the mall on payday to buy or trade new games for their PlayStation. When she wasn't preoccupied with work or the boys, she was at church or in prayer groups with her friends, usually other mothers who designated certain nights to pray for their children.

As my mother filled the void Rick had left with God and parental attentiveness, I was on the bus, shuttling between our apartment in Kalihi to Salt Lake. Moanalua became a daily annoyance, with the administration's vocal intolerance about my dress becoming unbearable. By the end of the school year, I was called out of class or lunch to Vice Principal Johnson's office at least a dozen times because my legs dangled out of skirts.

"You know our rules," Johnson would say, smirking as she wrote another red slip instructing me to go home and change, causing me to skip whole days of school. My mother soon noticed my string of absences and, surprisingly, sparked a conversation about why I was always home before her. I explained that the way I dressed was "distracting" and making people "uncomfortable," according to Johnson.

My mother wasn't confrontational, and I know a part of her felt it was her fault for not advocating for me at Moanalua. I couldn't explain to her that I was beginning to believe that maybe, just maybe, I deserved that treatment because I was different. I realize now that I was internalizing the administration and some of my peers' phobias, which would take years for me to undo.

My string of absences didn't affect my grades, but avoiding school was not a solution. With Mom's help, I finished the school year and transferred to Farrington, a five-minute walk from our apartment, joining Wendi and my brother. It was my mother, through her involvement with the athletic department, who helped ease some of the growing pains at my new school by asking the registrar's office to note my gender and name on the records. My mother's vocal advocacy for me, paired with the administration's openness, helped me skirt many of the awkward, uncomfortable moments I had faced during my two years at Moanalua.

Awkwardness still ensued as I reintroduced myself to classmates, many of whom had known me from middle school. "Nice rack," shouted William Phillips, the quarterback of the football team, whom I had let copy my pop quizzes in eighth-grade social studies. I rolled my eyes as his friends giggled at my growing bustline.

My breasts were certifiably bounceable, wrapped in a blue sweater with a deep neckline that captured my classmates' curiosity. I was in a rush to flaunt them, and the guys who took residence outside my first-period psychology class gawked at me. It amused me when they caught themselves staring and attempted to erase their lust with a quick, hurtful tease, squashing any confusion that my body presented them with.

As I walked into class, William asked, "Eh, you get your sex change or what?"

Luckily, our teacher, Mr. Tanaka, who had come to Farrington to coach football but ended up with a class of half-interested psychology juniors, heard him. "William, shut your mouth," he said in a stern voice, "or you'll find yourself benched."

A teacher had never stuck up for me in this way. It was teachers like Mr. Tanaka who led the way for acceptance campus-wide, ensuring that I was treated like any other girl in class. Farrington, which had a troubled, violent history due to Kalihi's poverty and gang presence, was experimental and forward in its strategy. The school led the way with a radical, holistic approach to meeting the needs of students. Farrington had a special center for teen mothers and moms-to-be; a groundbreaking English-as-a-second-language program catered to the growing immigrant community from the Philippines, Micronesia, and Samoa; and the Teen Center, an office run by two social workers and a nurse, where students learned about sex education, took advantage of peer mediation, sought LGBTQ services, or could find a safe environment to talk. The resources at the Teen Center changed my life.

Wendi, with whom I walked to school every day, introduced me to Alison, one of the social workers at the Teen Center. She cofacilitated a monthly support group for transgender students, called Chrysalis, with a transsexual woman in her early forties named April. With her fair skin and fluffy blond hair, April was the first everyday trans woman I had ever met. I had seen trans women only at night, on the streets or performing in pageants or clubs. April was married to a businessman and worked as an HIV/AIDS prevention outreach worker in Honolulu, where she regularly tested the girls. She always carried bags of lube and condoms in her handbag, which she gave to us at the end of Chrysalis meetings. It was April who administered my first HIV test at sixteen. She swabbed my mouth in the parking lot outside our school library and called me two weeks later with my negative test results.

Chrysalis was a safe place where we could openly be ourselves without the commentary of the outside world. We discussed our struggles (Alex's fear of being disowned by her Mormon parents if she came out), our successes (Wendi's early admission to cosmetology school), and our dreams (my goal of getting a scholarship to college). We snapped our fingers at one another's fierceness, quoted *Golden Girls* at the drop of a hat, and read one another when it was necessary, as with Paula's inability to give herself a good tuck. ("Girl, did you bring your camel with you?" Wendi would tease, making us all laugh.) The most powerful feature was April's guest speakers, who showed me that having an everyday life out in the world in the daylight was a possibility. April brought in trans women who worked as lawyers, store managers, teachers, and community outreach workers, like Hina and Ashliana, who were in their mid-twenties and giving back to girls like us through their nonprofit, Kulia Na Mamo. Chrysalis was a sanctuary of our own creation where we let our members know they were not alone. It was also where we asserted that we deserved to be here, that Farrington was our school, too.

Farrington had a history in my family. It was where my mother met Rick, where she graduated with Cori on her hip, where Uncle Toma threw the touchdown pass that won Farrington the state title in 1990. Chad upheld our uncle's sportsman legacy, running track, playing basketball, and catching passes as a wide receiver on the football team. It was my brother's teammates who often gave me the hardest time. My only reservation about transferring was Chad. I felt bad that my presence disrupted the world he had carved out for himself. We didn't discuss my transfer, and if Chad was bothered, he wouldn't have told me. He was kind that way, more considerate than I would have been. Even though Chad accepted and respected me, I know that a part of him didn't want me at his school. He didn't want to hear the guys whispering about what was in my bra and my panties. But Chad, the sensitive, caring one, shared his school with me, and it became mine, too.

Though my family in Hawaii grew to accept my gender over the years, the same can't be said for my father, whom I hadn't seen in the nearly five years we'd been with Mom. Despite his absence, he was very much present to me, especially when he called the apartment, here and there, to speak with Chad and me. I usually sat next to Chad, sharing the receiver as he asked about school, the family, and sports. When he asked for me, Chad knew to say I wasn't there; it was the only time he ever referred to me as "he" or Charles. I hadn't told my father that I was a girl. I was afraid to do so. He still had an intimidating presence in my life. After a year of this charade, when I was in my junior year, Dad asked for pictures. I finally sent him my yearbook photo and this letter:

Dear Dad,

I hope you're well. I want to say that I'm sorry I haven't spoken to you in a while. I've been going through a lot of stuff, things you probably will not approve of and probably will not understand.

Growing up, I've always felt different, like I was born in a body that didn't match who I was. With the help of Mom, Chad, and our family and my friends, I've realized that the reason I felt different was because I have always been a girl, just in a boy's body.

I'm sure you'll be angry about this and won't approve of it. I remember when I was growing up you scolded me for liking girl things, for not playing football and basketball like Chad. I'm sorry that I've disappointed you in the past and maybe now, but I'm trying to make myself happy.

I go by Janet now. I don't expect you to approve of this and I know it's a lot but I just wanted to be honest and stop hiding and avoiding you. I hope we can talk again, but I do understand if this is too much for you to handle.

I love you but if you can't accept who I am, then I can't talk to you.

Love,

Janet

After I wrote the letter, sealed the envelope, and dropped it in the mail, I wanted to take it back. I'd been too defiant because I had been avoiding all contact and conversation with my father for over a year. I had a lot to tell him, yet stubbornly told myself I didn't need his approval or love. A piece of me had something to prove to him: that despite his years of frustration over who I was, I was a happy and healthy teenage girl and there was nothing he could do about it. I knew that the physical distance between us kept me safe. The odds of him having the money to fly to Hawaii to reprimand me and cuss me out were slim.

A week later, I got a letter in the mail from Dad, which surprised me. In it, he complimented me and said that I "looked nice." He said it would take him a while to get used to calling me Janet and seeing me as a girl, but "I will try my best." He used the latter part of his letter to address my "ultimatum":

Your disrespect for me is apparent. You never respected me when I think about it and you never liked me. But I'm the parent and you're the child and it is not your job to love me the way I love you. My love for you is unconditional and no matter what you decide in your life I will love you. Doesn't mean I have to like it, but I will always love you.

Love,

Dad

When I look back on this exchange, I realize that I didn't give Dad the chance I gave my mother, who had time and experience, seeing me take all the baby steps I took to reveal myself, from Lip Smackers and tight jeans to name changes and hormone treatments. My mother and I didn't consult him when I started hormone therapy, I avoided him when he called, and Chad kept him in the dark. I realize now that I shocked my father into submission by giving him an ultimatum that proclaimed: *Accept me as your daughter or pretend that I do not exist.* When a person transitions, it doesn't affect only the person undergoing the change but all those who love that person. I didn't take into account the mourning that my father, my mother, my siblings, and my family would undergo as I evolved, and in my father's case especially, I didn't take into account his love for me as his child, a love that has given me a solid core, knowing that no matter what I go through, even if he has nothing else to give, I have his love.

By the end of our junior year, Wendi considered Farrington a waste of her time. I can't count the number of times she stood me up on the intersection of Gulick Avenue and King Street, the meeting spot for our morning walks. She overslept with little regard. She spent most of her time with older girls like Shayna, who schooled her in the ways of Merchant Street and got her into the straight clubs in Waikiki. For a seventeen-year-old girl, fast money, parties, and boys were an appealing alternative to algebra and English. I remember her coming to school at lunch with no makeup on, big sunglasses, jeans, and a hoodie. She was just going through the motions, showing her face so the vice principal wouldn't call her grandmother for truancy.

I swiftly judged Wendi. She was becoming a night creature, like the older women we knew who came out only at night, when they knew getting clocked would not be an option. The night shielded them from obligations, from what I saw as the "real world." I wanted Wendi to be better than they were, to rise above them. I was also bitter because she was a deciding factor in my decision to transfer to Farrington. I had wanted us to eat lunch together, to go to prom together, to strut down the aisle in our white graduation gowns together. But school was never Wendi's thing, and I never told her I was angry with her for what felt like abandonment. We were best friends who became young women together, pooched rides together, learned the tricks of the streets together, and dreamed together. Her leaving school created a wedge between us, one that in hindsight was a gift.

Throughout my adolescence, I was compared to Wendi, the louder, more flamboyant half of our relationship. I was envious of the attention that she commanded, of her long and silky hair and equally lengthy legs—fitting so perfectly into Hawaii's standard of mixed-Asian beauty—and, most striking, her unapologetic air. Wendi always seemed light and free, operating without obligation, without a filter, without the sense of impending judgment that I admittedly had. She didn't care what people thought or said about her, and I respected her for that. I had hoped, ever since we met in the seventh grade, that some of her would rub off on me. Ultimately, she decided to drop out on her eighteenth birthday, at the end of our junior year. She fast-tracked her GED and went to cosmetology school as I continued on alone in my senior year, a time that allowed me to step out of the shadow of our friendship and find myself. I made new friends, like the cool-girl clique Allure Ladies, who embraced me, welcomed me to their table at lunch, and invited me to parties on the weekends. I also joined peer mediation at the Teen Center under the guidance of Alison, who became one of my first allies. She took me to conferences where I trained middle school students on conflict resolution and the benefits of creating LGBTQ student alliances. I talked to her about the complex issues in my life, including my gallivanting on Merchant Street.

"But I don't do what they do," I lied, not wanting Alison to know that I had an arrangement with Max and a handful of loyal regulars. I knew she was acquainted with Merchant's because our Chrysalis co-facilitator April did outreach there. "A lot of young girls go to just hang out. It's like Chrysalis, a place where we can be with our own."

"It's important to be around people who understand who you are," she said, looking at me as I picked at the bowl of Chex Mix in front of me. "Do you ever worry about money?"

"Only when I think about the cost of surgery and stuff," I said, feeling a bit defeated. It was the first time I had told anyone besides Wendi about my desire to have bottom surgery.

"That doesn't make you a girl, Janet. You are complete just as you are," she said, trying her best to lighten the burden I felt as a seventeen-year-old with no money to reach such a goal.

I first became aware of the fact that genital reconstruction surgery (GRS) was a possibility when I was thirteen, lying in Wendi's bed, hearing stories of older girls who had undergone the procedure. Now they were in front of me on Merchant's, living possibility. In my gut, I knew that I was a woman regardless of what lay between my legs. Most of the women I knew hadn't undergone GRS; some had been saving for years but life got in the way, while the majority chose not to have it. I knew that their genitals didn't dictate their womanhood, and I knew there were many paths to womanhood. My path and my internal sense of womanhood included a vagina, and that does not negate anyone else's experiences. I was determined to have GRS. It was never a question of *if* but *when*. *When* depended on how fast I could attain those resources.

"I want other things, too, like I want to go to college as a girl, and I want to move to the mainland and just live my life," I said. "But I can't do all of that without first getting over this. It's like the first big step I have to make."

Alison nodded in the assuring way she always did, telling me that she was confident I would do everything I wanted and more. Years later, when I replayed this conversation to her and told her that I had crossed the threshold into sex work while at Farrington, she was surprised. She told me that she'd had an unwavering faith that I had dodged that fate. "You were always so smart," she said. "So I just knew you would find a way. I just hate that it had to be that way."

It was Alison who urged me to get a work permit so I could nab an after-school job and start saving for my dreams. I soon landed at a popular urban clothing boutique called Demo at Pearlridge Mall in Aiea, known for its crew of fly salesgirls. I felt honored to be one of them, in cropped graffiti tees and embellished low-rise jeans. This distinction made up for my pathetic paychecks, about a hundred and fifty to two hundred dollars for thirty to forty hours of work, an amount that I spent on employee-discounted Baby Phat. The girls on Merchant Street would've laughed at my salary. When your self-identity and worth are tied up in how much you can make and how many men want you, it can be hard to see value in doing anything else. Though I knew I earned more with sex work, I wanted to prove I could do something else, to prove that Merchant Street wasn't my *only* option.

I took pride in the fact that I could get a job, that I could be out in the daytime, that I could spend my humble earnings on Taco Bell Mexican pizzas in the food court, that I could be visible, out of the darkness. Some people in the mall knew I was trans, but most did not. It was a taste of the freedom I would experience as a young woman in New York City. Those paychecks weren't going to get me to New York, though. That was real. No matter how much

I loved working at the boutique, I knew it couldn't ease the urgency prompted by the clock that ticked within me, reminding me daily that it would take money for me to get where I needed to be. I couldn't ignore the fast money available to me. The survival sex trade economy and the women of Merchant Street would lead me to realize those dreams.

It was the sight of Kahlúa's newly stitched-up vagina during my final year of high school that put me in touch with possibility, just a few thousand dollars away. Kahlúa, who was in her late twenties, came to Merchant Street for one reason that night: to flaunt her new Lexus, boobs, diamond ring, and vagina, fresh from Thailand.

"Honey, I'm getting married next spring," she said, extending her knotty knuckled hand, which sparkled with an emerald-cut diamond. "Congrats, girl!" was said all around. We wanted to ask how she'd funded this quick transformation and knew it had to be the guy who had proposed. Just a year before, Kahlúa had seemed like all those other butch queens, who'd put on a wig, a dress, and some heels on the weekend to attract cute guys who wanted a girl with something extra. I didn't even know that Kahlúa was living her life as a girl, and she knew any girl would be envious of her progress, so she came there to make us gag. And gag we did.

"I met this guy at Hulas about nine months ago," she said, prompting Rebecca to walk away because Kahlúa's Cinderella story was already too much for her. Rebecca believed you had to earn your womanhood. She was out on Merchant Street nearly every night, and no one gave her anything; she worked for it.

"Girl, never mind her," Shayna said, consoling Kahlúa, who was obviously hurt by Rebecca's shade.

"Well, we began dating, and he told me that I looked good in drag," she said. "I told him I actually wanted to be a woman but didn't have the money, and he said he would help me because he loved me. Next thing you know, I was flying to Bangkok to do it with Kalani's doctor. I went in January."

"And he paid for everything?" Wendi said as a crowd of girls zeroed in.

"Yes, girl. All twelve thousand dollars of it," she boasted.

This ignited the fairy tales of all the girls on that block, the urban legend we'd heard our entire lives: Some handsome or at least decent man would swoop in and pay for your pussy without asking for anything in return. And you would live happily ever after as a legal female or, as Octavia St. Laurent said in *Paris Is Burning*, "a full-fledged woman of the United States." Despite my jealousy over Kahlúa's swift transformation, I knew that having some man pay for your surgery involved sacrifice. Nothing is given to you for free. There's a level of ownership when a man sponsors you, as the girls called it. I always wanted to say that I did this for me, that this was and is and will always be mine.

"Girl, we like see," Shayna said, not even feigning propriety. She had seen it all.

As if she'd been practicing this choreography her entire life, Kahlúa crouched down, lifted her skirt, and spread her lips. I had never seen a vagina this close before. I had seen porn only through cable stations we didn't have access to. It was always behind a haze of black-and-white moving pixels, and the vaginas I saw in *Playboy* were always prettily posed, with soft lighting and retouching. They looked more like illustrations. I naively thought there was one uniform vagina template, and Kahlúa's looked nothing like that. It looked like a gruesome scene from *Law & Order: SVU*.

"Ohhhh, it's healing really well," Shayna said, and the older girls nodded in unison. "Girl, that looks really good!"

That was when I decided I knew nothing when it came to vaginas, despite my determination to have one of my own, straight from Thailand: just one of a handful of far-flung places (Morocco was once a hub; now Brazil, Iran, Serbia, and Thailand reign) where trans people travel for affordable gender affirming surgeries. Genital reconstruction surgery in the States can cost upward of thirty thousand dollars, whereas in Thailand, at the hands of surgeons who have performed significantly more procedures due to high demand, it can cost about a third of the price. In 2001, GRS was offered for about seven thousand dollars plus travel. The cost of surgery is the sole responsibility of transsexual patients, who are often already grappling with social and economic marginalization. Most trans people cannot afford to pay these expenses.

Though I hadn't saved enough money to pay for a ticket and hotel stay in Thailand, I asked Kahlúa for her surgeon's contact information. Her positive experience and results presented me with possibility. Kahlúa wrote her surgeon's name and Web address on a napkin, which I held on to tightly. It became my ticket to freedom.

Chapter *Fourteen*

S ome of my most pivotal moments rose from pop culture. As a child who grew up in front of the television, I spent my adolescence blanketed in images from the late-nineties pop boom. I watched MTV's *Total Request Live* (*TRL*) faithfully every day after school, and it was seeing the premiere of "Bill, Bill, Bills" on the countdown that shifted how I saw myself. I was in awe of one girl, waving a hot comb in the air at her mother's Houston, Texas, salon while lip-synching Destiny's Child's outspoken lyrics. Her name was Beyoncé Knowles.

Oprah Winfrey talks about the moment she saw Diana Ross and the Supremes on *The Ed Sullivan Show* in the sixties. She has said that seeing Diana Ross being glamorous "represented possibility and hope . . . It was life-changing for me." That's what I felt as a teenager in front of my TV in a lower-middle-class apartment: no real possibilities beyond school, no images of any girls like myself in the media; it fed me to see Beyoncé in that video and, later, on magazine covers and at the Grammys and on my bedroom walls.

I was a mixed black girl existing in a Westernized Hawaiian culture where petite Asian women were the ideal, in a white culture where black women were furthest from the standard of beauty, in an American culture where trans women of color were invisible. I was not represented in the media, but Beyoncé and Destiny's Child validated me. If I was working at the mall, Chad and Jeff dutifully recorded Destiny's Child's TV appearances; they knew how serious I was about DC3. When Mom went to the drugstore, she'd pick up *Teen People* or *Vibe* if she saw Destiny's Child on the cover. I still remember the black-and-white *Vibe* cover featuring Beyoncé as Diana Ross after three members of Destiny's Child were booted from the group. If I went to the hair salon, I asked for a blond weave, steadily rocking those loose braids Beyoncé wore in the "Bug a Boo" and "Say My Name" music videos. She was my style icon, the epitome of a graceful, talented, strong woman. She was the mold for me. She made me love being brown, she made me love my adaptable curly hair, she made me love that my thighs touched.

All that admiration didn't translate to those around me. No matter how much I loved myself, my growing self-confidence didn't shield me from intolerance and ignorance. Some of my classmates refused to let Charles go. I'd hear my given name thrown at me in the hallways, at assemblies, at dances, or as I was walking home from school. It was a sure way of putting me in my place, of letting me know that no matter how much I evolved, they clung to the way things were. The past was more than prequel; they remembered and made sure no one forgot.

One day when I was walking home from school, a group of kids from the KPT housing projects, where Cori lived, were trailing me. I was wearing heels, slightly wobbly and unsure on the unpaved path that led to the bridge over Kalihi Stream. As I neared the bridge, I heard the kind of obnoxious group cackle that's meant to arouse fear in someone not part of the clique. A chant soon began: "Chaarrrlesss! Ohhh, Chaaaarles!"

Keeping my eyes on the rocky path, I carefully sped up and widened my stride. I had to be careful. If the thin wedge of my sandals met a rock at a bad angle, my ankle would buckle. I noticed one pebble, then another, and a few more hitting the ground around me, bouncing like Rice Krispies in milk. Then one hit the back of my head, and another my back. The rocks didn't hurt, but they shook me, crumbling my pride. I wish I had been brave enough to turn around and confront them. Instead, I took the rocks on my back and my head until I crossed that bridge to my apartment while they laughed past me. When I got home, I collapsed onto my twin mattress and committed to traveling further than any of these idiots ever would. I found solace in the fact that nothing was wrong with me. Instead my audacity to be seen, to dare for greatness, moved those without that same courage toward defense. Feminist theorist and cultural critic bell hooks wrote, "Sometimes people try to destroy you, precisely because they recognize your power—not because they don't see it, but because they see it and they don't want it to exist."

Though I lost that battle, I did win others, including the grand prize in a speech contest where I fiercely recited Maya Angelou's "Still I Rise" and "Phenomenal Woman," words that served as fuel, enabling me to recognize a legacy of resilience that lay deep within me. Then Alison told me with the biggest smile that I was one of four finalists for a full-tuition scholarship to the University of Hawai'i at Mānoa. I wasn't thrilled. I dreamed of going to NYU, like Felicity (or UNY, as it was called on the WB series), but I'd applied to UH because I didn't want to leave Hawaii without having had bottom surgery. Alison told me that members of the faculty had nominated me, and the W. R.

Farrington Memorial Scholarship committee would interview me in a few weeks. The award was worth sixteen thousand dollars, covering tuition, books, and other expenses.

On the day of the interview, I knew the odds were stacked against me. When I saw Elaine, a Vietnamese girl who was by far the most academic girl in our school, I knew the interview process was just for show. The award had to be hers. We four finalists sat in the teachers' lounge near the front lawn of the school, facing the circle sculpture by artist Satoru Abe. Called *The Seed*, it boasted bronze and gold leaves reaching out to the sun. I wasn't nervous about the interview until I meditated on the cluster of three seeds at the bottom of the statue. The piece's energy was in the reaching leaves, but they all emanated from those seeds. I thought about how this money could help me, how I'd be the first person in my family to attend college. I thought about accepting my scholarship and how it would be the seed money for my future.

When one of the counselors facilitating the interview called me in, I was surprised by the number of committee members in the room. There were three women and four men, one of them the publisher of the local newspaper, the *Honolulu Star-Bulletin*, and another the great-grandson of the namesake of the scholarship and our school, a former governor of Hawaii. I sat at the head of a long table, in front of the eyes of all of these adults. My hands were uncomfortably placed in front of me, one of my acrylic nails missing and my French manicure chipped slightly. I wore black wide-legged trousers and a white button-down blouse. My hair was auburn with two blond strands in my front layers, mirroring Beyoncé's signature highlights.

"So, you want to study law and be a certified public accountant as well?" one of the men asked, skeptical in the way that adults are when young people's goals seem unrealistic. Quirky Ally McBeal had made me want to be a lawyer, and my business accounting teacher, who treated me with kindness, had made me want to be an accountant. I didn't tell the board that. I told them I appreciated the certainty of numbers and the uncertainty of the law's interpretation.

They asked me other standard questions that spanned my involvement as a peer mediator and a member of Chrysalis. I effortlessly answered those questions because I expected them. As the interview was closing, one committee member gently inquired about what it meant for me to go through "the changes" I had gone through so publicly. I told her that I had transferred to Farrington to find the support that I needed, and though some students teased me, my experience had been mostly positive. Then she asked, in an unscripted moment of awe, "How do you do it all?"

That was the first time an adult besides Alison looked at me with genuine wonder, as if I were something to be marveled at. I didn't give myself a moment to think about how I was an honor student, a trans girl, a mall employee, a part-time sex worker, and a soon-to-be college student dreaming of a sex change. Like Beyoncé on my walls and Janie in *Their Eyes Were Watching God*, I felt validated, reflected, understood. Her recognition of my struggle, my circumstance, and my tenacity overwhelmed me with emotion. I didn't know if there was a right answer. I just knew I had to be honest.

"I don't think too much about how I do it all, because I have no choice but to do it all," I said through mascara-stained black tears, resembling Lauren Conrad on *The Hills*. "I think it's hard being any of us, and the only thing that makes it a bit easier is being okay with who you are. Some days are easier than others, but every day I am really happy to be me, and I think that helps a lot."

That May, with my family, Wendi, and Alison cheering me on, I accepted the sixteen-thousand-dollar scholarship. I received a lei and an award certificate as the applause of three hundred of my classmates and their families and friends roared in front of me. In my white cap and gown, I took in the sea of white and maroon filling our school's amphitheater, feeling victorious and humbled and affirmed in a holistic way. These people believed in me, which made me believe in me even more. I felt nothing could stop me. We celebrated over Chinese food that weekend with Papa and Grandma Pearl and my aunts and uncles, whom Mom had reconnected with after her breakup with Rick. I received cards of congratulation and leis and school-supply money. I landed on the front page of the life section of our daily newspaper, which cited me as Janet Mock, not Janet Mock the transgender girl. I was Janet Mock, "the UH-bound daughter of Elizabeth Mock of Honolulu."

College began that fall in the wake of much mourning. On my way to my first day of school, I heard on the radio that the singer Aaliyah had died in a plane crash in the Bahamas after a video shoot. She was only twenty-two, four years older than I was. I had known her through her music since she was fifteen. Having never known anyone close who had died, I cried those first few nights of my freshman semester to the songs of her self-titled final album, released just a month before her death.

Two weeks later, Mom shouted from the living room at six A.M., telling us to get up. I joined my family in front of the TV, where we watched the footage of the World Trade Center on fire. We sat mere miles from Pearl Harbor, where sixty years earlier it was blazing by foreign attack. The world felt chaotic, the future uncertain, and the first thoughts in my head were selfish ones: *I do not want to die before I get a chance to be truly myself.* There were vigils at school, a march, and blood drives. Everyone wore American flag pins and ribbons on their cars. Hawaii felt so far away, so detached from the mainland, from New York, that the attack's impact felt as if it had happened to some foreign country. That sense of mass loss, though, made me think about my own death, about how my youth didn't guarantee that I'd be here forever, and in the limited time I had left, I wanted to be fully me.

A flame of determination and urgency rose up, rivaling my internal angst and desperation about my body. I could not look at the mirror without panties on, and when I lay in bed, I was always tucked. There was never a free moment when I allowed my genitals to just be beyond the shower or in some man's hand or bed for money. Even then, I cringed. *What woman lets a man touch her like that?* I thought. Not the kind of woman I saw myself as. That cycle of desire, the desire to be touched and loved and appreciated for exactly who I was and the messages that I sent myself about who I was and how I looked, sent me into a tailspin.

I never resorted to physically hurting myself, which seems to be a common thread among trans youth grappling with issues of identity, body, and the angst of being teenagers. I've heard stories from people who were so disgusted by their body, with the dissonance, incongruence, and conflict it presented to their sense of self, that they mutilated the parts that they wished they could be rid of. It seemed like it was the only way out.

I was willing to make any compromises to get my surgery, and those nighttime thoughts birthed a plan that would get me to my goal by the end of the year. I made the decision to engage in the sex trade full-time on Merchant Street to save the money I needed to fly to Thailand by the end of the year. It was a plan for my own survival. It was my decision, one of the only viable choices for me to get what I needed. Many people believe trans women choose to engage in the sex trade rather than get a *real* job. That belief is misguided because sex work *is* work, and it's often the *only* work available to marginalized women. Though we act as individuals, we can't remove ourselves from the framework of society. Systemic oppression creates circumstances that push many women to choose sex work as a means of survival, and I was one of those women, choosing survival.

Pulling out the napkin Kahlúa gave me with her surgeon's name, I found his website, which detailed that he had performed more than a thousand genital reconstruction surgeries and had studied under Thailand's most acclaimed surgeon. His portrait was amiably confident. He stood in a black suit with his arms over his chest, flaunting a welcoming smile. I wrote him a detailed e-mail about my journey: I had been living as a girl for the past four years, three on hormone therapy. I told him I was interested in undergoing surgery in December, three months from now. He wrote back a day later, requesting that we consult over the phone and to ready myself with a letter from my physician.

During our phone call, Dr. C. said that he remembered Kahlúa and would be delighted to help me. He detailed the procedure, the recovery process, and my stay in Bangkok. He said he could schedule me during my winter break from school. I was certain he was the surgeon for me: He was kind and patient; I could examine real-life examples of his work; and he was well versed with any operating room complications. I e-mailed him that weekend to set my surgery date for December 20, 2001, wiring seven hundred dollars from my checking account: a 10 percent deposit for the surgery and seven-day recovery.

Days later, I was surrounded by screaming girls at the Neal Blaisdell Center. It was September 21, just ninety days until my trip to Thailand. The most beautiful woman, my real-life dream girl in white sequined shorts and a cutout top, took the stage. Brown-skinned beauties flanked her, one a redhead, the other brunette. All my focus was on the girl in the center. It was Beyoncé, the woman I had looked up to since I was fifteen. As part of the *TRL* tour, Destiny's Child, complete with Kelly Rowland and Michelle Williams, held firm to their concert despite uncertain times. Rappers Eve and Nelly were supposed to join them on the tour, but they canceled in the wake of September 11.

Destiny's Child opened with their single "Independent Women," from the *Charlie's Angels* sound track, and closed forty-five minutes later with a cover of Bob Marley's "Everything's Gonna Be Alright" and their megahit "Survivor," fitting tributes to our nation's mourning and my feelings about a future that seemed to be looking up. I had started to study my horizon, energized by the possibility of what was to come. "The dream is the truth," Zora Neale Hurston wrote. So I would go on to "act and do things accordingly."

Chapter *Fifteen*

Working on Merchant Street was a nonevent at the time. Keeping secrets in the darkness of Derek's bedroom all those years ago had prepared me, it seemed. After I'd jumped in one man's car, jumping in another wasn't anything of note. The cars of strangers became my evening cubicle, my first office of sorts. Serving men and taking their money were the only requirements of the job, and I was a natural.

The bulbous gearshift of a date's car was always in the way, no matter if it was a Lexus or a Honda. I draped my body over it or the center console in a way that flattered my exposed ass and comfortably placed my face in his crotch. Most times I jerked and sucked wearing my thong, unless he paid extra for me to be exposed. I filled every condom with a packet of lube and slipped it onto his penis. The lube made the latex softer and suppler, thus speeding up ejaculation and decreasing my time and effort. I rarely pleasured a man in the backseat because it gave the date too much freedom to touch and move around and make demands I didn't feel like fulfilling. I preferred him confined to the snugness of the driver's seat. Whether we were parked in a nearby lot or on a dark, tree-lined residential street, the men were all the same. Some were gross, some were not. Attractiveness was irrelevant. All I cared about was that they were respectful, clean, and had the cash in hand.

Time was money, and all the money we made was ours. We spent it on necessities, from rent and car payments to food, clothes, hormones, and surgeries. None of us had a pimp for protection; we didn't need a man because we looked out for one another. It was the women on Merchant's who taught me the lube-in-condom trick, who made sure my purse was filled with condoms, who whistled when an undercover cop was stopping for a girl, who rounded us all up when outreach workers were on the block testing for HIV and other sexually transmitted infections.

I had made rules for myself on Merchant Street, things that were absolutely off-limits: no anal, no kissing, no topping. Setting and articulating these rules gave me the illusion that I was in control of the ridiculous situation. The underground economy predated me. The Merchant Streets of the world were there long before I came into being and would be there long after I retired that December. It was an ecosystem with its own rules. As desperation sank in and my surgery date encroached, I bent many of my rules, depending on the money offered.

One rule none of us broke once we crossed over into working-girl-dom: Don't ever do freebies or lower your prices for any date. If someone lowered her prices, she would be found out, because a date was never loyal. He would tell you, in an effort to haggle with you, who let them penetrate for sixty dollars or blow for forty or jerk off for twenty-five. Girls who dropped prices were shunned, looked down upon, called desperate.

"Oh, nay, Mary, he's a cheap *kane*," a girl would scream to you as you leaned in the car's window. "No date him. Scram, you chaser!"

No girl would jump in that car and be able to return to the block with her head held high. We spilled the tea about good dates and bad dates, about guys who were shady or sketchy or high, about the ones who took way too long for the amount of money they offered. We also knew who was a cop who liked to date and actually paid, versus the ones who liked to date but would threaten to arrest you if you made him pay.

To avoid getting arrested by undercover cops (or *maka'i*) and sting operations—which usually happened at the end of the month, when the police department needed to meet quotas—we developed a code based on the experiences of the older girls on the streets. Word was that if you said *gift* or *donation* instead of *price*, *money*, or *cost*, you couldn't be arrested because you hadn't attached a dollar value to sex acts. Another safeguard was asking a date to let you touch his penis. If he willingly whipped it out, that meant he wasn't a cop, because a cop wouldn't cross such a line. Some girls would go as far as telling a date to lick her breasts or genitals to be completely sure he wasn't an officer. This was all dependent on the cop's trustworthiness. This system helped me to never get caught, unlike Wendi, who was impatient and took risks. She got popped a few times on Merchant Street. Luckily, she was a minor at the time, and her arrests were expunged from her record.

Most trans women engaged in survival sex work are not as lucky as Wendi. Poverty is the key factor that drives trans women of color into sex work. The sex industry is filled with women of color, and so are our prisons. Race, class, and gender are all factors that frame the harshness of sentences, and, more likely than not, a trans woman of color arrested on solicitation will be treated as a criminal with little regard to the systemic oppression that has led her there. Our society criminalizes underground economies like sex work, and deep moral biases and stigma make even the most liberal folk believe that these actions are a moral failure of the individual rather than the workings of a system.

When a trans woman is arrested, she is charged with an act of prostitution, a non-violent offense committed by consensual adults, and placed in a cell with men, because prisons are segregated by genitals. A trans woman in a men's prison or jail is vulnerable to sexual assault, contracting HIV, and being without hormones and trans-inclusive health care during her incarceration. Yes, this is cruel and unusual punishment.

While working on Merchant's, I didn't have the luxury to analyze the ways of the world. Weekdays were hit-or-miss; you couldn't predict how busy you'd be. Usually, I'd be out on the street from ten P.M. to two A.M. Weekends were more reliable, dating consistently from ten P.M. to five A.M., since the nightclubs, mostly in Waikiki, closed at four. I averaged anywhere from $600 to $1,000 a weekend, giving $60 blow jobs, $40 hand jobs, and $20 to $40 upgrades (if they wanted to see, touch, or suck my penis). Occasionally, if the guy was cute enough, anal sex was on the menu for $120, but only if I was receiving it. I never topped because my very personal definition of womanhood didn't involve exerting myself in that way. Plus, I couldn't guarantee an erection due to years of hormone therapy. It seemed too messy and time-consuming anyway.

Most of the guys who dated me didn't care about an erection as much as they wanted to be pleasured by a woman who had something extra, something that made me a rare sex goddess in their eyes. Sexuality and people's desires, preferences, and fantasies are difficult to define. But what I know for sure is many men are attracted to women, and trans women are among these women, and our bodies in all their varying states of being are desired. Yet it's the bodies of women with penises who are made to feel that their bodies are less valuable, shameful, and should be kept secret.

As long as trans women are seen as less desirable, illegitimate, devalued women, then men will continue to frame their attraction to us as secret, shameful, and stigmatized, limiting their sexual interactions with trans women to pornography and prostitution. And if a trans woman believes that the only way she can share intimate space with a man is through secret hookups or transactions, she will be led to engage in risky sexual behaviors that make her more vulnerable to criminalization, disease, and violence; she will be led to coddle a man who takes out his frustrations about his sexuality on her with his fists; she will be led to question whether she's worthy enough to protect herself with a condom when a man tells her he loves her; she will be led to believe that she is not worthy of being seen and must remain hidden.

For many dates, I was the first trans woman they had sex with. They were men who had spent years looking at transsexual porn or cyber-sexing with trans women through webcams but had never met a trans woman in real life. Honestly, many didn't even see me as a *person*. If I hadn't had a penis, I would not be as attractive to many of the dates I profited from. My allure and income on Merchant Street was dictated by what hung between my legs, and some of the men who became my regulars sexually evolved beyond me, preferring a girl who could top them or give them sexual experiences that aligned with their imaginings and fantasies.

It was empowering to not feel shameful about my body and sexuality, but it was under the guise of doing a job that was full of stigma. I was not proud of this work. I was grateful it existed, but that doesn't mean I was grateful for the lustful gaze and touch of older men. They didn't know me; they wanted to occupy me. And frankly, I was grossed out by the dates and had zero compassion for them.

Kindness and compassion are sisters but not twins. One you can buy, the other is priceless. To have compassion for these men would mean that I'd have to know them and they would have to know me, and this wasn't part of the sexual contract.

It was a bit different with regulars. There was more kindness there, something that almost resembled respect. Regulars grew to become part of my everyday life, like a neighbor you share an elevator with from time to time: He gets off on seven, you on twelve. You smile, you press the button for him, he for you, and then you never see each other until that chance meeting when he happens to ring your elevator. You smile, he presses the button, and you say bye. You don't know his name, he doesn't know yours, you treat him with kindness, and you appreciate the time you spend together, but you don't dwell on it and think, *Hmmm, I wonder how he's doing.* There's no longing, just a sense of the inevitability of the exchange.

For me to know or care for my dates would mean admitting that I accepted the cruelty of the situation. Let's be clear: A world in which a young girl uses her body, her most intimate asset, in order to survive is unconscionable. But I did and still do have hope. In the small denim handbag that held my condoms, lube, baby wipes, hand sanitizer, scented lotion, and lip gloss, I carried a folded piece of paper with words from Maya Angelou's *I Know Why the Caged Bird Sings*: "I didn't come to stay."

When I wasn't on Merchant's or at home, I was on campus at the University of Hawai'i. I adapted to college life effortlessly and thrived on the independence of my course schedule. I attended lectures on philosophy, English composition, religion, and political science during the day and spent my late afternoons completing my coursework. Wednesday through Saturday, I juggled my academic load and my evening shifts on Merchant Street, where the older girls like Rebecca and Shayna cheered me on, ensuring I had a ride home early enough to make it to my morning classes. It was understood in our sisterhood that I was making something of my life, that I was reaching heights that most girls and women like us were unable to grasp, and that my time on Merchant's would be short-lived.

I now know that I survived the dissonance of my daytime and nighttime lives through compartmentalization. Psychologists define compartmentalization as a defense mechanism or a coping strategy, one that enables a person to deal with opposing situations simultaneously. I employed it for over three months. I saw myself as a college student by day, diligent about classes, study groups, and library hours, and a teenage sex worker at night, diligent about being professional, quick, and smart with fast money. These two worlds, in my mind at the time, had nothing to do with the other. I applied extreme focus on getting good grades in the day and making the money I needed for my surgery at night.

When I was watching TV with my brothers or typing my term papers at the computer lab, I didn't think about my dates or the girls on Merchant Street. It was a short-term coping mechanism that allowed me to survive the intensity of the situation. It gave me the freedom that I needed to believe that I was still just any other college coed with plans and promise, though I broke the law four nights a week. I realize that I was able to make it through and actually succeed despite many traumatic situations, from sexual abuse to my father's drug addiction to our family's homelessness, because of compartmentalization. What I had done with my body issues, my family's economic struggles, and my academic success was place them all in compartments. I isolated each from the other as I dealt with them separately.

In the evenings, as Chad, Mom, and Jeff were saying their good nights, I was preparing for my nights out. One of my friends who also worked the streets would pick me up on her way to Merchant Street (I usually filled up her tank once a week by way of thanks) at about nine-thirty P.M. When we arrived downtown, I always greeted the girls who were out, and we'd have small talk about whether it was slow, dead, or busy and how their previous night went. We'd swap stories about the randomness of the streets, like the guy who'd approach a girl and ask her to pee on him in the alleyway for forty dollars. Or some poor girl, her arms bruised, would detail her unfortunate run-in with one of the tax-collecting queens. They were trans women, most likely high on meth, who worked for cheap or for drugs on the "back streets," a seedier area at River and Kukui Streets. They randomly made their way to Merchant's, asking girls for twenty here, fifty there. If you didn't give them money and they thought you were lying, they would attack you. Fortunately, I never crossed paths with those vicious queens.

At home, though, with the exhaustion of the streets and my course workload, I was turning into a vicious queen myself. I didn't really try to hide the fact that I was on the streets nearly every night. Frankly, I couldn't care less what my mother thought at the time because she had no right to pass judgment on my life after what she had put us through. I remember one day Mom was complaining about the electric bill, scolding me and my brothers for leaving lights on in empty rooms. She had these outbursts, when she cursed and slammed cabinets in the kitchen while cleaning, once every few months. Rightfully, she was stressed, overburdened, and underappreciated. Tired of hearing that particular woe-is-me monologue, I lifted myself from the couch, walked into my room, grabbed $120, and placed the cash on the kitchen counter. When I returned to the couch, Chad's eyes went from the twenties to my face. He wore a look of shock and suspicion that asked, *Where'd you get that?*

I watched my mother closely. She dried her hands on the striped dishrag and turned toward the money. She paused on the bills lying on the counter for a few seconds. I waited for her to ask me how I got that money. I wanted to confess to her about what I was doing. I wanted to cry into her chest and tell her that I rented out my mouth and sometimes my ass to men to make money for the things she couldn't afford to get me. I wanted to tell her I was tired and I needed help. I needed her. Instead, she picked up the six bills and went to her room. Even then I knew that I was never a priority for my mother. It was the curse of always excelling. I never got in trouble. I always took care of things, and this was a blessing for my overstretched mother, who knew I had a handle on things.

I wanted her to be the parent in that moment and demand that I stop. I wanted her to shake me and tell me that she'd find another way for me. But we both knew that she had no solution, no money, no resources that would stop me. She wouldn't be saving me, so she remained silent and paid the electric bill.

Chad, seventeen and a senior in high school, was worried about his sister. His look let me know that he knew where the twenties came from, why I was rarely home at night, and why I had new clothes and hairstyles. I wish I'd been empathetic enough to lie to Chad and say I had a rich boyfriend whom I spent nights with, who bought me things. At the time, I didn't have the capacity to care what others thought. I was going to do what I needed to do regardless of anyone's input.

Chad recently told me he became suspicious after he heard whispers at school from his jock friends about seeing me on Merchant Street. His friends were among the caravan of guys who'd drive by, throwing obscenities, pennies, or eggs at the girls. They were the same guys who'd drop their friends off and return alone to date the girls. Chad also told me that he woke up a few times a night when I was out, checking my room periodically to see if I was home. "I couldn't really sleep if you were out," he said. "I was scared something was going to happen to you."

It broke my heart hearing this because I loved my brother, but I felt alone and was angry at the world. It was an anger and despair that blinded me to the genuine concern he had for me at a time when I was reckless and arrogant enough to think that I could handle it all.

"I didn't like some of the decisions you were making," Chad told me recently. "I hated the fact that you were out there doing whatever you were doing. But I knew that you were doing it to be who you are today."

The woman I am today has sensory triggers that transport me back to late 2001. The smell of latex never fails to place me naked in the passenger seats of men's cars. Waiting for a friend alone on a dark street corner of New York takes me back to being eighteen, scantily clad and in high heels, waiting for someone to pick me up. Any woman wearing Victoria's Secret Amber Romance, the lotion I wore at the time, brings me back to the reflective windows on the buildings of that block where I'd primp myself between dates.

It took years of self-reflection and heightened political consciousness for me to look back on my time as a teenager in the sex trade with the same compassion that I easily extended to young girls I read about in articles or saw featured in documentaries on sex trafficking. I saw these girls as vulnerable, controlled by an abusive man who lured them under the guise of love into the commercial sex industry. They even called him Daddy. No one on Merchant Street had a pimp to blame. I operated under the illusion that I was out there on my own free will. I had no villain, no one person to blame for my circumstance, so for years I blamed myself. This lack of a villain initially made it difficult for me to look at my younger self with compassion. I've argued with myself for years that no one *forced* me to do it; no pimp wooed me with sweet nothings and gifts to work the stroll. I *chose* to do it. But how many choices did my younger self really have?

Selling sex seemed like a small price to pay in order to get what I needed. I did it for "free" my whole life, I thought, with Derek and Junior and the men I blew and fucked in my adolescence. I later learned that sexual abuse is a common pathway for many women in sex trade and work, with an estimated 66 to 90 percent of teen and adult women reporting that they were sexually abused prior to engaging in sex work, according to anthropologist Dorothy H. Bracey, who spent years profiling youth and women engaged in sex work. Uncovering that fact led me to realize that I was not alone, and there were many factors that made young trans women like me all the more vulnerable to the survival sex trade, whether by choice, circumstance, or coercion.

Trans youth, especially those of color, represent a large portion of young people engaging in survival sex, yet they are often erased from narratives of organizations serving youth sex workers. The greatest push factor for trans girls engaged in the sex trade is poverty, stemming from homelessness (often brought on by parents and/or guardians refusing to accept their gender identity) or growing up in already struggling low-income communities where resources are scarce. A young trans woman, especially a runaway with no familial support, may not find a job due to lack of education or prior experience, age, or no updated ID documents showing her appropriate gender markers, which can lead to further discrimination. Most likely, if you're a low-income trans woman of color, you don't have access to health care, which makes it difficult to cover hormones and surgeries. With this systemic lack of resources glaring in your face, your body aching for food and hormones, your mind internalizing the pressures of society that say you must look a certain way and that you don't matter, survival sex work becomes a tried-and-true solution that you've seen older girls survive on for years.

Without money of my own, I had no doctors, no hormones, no surgeries. Without money of my own, I had no independence, no control over my life and my body. No one *person* forced me or my friends into the sex trade; we were groomed by an entire system that failed us and a society that refused to see us. No one cared about or accounted for us. We were disposable, and we knew that. So we used the resources we had—our bodies—to navigate this failed state, doing dirty, dangerous work that increased our risk of HIV/AIDS, criminalization, and violence.

Fortune and luck were the elements separating me from the hundreds of vulnerable women killed every year for being poor, trans, feminine, and of color. I later learned that trans women of color are disproportionately affected by hate violence. In 2012 alone, the National Coalition of Anti-Violence Programs (NCAVP) documented twenty-five homicides of people in the United States who were murdered because of their gender identity and/or sexual orientation. Thirteen were trans women, all of whom were women of color, comprising an astounding 53 percent of all anti-LGBTQ homicide victims, despite representing only 10.5 percent of survivors who reported incidents of hate violence to NCAVP. These stark statistics point to the disproportionate and deadly impact of hate violence against trans women of color.

On a late night in November, just four weeks before my scheduled surgery, with my flight to Bangkok booked and finals around the corner, a white van pulled up to me on Queen Street. I had a rule never to date men in vans. I couldn't know what they carried in the back of their vehicle, like weapons or other men. Too much risk was involved. So I just kept walking.

"Can you please stop and talk to me?" the man said, heightening the pitch of his voice to sound less intimidating. "I've dated other girls before."

"Sorry, I don't date men in vans," I said as he continued to trail me slowly.

"I've dated Shayna, Rebecca, and Heather," he said, stopping me in my tracks. "Everyone knows me."

My guard went down a bit, and I asked him to turn on his overhead light. The yellow glow uncovered a chubby-cheeked man with brown shaggy hair under a Rainbow Warriors football cap. His eyes were bulgy, like a pug's.

"What do you want?" I said from the sidewalk, refusing to lean into his passenger window. I knew distance would keep me safe.

"I'd like you to suck me off while I touch your sweet titties," he said in the unabashedly horny way of horny men with no need for pleasantries.

"You okay with my eighty-dollar donation?"

He nodded while licking his lips. I had to do everything in my power not to laugh. I had become a professional at controlling my instincts and reactions in the pursuit of money. When I told him I'd follow him to the public parking lot on Beretania Street, he put his tongue back in his mouth. "Oh, just come with me," he pleaded. "I'm really fast, easy. I'll give you an extra forty." He pulled a fan of crispy twenty-dollar bills from his pocket. They looked fresh, like unhandled bills from the ATM, my favorite kind. They made the work appear less dirty.

Something in my core whispered, *Wait for another date.* But the sound of those crisp twenties in his stubby fingers was too loud. I jumped in the van and directed him to the parking lot where I took a lot of my dates. After he parked, he unbuttoned his cargo shorts and began stroking himself. "Help me out," he said. "Show me those sweet titties."

I couldn't stand men who said *titties*. It made me not want to have breasts. I lifted the bottom of my brown boobs out of my bra and began tweaking my nipples. He was hard, oohhhing and ahhhing as he kept stroking. I pulled a condom out of my purse and twisted the cap from my lube, filling the condom.

"Ahhh, no need condom," he said.

"I don't blow without a condom," I said.

"Okay, what about just a hand job, then?" he asked.

"I don't jerk without a condom," I lied, because he was starting to skeeve me out.

"Come on, I'll give you two hundred dollars," he said. "The easiest two hundred of your night."

"Money first," I said as he let his penis stand on its own and grabbed the bills from his pocket.

I put the money in my denim handbag and began stroking him. Under the beams of the moon, I could see the darkness of his dilated eyes. He looked at me with a focus that scared me. I realized that he was high on something. That internal whisper escalated to a shout: *Just leave the money and get out.* I ignored it, and he came within five minutes. I put my breasts away, handed him some wipes, and rubbed sanitizer on my hands, the smell of alcohol filling the car.

"Told you I was easy." He smiled as he turned the ignition. "Should I drop you at the same spot?"

I nodded as my anxieties about him left me. He came, I got paid, and we were on our way back to the block. As we approached the corner of Merchant and Bethel, I noticed more girls were out at the far corner and asked him to drop me near them. Instead, he pulled over and grabbed my arm.

"Give me your purse," he said calmly. Under the lights of the street, I could see the irritated pocks on his cheeks and the frightening intensity of his stare. He was definitely tweaking.

"No," I said, lifting the lever of the door while tugging my purse, which held about eight hundred dollars from two nights of work.

"Let your fucking purse go or I promise I'll gut you," he said as the glare of the pocketknife in his hand reflected slightly.

"Please, just let it go," I pleaded with him in my sweetest voice, hoping to ignite compassion in him, something absent in all of these exchanges.

"Bitch," he said, grabbing a handful of my hair and bashing the side of my face into the center console between our seats. "Let the fucking purse go."

"HELP! HELP! SOMEBODY FUCKING HELP ME!" I screamed. I didn't feel the throbbing of my head, just the rush of adrenaline.

Miraculously, I got the door open with my left hand gripping my bag, my right foot on the street, and some of my hair still in his hand. He was too strong and won the tug-of-war, speeding off with my purse and a hair extension as I fell on the street. The sting from the glued track stung my scalp as I lay there in defeat.

"GET THAT LICENSE PLATE!" I screamed when a couple of girls ran down the street to me. I called the cops from one of their cell phones, even though some of the girls predicted that they wouldn't do anything for me. I told the operator that I'd been robbed, describing the van, the license plate, and the incident.

Two police cars—the normal squad car and a single-rider golf-car-like vehicle—arrived within ten minutes. I sat on a bench in Fort Street Mall as three officers asked me to relay the details of the attack. I felt naked, unprotected without my purse or identification, and inappropriate, like a girl with no keys to any home.

"Why did you go in the van?" asked the officer writing the report.

"He was giving me a ride home," I lied, knowing that the truth couldn't be written in the report.

"Aren't you out here every weekend?" asked the officer who drove the cart, chewing his gum nonchalantly. I recognized him and his mustache. He never bothered us but did drive around the block every few hours, often stopping to chat with Rebecca.

I nodded with embarrassment. He wanted to squash this report and put me in my place as a prostitute unworthy of justice. His indignant tone said what all three officers were thinking: *There is no purpose in writing a report for you as you pretend to be a victim. You brought this on yourself.* I wanted to cry, because I realized the absurdity of my claims, of the fact that I had the audacity to report someone else's wrongdoing to the police when I was breaking the law on the regular. Still, I wanted to show them my worth, to say that I was more than just a teenage prostitute. I was different, special, worthy. I was a college scholar with promise and a 3.8 GPA. My cleavage-baring tank top and frayed denim miniskirt betrayed me. To them, I was nothing more than another hooker. No one would miss me if I went missing.

"Do you want to press charges?" the officer with the notebook asked in an exasperated tone.

I shook my head and watched as they drove away. I used one of the girls' phones and called one of my regulars, Sam, whom I had been dating since my junior year of high school, to pick me up. I didn't have the courage to return home. I felt unworthy of my own bed and stayed at Sam's high-rise apartment overlooking Ala Moana Beach. I relayed the details of the attack while lying in his Notre Dame T-shirt.

Sam was in his late thirties, with sandy blond hair and large green eyes that always took me in with a warm compassion that I rejected each time he hugged me, touched me, moved deep inside me. Sam was from San Diego and had lived in Hawaii for about five years, working as a lawyer. He moonlighted as a photographer, traveling to Brazil, Las Vegas, Los Angeles, and Thailand to capture trans women for his friend's popular pornography portal.

I cried myself to sleep that night and woke in the morning to the smell of eggs and coffee. He handed me a mug as I sat at his breakfast bar, where I saw the brightest blue ocean. I still marvel at the fact that I grew up surrounded by such powerful beauty, the Pacific Ocean nestling me in its majesty.

"You know, Janet, I was thinking," he started. He was my only regular who knew my name and where I lived. "You don't have to do this anymore."

"You think I want to do this?" I said, swishing the sweet bitterness of the coffee in my mouth. "I'm too close to bow out now."

"What if I gave you another option?" he said. "What if you let me pay for the rest of your surgery?"

"I couldn't let you do that," I said, tucking my knees to my chest, stretching his college shirt.

"Why not?"

"It just wouldn't be right," I said.

"What's the use of me having money if I can't help someone I love?"

His question lingered over breakfast. This was the dream of thousands of girls everywhere: for a man to love you, care for you, provide for you. It was the rescue, like Richard Gere climbing Julia Roberts's fire escape in *Pretty Woman*. Sam was the embodiment of that dream, a husband or sugar daddy who was attractive enough and generous with his wealth. I knew women like Kahlúa and many others who had fulfilled that dream of having a man provide for them, giving them surgeries and resources. I could not try on their dreams; they didn't fit me. To accept Sam's charity would involve the ultimate compromise of appropriating someone else's dream.

I realize this sounds contradictory, coming from the same girl who offered her body to men for half hours at a time. But I wasn't for sale in that way. Never was. I couldn't imagine looking between my legs and thinking of Sam's pity disguised as love for the rest of my life. I wanted to be able to say I did it myself, on my terms, my way. To accept Sam's gift would be to lie, and I had never lied to him or myself. I couldn't accept his gift because I knew he thought he loved me. It was a one-way affection I'd profited from for years. Sam was aware that I was hustling every night to raise the money for my surgery, and only now, as I was so close to reaching my goal, just twenty-five hundred dollars away, he had extended charity. Acceptance of his offer would cost too much. It would involve my freedom under the unspoken understanding that I would then be *his* woman.

I declined Sam's offer just a few weeks before I lifted off to Bangkok. I had finals coming up, though flash cards and all-nighters weren't really on my mind. I was sacrificing pieces of myself nightly for the bigger picture: to exist in a body that represented me more fully. Using my body was easy initially. I owned it and used it to benefit me. I was born with it and had to live, love, and suffer in this world with it. It was mine to sleep with, profit from, and modify. I grew up in a world where the sex trade, like the modifications we all went through, was part of the pact, a part of the journey we had to go through as trans women.

There's a level of competence and mastery involved in being good at hustling, and the constant attention from dates falsely boosts your self-esteem. The tragedy is when girls believe all they are good at is being some man's plaything. When your self-identity and self-worth are tied up in how much money you can make and how many men want you, it can be scary not to rely on that identity; it can be hard to let it go and not know how to define your worth for yourself. Unlearning all I had been taught about who I was, what I could imagine for myself, what I felt was possible, and my tenets on love and sex and trust have been my biggest lessons. I'm still learning.

Sitting in Sam's kitchen, I paused and experienced one of those check-in moments with myself. I sat there and thought, *You know you're a prostitute, right? That you sought comfort in a regular after being attacked by another date, and now this date is proclaiming his love for you, his go-to fetish come true.* I waited for some sense of shock, for some well of emotion. This wasn't the trans version of *Pretty Woman*. No one was going to climb my fire escape and rescue me. Nothing but a solution came. Not a good one, but it was a way out.

"How much do you pay those girls who pose for you?" I asked.

"That's not for you, Janet," he said with a skeptical look. "You can't take it back once it's out there."

Chapter *Sixteen*

I cringe at one thing when I look back on my adolescence. Reliving this decision, made over a dozen years ago, has been the most difficult part of my writing. I've thought honestly about softening it, maybe even erasing it from my history. My ego convinced me several times that I could deny it ever happened. But I know that excluding it from this chronicle of my life would be cowardly. It would mean I was actively erasing a part of my journey. Why tell your story if you're not going to tell it in its entirety?

My decisions are my decisions, my choices my choices, and I must stand by the bad ones as much as I applaud my good ones. Collectively, they're an active archive of my strength and my vulnerability.

I wish I valued myself enough to tell myself that there are in fact things you don't *have* to do to survive. You can say no, but that's the thing about vulnerability. I didn't know then that I was at my weakest, my most exposed. I was too much of a survivor to admit it. I was busy fighting and didn't have the luxury of weighing options and considering consequences. Instead, I quickly made the best possible decision available to me at the time and found relief in having found a solu-tion, something that would move me closer to my goal. I was fully in the moment of making progress, and it wasn't until I evolved beyond survival that I realized what I'd done. No matter how vulnerable, how young, how exposed I was, I still can't reverse this decision.

When I met Sam's friend Felix at the sex toy shop on Nimitz High-way, I picked out a black camisole and thong hanging on a white plastic hanger. Felix, a pudgy, chinless man with sparse blond hair covering his forehead, questioned my choice, dangling a white lin-gerie and garter set in front of me. It was wrapped in plastic, sterile, never worn. "How's this?" he asked in his jolly British accent.

"Cute," I said, shrugging. I couldn't care less about wardrobe; I had never worn lingerie before.

"Cool, we'll get this, and you pick out another outfit," he said. "Black is boring."

Felix's choice was sweet, innocent, virginal. I picked a Brazilian-cut bathing suit, which was more grown-up, like the seductress I felt men wanted in their beds. At the counter, Felix paid in cash, throwing a small pink dildo into the bag.

We drove his red convertible Jaguar, with a personalized license plate that boasted the name of his company, to a gorgeous house on the hilltops of Hawaii Kai.

"Would you like a drink?" he asked as he placed his keys on a side table in his living room.

"I'm fine, actually," I said.

"Cool. Mind taking this, though?" he asked, handing me a bottle of water and a diamond-shaped blue pill. The Viagra was another nod toward his professionalism. He'd obviously encountered girls who couldn't get erect because of estrogen.

I took the little blue pill in Felix's bathroom, standing barefoot on his beige-and-blue-tile floor. It was the prettiest bathroom I had seen, with a claw-foot tub framed by a glass wall with embossed leaves, something straight out of MTV's *Cribs*, and a separate shower. With the white teddy, thong, and garters on, I leaned over his sink, the cold marble meeting my barely covered belly, and lacquered my lips with a generous coat of MAC's Prrr Lipglass. I looked at myself in the mirror, as I'd always done when I got ready, and paused, hearing Sam's words: "You can't take this back."

As on those dozens of nights when I got ready for Merchant Street, this was no different. No wave of emotion, no ache in my belly telling me to get dressed and go home. Nothing came. I flipped my blond braids to one side of my face, smacked my lips, and smiled.

I took a seat in a chair opposite Felix and his camera, which stood on a tripod. The leather chair was whiskey-colored, a few browns darker than I was, contrasting my skin, barely covered in the skimpy, sweet lingerie. The cheap lace scratched the backs of my thighs. When the red light lit, I looked straight into Felix's camera and said my name and that I was eighteen. I resembled a teenage virgin bride on her wedding night.

"What are you going to give to us?" Felix asked, with his face shielded from the camera.

"Everything," I said cheekily, placing two fingers in my mouth while rubbing my nipples with my other hand.

"Is that a promise?"

"Oh yeah, most definitely," I purred, my glossed lips and legs spread wide-open.

"Why don't you stand up and show everybody your body."

I went on to pose in my lingerie, play with myself using my new toy, and blow Felix. We then moved to his bedroom, where he had sex with me, still unseen by the camera as I lay exposed.

"Baby, that was so fucking good," he said, his chubby-cheeked face sweaty and red. With his cum still on my chest, he proposed that we schedule another shoot, rounding out my fee to fifteen hundred. Accepting his offer was a no-brainer. It was the most money I would ever make at one time.

In Felix's shower, I washed all remnants of him off of me. As I scrubbed my body, a sense of accomplishment washed over me, rivaling the scent of Irish Spring. I was just weeks away from flying to Bangkok, where I'd be changed forever. Dry and in my own clothes, I looked at Felix gratefully as he handed me $750 for the shoot, which I nestled in the side pocket of my handbag. I showed him my ID, proving I was the age of consent, eighteen, to appear in this shoot, and didn't think twice about signing away the rights to my image.

Later that month, as promised, I returned to Felix's for the second shoot, where I earned the remaining $750. A weight was lifted from my shoulders. My surgery was paid in full. No one could take the money out of my checking account. All I had to do was board that flight to Bangkok. I know now that the weight didn't disappear. It was just replaced by another load, something I'm unpacking now. I've had to share that weight with Chad, with my mother, with Aaron. And each time I've revisited this decision, I've had to face myself.

All the compromises I had made created a crescendo of energy that led me to ultimately dishonor myself, to desperately create a situation where I was in front of a camera, smiling coyly. I've never watched the video in its entirety, but in the short clips I've seen, I can't look past the image of a little kid who is trying her best to be sultry. I thought I was in control of that moment. I thought I was so adult. What strikes me isn't the rawness of the shoot but my youth. My voice is undeveloped, high-pitched. I see how bad I am at being sexy. I see my impatience, how I desperately wanted Felix to come so I could get my money. I see Thailand and the proximity of a fulfilled dream in my eyes. I see that I'm still becoming comfortable with myself, and there I lay in a leather chair, sharing my half-formed self with this stranger, his camera, and the objectifying male gaze, immortalizing the one part of my body that brought me so much anguish. I put it out there for the entire world to see.

I didn't foresee the growing reach of the Internet, which now enables millions of people to download my image for a small fee and share it with thousands of others. As I write this, I think about those who will be able to access these images, screengrab them, and repost them for others to see. I didn't think about the fact that when you put something out there, you can't get it back. Sam had warned me. All I knew for sure at the time was that no one was going to do anything for me. So I did everything in my limited power to get what I needed in order to attain my not-so-simple dream. Limited resources, being backed into a corner, being told that you can do anything when nothing is really given to you, all breed desperation.

What I cringe at is not the act of sex or my young, undeveloped body. I'm not ashamed of my form as much as I was when I was a teenager. I can recognize the beauty of that girl. I can see what makes her beautiful, but what makes her tragic is the desperation. Immortalizing my desperation for the world to see, that hunger, that starvation, are what makes me ache now.

I initially wanted to paint Felix as the villain who wooed me, urged me to do something, taking advantage of my youth, my lack of resources, my desperate situation. But I can't put all of that responsibility on him. He profited from the facts that I was poor, desperate, immature, impatient, that I didn't have the foresight to know that the Internet would become a platform for pornography, most of which objectifies women's bodies for the male gaze and pleasure. At the same time, I profited throughout adolescence on my beauty and my body. I used what I had at the time to get what I needed.

No one can destroy their past. You can try your best to cover it up, edit it, run away from it, but the truth will always follow you. Those parts of yourself that you desperately want to hide and destroy will gain power over you. The best thing to do is face them and own them, because they are forever a part of you. In writing this, I am facing the consequences of a decision I made as a teenager, a decision that afforded me the resources to exist, live, and dream in my body. I compromised my integrity by exposing the one thing I hated most about myself: my unconquerable desperation.

Chapter *Seventeen*

P eople often describe the journey of transsexual people as a passage through the sexes, from manhood to womanhood, from male to female, from boy to girl. That simplifies a complicated journey of self-discovery that goes way beyond gender and genitalia. My passage was an evolution from me to closer-to-me-ness. It's a journey of self-revelation. Undergoing hormone therapy and genital reconstruction surgery and traveling sixty-six hundred miles from Hawaii to Thailand are the titillating details that cis people love to hear. They're deeply personal steps I took to become closer to me, and I choose to share them. I didn't hustle those streets and fight the maturation of my body merely to get a vagina. I sought something grander than the changing of genitalia. I was seeking reconciliation with myself.

Arriving in Bangkok on the night of December 19, 2001, with sixty-five hundred dollars in cash as my only travel companion, I was aware that I was so near my lifelong goal, yet so far from home. I was alone and eighteen in a distant pocket of Asia. My first thought was bittersweet: *I made it on my own.* It was apt, though, that I was alone in a foreign country. In reflection, it's symbolic of my solitary journey to accept, adapt, and adore myself, an expedition that would be deemed just as foreign as Southeast Asia was to me my first evening in Thailand.

The custom lines at Don Mueang Airport were all kinds of wet hotness. Steamy heat moistened my face in a way that Hawaii's humidity never did. With my new passport stamped, I pushed through a crowd of men looking for their next fare, past the bustling baggage claim area. I saw a white card with my name on it, held in the air above two smiling Thai women, both just above five feet with matching dark, chin-length hair. One wore a vibrant purple and orange wrap, colors that reminded me of Grandma Pearl's garden. When I approached the women, they were delighted to see me, as if I were an old friend. The woman in the wrap introduced herself as Jane. She was the surgical nurse and office manager for Dr. C.'s clinic and spoke fluent English. The other woman, Fern, was all smiles and nods and tasks, grabbing my bags and taking on the streets of Bangkok from behind the wheel. She didn't utter a word as we drove about an hour to the doctor's office, where I was scheduled to have my presurgical consultation that evening.

From the leather backseat of the sedan, the unplanned juxtaposition of wealth and poverty struck me. I noticed sparkling glass highrises and luxury car dealerships adjacent to tarp-covered, tin-roofed homes and people eating street meat under twinkling neon signs advertising "Girls! Cocktails! Good Times!" Fern, her fellow motorists, and pedaling pedicab drivers ignored the lines painted on the road, merging at a rapid pace in the dimly lit darkness. I dug my palms into the champagne-colored leather seats, trying to maintain some semblance of control.

I was nauseous when Dr. C. held both my hands in his and kissed me on the cheek. He looked even more boyish than the photo on his website, with a kind face and an unfaltering smile. He called me Miss Janet, and his sweetness eased what little anxiety I had about placing my life in the hands of a stranger. We had communicated through a series of e-mails over the past four months, and I knew instantly, from the kindness of his staff, the cleanliness of his clinic, and the genuine respect and empathy he exhibited, that I had chosen the right person. I lucked out to have been treated by Dr. R. and Dr. C. I've since learned that it is rare for trans people to have access to medical professionals who are skilled, respectful, and sensitive.

With Jane standing close by, I sat on a paper-covered exam table in a thin pink medical dress. Dr. C. took my blood pressure and monitored my heart and lungs with a stethoscope. He then asked if I would mind lifting my dress. I nodded, slowly gathering the hem of the garment to my stomach.

"This is good, very good." He smiled upon touching my hairless genitals with gloved hands, his slim eyes twinkling with delight. "We're going to achieve very good depth."

"How many inches do you expect?" I asked.

"I can promise seven inches, but I know we can get eight, maybe even more with good dilation when you go home," Dr. C. said. He went on to explain the details of what would happen during the following morning's procedure, which would involve him refashioning the skin, nerves, and tissue of my genitals (except erectile tissue and testicles) into a vagina of my very own.

"Will I be able to have an orgasm?" I asked.

"Yes, the majority of my patients in time achieve good orgasm." He pulled the hem of my dress back to my knees.

Jane handed me a consent form that reiterated the details of the surgery, listed the cost and one-week recovery stay at the surgery center, and the long list of possible complications, including death. I paused for a beat over that five-letter word and realized that I could die alone in a country many miles from those I loved. I reflected on the fact that I never asked my mother or father if they were okay with this, that I barely said a proper good-bye to Chad, Wendi, or Jeff, that I boarded the plane never thinking, not once, that I wouldn't be on the return flight home.

I didn't dwell on the risks because there was no other alternative for me. This surgery in this foreign country was the step I'd known I had to take ever since I was old enough to know it was a possibility. Death was guaranteed for all of us, and I was young and naive enough to believe that I had more living to do. So I signed my life away, handing Jane the consent form. She added it to my file, which included my blood tests, chest X-rays, and endocrinologist's letter, verifying that I had been living as a woman and under his care for hormone therapy since I was fifteen.

"Thank you, Doctor," I said as I handed Jane sixty-three hundred dollars in cash, the outstanding balance for my surgery.

"*Kop khun krap,* Miss Janet," he thanked me in Thai, reaching for my hands. "I want to thank you for trusting me to help you in this next step of your life. It's a blessing that I get to make people like you more happy."

I paused on his sentiment of "more happy." I liked his acknowledgment that the surgery wasn't finally making me happy; it was a necessary step toward greater contentment. Having genital reconstruction surgery did not make me better. The procedure made me no longer feel as self-conscious about my body, which made me more confident and helped me to be more completely myself. Like hormones, it enabled me to more fully inhabit my most authentic self.

The hospital, my home for the next week, was just a few miles away. It resembled a hotel, with a doorman who grabbed my bag from

Fern and escorted us to my room, marked "Miss Janet—Hawaii" on the placard. It was a single room with a full bathroom and balcony that overlooked the city, my closest neighbor a mosque. As instructed, I hadn't taken hormones for the past two weeks, and I blamed this hormonal imbalance for my teary farewell to Jane and Fern when they bade me good night.

As I unpacked my bags, a smiling nurse came into my room to administer an enema, which cleared my bowels for the surgery. I showered, settled into my bed wearing an oversize tank top, and called home. Mom was more than half a day behind me and was already at her office, working one of her last days before the Christmas holiday. I let her know I'd arrived safely and my surgery was scheduled for seven A.M. and I would have someone call her when I woke up. We exchanged "I love yous" and hung up as if I were down the street, spending the night at Wendi's.

After a restless night, I sat up on my bed at about six A.M. to the sound of the mosque's morning call to prayer blasting through the speakers. Shortly after, Jane, in green scrubs, greeted me with a smile and a surgical gown. Slipping into the white cotton dress, I lay on my back in the rolling bed outside my door. Jane and another nurse took me in an elevator up two floors to the operation room, where Dr. C., an anesthesiologist, Jane, and the other nurse stood in matching green scrubs. They were wearing sandals, and this reminded me of home.

"Today's your new birthday, Miss Janet," Dr. C. greeted me, his eyes twinkling from behind his surgical mask.

I smiled as Jane placed an IV in my arm and the anesthesiologist rolled his chair to the head of my bed. He introduced himself and said that he'd be monitoring me during the surgery and that I had nothing to worry about.

"Now count backward from a hundred," he instructed.

"Ninety-nine, ninety-eight, ninety-seven, ninety-six . . ." I counted, my last sight being the cream-colored ceiling of the operating room.

I woke up a bit groggy in the recovery room with my knees spread apart at a forty-five-degree angle. I immediately felt like I had to pee, though the attending nurse said I had a catheter and my urine would release itself. I was puzzled because the need-to-pee sensation didn't leave me for that first hour. I didn't feel any pain because I was given a Demerol drip intravenously. Discomfort from bed rest was a reality that no narcotic could ease. I wasn't able to get up from my bed for four days because my vagina, covered with an ice pack to reduce swelling, was packed tightly with petroleum gauze to maintain its depth.

It was a relief when Dr. C. arrived in the room to visit me. Standing at my bedside, he placed a hand on my shoulder and smiled. He then made his way to my propped legs. Examining his handiwork, he said the surgery had gone well and that the packing would be removed in four days.

"Your job is to rest," he said. "The nurses will take good care of you."

"*Kop khun kha*," I thanked Dr. C, feeling sleep drape upon me.

I was awakened every hour or so by two alternating and attentive nurses who seemed omnipresent. Neither spoke fluent English, so those first few days were full of mimed gestures, intermittent naps, blood pressure and temperature checks, sponge baths, and morning and evening calls to prayer.

My first thoughts during those initial post-surgery immobile nights were about Dad. *He was right,* I told myself as the mosque's speakers set the city abuzz for evening prayers. I thought of my father because I knew that though he would be uneasy about the surgery, he'd respect my independence. I thought about his way of doing things, how he'd taught us to ride our bikes without training wheels, and how he'd thrown me in a pool to teach me to swim. I'd screamed at first in protest out of fear that I'd fail, but he told me with such assurance and authority, "Keep paddling, man!" I moved my arms, stayed afloat and didn't drown, and eventually moved forward.

Those intense months before my surgery, I kept afloat as Dad had taught me, blindly moving toward my destination. After all the work, the anger, the desperation, and the compromises and pain, I was able to pause because I had made it. After eighteen years, my body mirrored me. The weight of that dream realized was on me as the medicine let me sit with my thoughts. No longer was I numb emotionally, and I realized that there was no celebration because I was alone.

"Out of all my kids, man," Dad told me recently through a smile, "you're the most like me. That's why we butt heads. You're just like your selfish, big-headed ass daddy."

I initially took offense at his statement about our mutual selfishness. I felt my decisions weren't hurting anyone but me, whereas his hurt those who loved him most: His adultery hurt Mom, his drug addiction put Chad and me in jeopardy. Upon reflection, I saw that the people I loved most were slighted in my quest. I left home without really speaking to Mom. I missed the majority of Chad's football and basketball games. It had been years since I last walked Jeff home from school, and now he was big enough to not even need me. Once I'd made the gradual decision to reveal myself, I began alienating myself from those I loved, a decision that made it easier for me not to be accountable to anyone. It was a solitary journey, one I'd take again to reach contentment, but the isolation I felt in that bed hurt.

As I rested, a nurse came in, asking if I'd mind a visit from another patient in recovery. The only people to visit me were the doctor in the mornings and the nurses and the room attendant who wore a black hijab and brought me juice, water, and fruit on a mauve food tray. I nodded, and a six-foot-tall blonde made her way through the door.

"Hello, sunshine," she said with an Australian accent. "I hope you don't mind me barging in here."

"Not at all." I smiled, delighted by her familiarity. "I could use some company."

She introduced herself as Genie and took a seat in the leather armchair near my bed. Her lengthy, sturdy limbs were covered in freckles, matching the smaller constellation on her nose, which gave her a youthful look. She was striking and sun-kissed, with blue eyes that looked slightly catlike from the pull of her high ponytail.

We exchanged niceties about our hometowns, trips, and procedures. She told me she'd undergone GRS five days before me and was accompanied by her girlfriend, who had returned to Australia earlier that morning, prompting me to ask if she'd ever seen a kangaroo. Genie was the kind of sweet that answered my cliché with a spark of newness, as if it were the first time a foreigner had asked that question.

She was in her mid-forties, but her sunny demeanor made her appear a decade younger. Sadly, the details she shared with me about her life didn't match her light disposition. Before transitioning, Genie worked as an engineer, was married for nearly twenty years, and had a teenage son.

"My family was my everything," she told me with a hint of nostalgia. "That's why I tried so hard to hold my feelings at bay. I wanted to be the best parent and partner I could be."

After deciding to transition three years before, she swiftly lost all the things she loved: her career, her home, her wife, and her son, who she said was figuring things out. "People say that I'm being selfish, that I haven't thought about what this is doing to my son," Genie said.

"But I thought about what this would do to my son every day. I put my family's needs first for fourteen years. I just couldn't keep hiding anymore."

Sadly, living your truth has consequences. The social cost of transitioning can be astounding. Genie had been working as an accomplished engineer, but when she announced that she was trans, she was asked to step down from a job she loved, and in turn lost her only source of income. Because of stigma and discrimination, it can be difficult to get a new job, which impacts the ability to pay for health care, food, shelter, and other necessities. Luckily, Genie had savings that she could rely on, but this didn't compensate for the rejection of those closest to her.

Genie met new friends in trans support groups in Sydney, which was where she met her girlfriend, another trans woman. She had held Genie's hand over the past few years, the only family she'd been able to rely on. I'm still struck by how many trans and queer people around the world are flung out of their homes, ostracized by intolerant families, and go on to reconstruct the idea of family by creating a network of kinship.

"We became fast friends and eventually a bit more," Genie said. "She's been my angel."

When I think about Genie's story, I can't help but marvel at the resiliency of trans people who sacrifice so much to be seen and accepted as they are. Despite those sacrifices, trans people are still wrongly viewed as being confused. It takes determination and clear, thought-out conviction, not confusion, to give up many of the privileges that Genie did to be visibly herself, though her experiences varied from my own.

I was a young person who grew up poor, brown, and trans. I didn't calculate loss because I had no job or money to lose. Luckily, my family, despite their messiness, was an asset. They embraced me in a way that Genie's family did not. This lack of social capital instilled an "I have nothing to lose" blind determination that made it easier for me to be true to myself at an early age. I was unabashedly brave, taking risks because I had no experience. Genie, on the other hand, had so much to lose. She had lived most of her life being perceived and awarded as a heterosexual white man—the epitome of power in our white patriarchal society—but when she announced that she was trans, she paid many costs. She had access to funds, though, that allowed her to seek medical intervention swiftly, whereas my lack of resources led me to risky sex work.

I was admittedly bitter about Genie's economic stability, about the fact that the monetary costs of this trip to Bangkok would not affect her bank account. I was broke: not a cent in my account until my scholarship checks were deposited in the New Year. In turn, I noticed that Genie made it a point several times to marvel at my appearance and the fact that I was able to transition early. I distinctly remember her telling me over spicy tom yum soup that I had a lot to be grateful for because I was a "freaking babe."

She looked at me in awe, marveling at how well I could "pass," as if I had everything because the world would read me as a desirable woman: young, attractive, *and* cis. I knew through various experiences that when I was presumed to be a cis woman, I was still operating in the world as a young black woman, subject to pervasive sexist and racist objectification as well as invisibility in the U.S. media, which values white women's bodies and experiences over mine.

Genie's persistent reference to my appearance reflects many people's romanticized notions about trans women who transition at a young age. I've read articles by trans women who transitioned in their thirties and forties, who look at trans girls and women who can blend as cis with such longing, as if our ability to "pass" negates their experiences because they are more often perceived to be trans. The misconception of equating ease of life with "passing" must be dismantled in our culture. The work begins by each of us recognizing that cis people are not more valuable or legitimate and that trans people who blend as cis are not more valuable or legitimate. We must recognize, discuss, and dismantle this hierarchy that polices bodies and values certain ones over others. We must recognize that we all have different experiences of oppression and privilege, and I recognize that my ability to blend as cis is one conditional privilege that does not negate the fact that I experience the world as a trans woman (with my own fears, insecurities, and body-image issues) no matter how attractive people may think I am.

Regardless of our differences, Genie and I grew close, and she was by my side on that fourth day when Dr. C. removed the gauze and catheter, assisting me in taking my first steps. I dangled my legs on the side of my bed and smiled at Dr. C., Jane, and Genie, who surrounded me.

I touched my feet to the cold tile and steadied myself, waddling a bit uncomfortably to the bathroom to pee. My urine sprayed wildly, wetting my butt in a way that I wasn't used to. Dr. C. said it was natural and that it would settle into a more controlled stream. Looking at my reflection in the bathroom mirror, I noticed the gap between my legs. I had been reshaped, and I felt closer to whole for the first time in my life. I had an overwhelming sense of lightness, as if I had let go of a burden so heavy, a burden that I had wished and prayed would just go away, and finally that burden was gone. I felt authenticated, similar to Sula after having sex with a man, basking in a "privateness in which she met herself, welcomed herself, and joined herself in matchless harmony." Now I felt I could go about in the world just as Janet.

Later that afternoon, Jane and Genie demonstrated the most laborious part of the recovery process, dilation. Handing me two white eight-inch stents—one was two inches in diameter, the other three—Jane applied lubricant to the thinner one and helped me guide it in. She told me to hold it there for twenty minutes. It was a process I'd have to repeat twice a day for the next six months, gradually increasing the size of the dilator to ensure that I maintained the depth Dr. C. had created. The healing process took six months, with the sutures and swelling disappearing. After a year, I stopped dilating altogether.

Still, it would take me years to feel at ease in my body. I was able to have pleasurable, comfortable sex with men, and I even learned to share my body in an intimate way, beyond transaction, with a partner for whom I cared deeply during my years in college. Unfortunately, having a successful operation did not relieve me from the universal awkwardness of first-time sex. Having the body I had always wanted helped me feel liberated in bed, but I was still wracked with insecurity about the size of my thighs, the attractiveness of my vagina, the diameter and darkness of my areolas. These insecurities are the same that any person experiences when exposing their body in intimacy.

All showered for the first time in Bangkok, I had my final meal with Genie over noodles. We promised to stay in touch through e-mail and bade each other a fond farewell. I assured her that I knew she would rekindle her relationship with her son, and this made her teary-eyed. She checked out from the hospital that night and relocated to a local hotel, where she explored Bangkok for a few days before returning to Australia.

Alone again with my thoughts, I reflected on happy beginnings, on starting anew, on the thought of rebirth. Unlike a new baby, I was branded by situations and people and decisions. Forgiving myself would give me the power and strength to move forward and truly have a new beginning, full of promise. It would take me years to do that work and release myself from the shame attached to the actions that had led me to Thailand.

The next day was Christmas morning, and I called home to check in with Mom, Chad, and Jeff. I wished them a merry Christmas and told them that I was healing fine. Jeff asked me if I'd had the chance to see the golden and bronze Buddha statues we saw on the Travel Channel. I remember laughing and telling him I had seen nothing but my recovery room, deflating his visions of sightseeing. Chad and I didn't talk long, but he told me that he missed me. It was the first time I had heard him say that since we were six and seven—the last time we were separated by an ocean, he in California, me in Hawaii. I found myself homesick and grateful that I had people to go back to. I also felt selfish for not giving them an opportunity to say they were afraid for me; for not even realizing that I was missing Christmas. As I went to sleep that night, I reflected on the gift of affirmation and love that my family had given me unconditionally, which enabled me to give myself the best gift ever: self-actualization.

I returned home on December 28, wrapped in the airline's blue blanket. Mom, Jeff, and Chad greeted me at the baggage claim. I noticed my mother was visibly shaken, her eyes swollen as she rushed toward me, embracing me for what felt like the first time in a long time.

"I'm sorry, Janet," Mom wept into my ear, her tears collecting on the side of my neck. "I should have been there with you."

My mother had never cried for me. I'd seen her hurt many times by men who failed her, from the night she slit her wrists as a cry for help to the time Rick hurled her onto the oily pavement of the parking lot. Her apology was the start of a more honest chapter in our relationship, one where I finally began seeing her not as my mother but as a woman with her own dreams, wishes, failed expectations, and heartaches. I had faulted Mom for not living up to the image that I had projected onto her, the image of the perfect mother I felt she should've been for me. No one was able to live up to that ideal because that woman did not exist.

What I appreciate now is that my mother never projected such an image of the perfect child onto me. She never made me feel bad about being feminine, about ingesting hormones behind her back, about taking the steps I needed to reveal myself fully. She knew her limitations. She knew what she was and wasn't able to give. In her quiet way, she stayed out of my way; she could give me that. She accepted me. She trusted me. She let me lead the way toward my own dreams of self. But my mother recently told me that she carries guilt about not having the means to pay for my surgery or at least to travel to Thailand with me. "I feel I failed you," Mom said, "but out of all of my children, I never have to—and still don't have to—worry about you. You always had a plan on how you would accomplish the things you have in your life."

I can't imagine having such blind confidence and trust in a teenager, but my mother must've seen *something* in me, something that comforted her and told her things would be okay. The guilt my mother carries about Thailand is not necessary to me, because I never expected it of her; I don't feel she should have been there with me. Though I kept my expectations of my parents low, I felt and still feel it was my own journey to take, a journey of self-revelation, mirroring that of Janie returning home from burying the dead in the beginning of *Their Eyes Were Watching God*.

"There is an expiry date on blaming your parents for steering you in the wrong direction," author J. K. Rowling said in a commencement address. "The moment you are old enough to take the wheel, responsibility lies with you."

I took responsibility for my life at a young age because my mother and my father steered themselves and me in the wrong direction. The choices they made were fueled by their own desires, good and bad, and taught me that I, too, must follow my own. My father loves reminding me that we are so similar, yet our likeness is what maintains the distance between us. Though we have healed and made vast improvements over the years, I am still learning to accept that I don't have to like him all the time, and he doesn't have to like me, but we will always love each other. Our relationship is composed of love and friction, nostalgia and expectations, respect and contradictions. My father holds a grudge against me for not consulting him about my journey to Thailand, yet he's unapologetic about his absence through those formative years. I, on the other hand, long to be close to him but can't help silencing my ringer when he calls. That's the *is*ness of us.

Regardless, I would not be the person I am today without him or my mother. I'm grateful that they lived their lives on their own terms, that they instilled in me a sense of personal responsibility for *my* life, and that they always let me know that once I attained whatever it was I sought, they'd always love me.

When I returned to my twin mattress on the floor in our apartment, it was my mother who helped nurse me back to health, preparing meals and filling my prescriptions. It was the first time in my life that I remember her doting on me. We would both heal and grow closer over the years, years in which my mother would have other chances to dote on me. I still smile when I get my monthly care packages filled with my favorite Hawaiian delicacies, *li hing mui* gummi bears, *furikake* popcorn, and bags of vanilla macadamia-nut Kona coffee.

My mother often claims that I was the parent and she the child. I like to think that we were growing in life together, figuring out who we were in the context of our relationship and our relationships with ourselves and other people. I can honestly say that my mother, who has been happily single for more than a decade, has settled into herself, into a point of contentment that has allowed the two of us to be more than mother and daughter but actually friends. When I think about my relationship with Mom, I think about what Maya Angelou said about her mother: "My mom was a terrible parent of small children but a great parent of young adults."

One of my fondest memories of my mother as an adult was at Chad's wedding to his wife, Jane. At the Catholic ceremony in Schenectady, New York, Jeffrey, twenty-two, stood by Chad, twenty-eight, as I read Paul's first letter to the Corinthians. I was struck by a "patient" and "kind" love that "takes no account of evil" and "endures all things." Most important, I realized as Jeff, Mom, and I witnessed Chad's expansion of our family, love doesn't ever fail. The memory that stuck with me is Chad's dance with my mother, where I bawled like a soap opera actress as my brother held my mother in his arms and lip-synched Boyz II Men's "A Song for Mama." I realized the journey it took for the four of us to be there together, for Jeff to be all grown up and married, for me to be there with the love of my life, for Chad to celebrate my mother, letting her know that she, despite her guilt, had been the best mother she could be. She was enough. We were all enough.

There was a resounding peace that day, one that mirrored my first night back home after Bangkok. Lying on my twin mattress where, just weeks earlier, I had wept myself to sleep, I heard something unfamiliar, something so foreign that it felt right: tranquillity. I relieved myself of the tears and the sobs and the prayers for miracles, and realized myself. And that realization lulled me to slumber, serving as a backdrop to more far-reaching dreams.

You are a composite of all the things you believe, and all the places you believe you can go. Your past does not define you. You can step out of your history and create a new day for yourself. Even if the entire culture is saying, "You can't." Even if every single possible bad thing that can happen to you does. You can keep going forward.

—OPRAH WINFREY

An unbearable silence draped over me as I clutched Aaron's pillow, the only thing I felt would ever embrace me in his room. Aaron stood in front of me, tall, immovable, processing all I had told him about my journey. I had to stop myself from filling the void between us, from reaching out to him, from begging him to love me. I wasn't sure of anything but the fact that I was no longer merely the veneer I had cautiously constructed since leaving Hawaii for New York. I could no longer maintain the shiny, untarnished, unattainable facade of that dream girl, the mixed one with the golden skin and curls and wide smile, the one wielding a master's degree and an enviable job.

In mere moments, through the intimate act of storytelling, I'd shattered that shell and replaced it with the truth, and I witnessed Aaron's awakening to the reality of me. We were two people facing ourselves and each other, not sure what the future held. Those silent seconds after my mouth stopped moving, I didn't know if he saw me in his future, and that uncertainty hurt and gave me an overwhelming sense of premature loss.

I thought about Janie in *Their Eyes Were Watching God*, about that evening on her back porch when she sat in the darkness and told her best friend, Pheoby, her life story. She talked about the pear tree blossoms, about kissing Johnny Taylor over Nanny's gate, about being forced to marry old Mr. Killicks, about running away with Jody and then Tea Cake, about experiencing and burying soul-crawling love. Like Janie, I didn't want to meditate on the horizon; I wanted to conquer it, wrap it around me like a shawl. Like Janie, I wanted to be fully known, and I had finally told my story to someone I deeply felt for.

His brown eyes were flung wide open, looking at me in all my bare honesty. Then Aaron stepped toward his bed and parted his lips. "Can I hug you?" he asked, resting one of his knees on the foot of the bed.

I rose to my knees as he leaned toward me, and I fell into his arms, exhaled heavily, and cried. For the first time in my life, I was recognized in totality. Not in spite of my experiences but because of my experiences. Aaron embraced me, though I knew, with his smooth, solid, sunburned arms surrounding me, that my challenge would be embracing myself. How could I expect this man to love me when I didn't know what it meant to accept, embrace, and love myself?

When I left Aaron's arms, I flung myself onto the streets of downtown Manhattan, the home of my choice, the place I had entered nearly five years before, representing a new beginning. After graduating from the University of Hawai'i in 2005 with a degree in fashion and media studies, I moved to the East Village, where I roomed with two other New York University grad students, met new friends at magazine internships, tipsily kissed boys on St. Mark's, and cautiously kept my distance from people. Detachment allowed me to know people on my terms.

I had been openly trans from the ages of fifteen to twenty-two, in the midst of finding who I was and revealing my findings to my loved ones and the community I grew up in. I went to bars in Honolulu with girlfriends and flirted with guys. There were numerous times when the man I was dancing with would be tapped on his shoulder or pulled away. He would return with a look of confusion, detection, or disgust, as if he had lost something, as if he had been blind to something, as if he were the only person in that bar who didn't know. The moment of forced disclosure is a hostile one to experience, one in which many trans women, even those who have the conditional privilege of "passing" that I have, can be victim to violence and exiling. In Hawaii, my home, disclosure was routinely stripped from me. People would take it from me as if it were their duty to tell the guy I was flirting with that I was trans and therefore should be avoided. It's these societal aggressions that force trans women to live in chosen silence and darkness, to internalize the shame, misconceptions, stigma, and trauma attached to being a different kind of woman.

No one in New York City knew I was trans because I chose not to lead with that fact. It was the first time in my young life when I was able to be just another twenty-two-year-old living in the big city, shedding the image that my hometown had assigned me. E. B. White, in his love letter "Here Is New York," wrote that it is the New York of "the young girl arriving from a small town . . . to escape the indignity of being observed by her neighbors" who gives the city "its incomparable achievements." For me, New York was "the city of final destination, the city that is a goal," and my goal was independence.

In New York, I had the freedom to declare who I was, discover who I wanted to be, and choose who I wanted to invite into my life. It was freeing to be another girl in the crowd, enjoying and experiencing life. I was able to learn about storytelling from some of the nation's best journalists at NYU. I nabbed internships at magazines I had torn pages from growing up and rubbed elbows with editors whose letters I had read every month for as long as I could remember. I earned my master's degree and landed a coveted online position at *People* magazine.

My past wasn't something I thought of in my early twenties because I'd fought hard to be in the present I created. I *chose*, because it was my decision to make, not to announce I was trans. My transness felt irrelevant to most of my informal, passing relationships. It was not something I discussed upon meeting someone. It was not my editor, my coworker, or my colleague's right to know that I had been born a boy. I also felt that if I told people I was trans, the hurdles that I would have to climb to get to where I yearned to be would become even more insurmountable. Being trans would become the focus of my existence, and I would be forced to fight the images cataloged in people's minds about trans people. Trying every day to combat preconceived ideas and stereotypes learned from popular culture was not on my priority list at the time. I was trying to survive, in addition to figuring myself out and unpacking who I was beyond the gender stuff.

This took work that involved me excavating what it meant to me to be *me*, to be a multiracial trans woman, or at least the kind I embody: one who's most often read as a cis mixed black woman; one with no discernible accent reflecting my father's Texas twang or my mother's Hawaiian pidgin roots; one with an advanced degree, the kind of education that my teen-mom mother and sisters didn't have access to; one with large, curly hair called "good" by my father's sisters, even though the kids in Hawaii teased that it looked like *limu* from the bottom of the sea; one with skin brown enough to be called out but light enough to be deemed not *really* black; one who was taught to identify as black because that was visible and the world would judge me accordingly.

I was raised by my parents to be visibly black and raised myself to be a visible woman. It took me years to stand firmly at the intersection of blackness and womanhood, a collage of my lived experiences, media, pop culture, and art. I had come to blackness through Clair Huxtable's swift didactic monologues in reruns of *The Cosby Show*; through the anger I felt when I was prettily invisible in clubs in New York's Meatpacking District, where guys looked through me in search of white girls; through the uh-oh dance in Beyoncé's "Crazy in Love"; through the sounds of bottle-popping douches who called me "exotic" and said "You're really pretty for a black girl!" and "I'm usually not attracted to black women"; through the revolutionary words of Audre Lorde; through the vision of Michelle Obama's fist bump; through the consensus of the black-girl interns who said I was different because "You're the right amount of black," the kind white woman editors aren't intimidated to work with; through the raw brilliance of *This Bridge Called My Back*; through the beauty of Marsha P. Johnson's flowers, smile, and S.T.A.R.

I am aware that identifying with what people see versus what's authentic, meaning who I actually am, involves erasure of parts of myself, my history, my people, my experiences. Living by other people's definitions and perceptions shrinks us to shells of ourselves, rather than complex people embodying multiple identities. I am a trans woman of color, and that identity has enabled me to be truer to myself, offering me an anchor from which I can uplift my visible blackness, my often invisible trans womanhood, my little-talked-about native Hawaiian heritage, and the many iterations of womanhood they combine.

When I think of identity, I think of our bodies and souls and the influences of family, culture, and community—the ingredients that make us. James Baldwin describes identity as "the garment with which one covers the nakedness of the self." The garment should be worn "loose," he says, so we can always feel our nakedness: "This trust in one's nakedness is all that gives one the power to change one's robes." I'm still journeying toward that place where I'm comfortable in this nakedness, standing firmly in my interlocking identities.

Like identity, my not-so-relationship with Aaron was a complicated matter that was finding its way. Aaron refused to commit to me, and I refused to let him go. That romantic, dizzying feeling of infatuation was no longer in his belly after I told him I was trans. Those fleeting, fluttery feelings in mine were replaced by something deeper, something resembling love. The unevenness of our feelings filled me with insecurities. I told Aaron several times that I felt demoted, and each time he told me, "I never not want you in my life."

I trusted Aaron with my vulnerabilities because of his reaction that night in his bedroom. He showed himself to me as well, validating every instinct I had about him. Aaron recognized that opening up to him must've been difficult, but it was difficult for him to think about what was next because he didn't even think that my being trans was a possibility. His initial instinct was to comfort me.

"It wasn't about *me* and how *I* felt," Aaron said, reflecting on his reaction. "It took me a while to process all of it, but immediately I wanted you to know that there was nothing wrong with you and that I valued what you shared with me."

Aaron told me that he hadn't internalized what I'd said. My story didn't make him question his gender or sexuality, an assumption many people think must have been difficult for Aaron, a cis heterosexual man. My identity as a trans woman didn't make him doubt his manhood or my womanhood. He said it actually made him feel closer to me and made him see the parallels in our journeys, specifically with the isolation of having grown up visibly different, the only black kid in rural North Dakota and Maine.

"I was out there all alone, questioning who I was and what it all meant at a young age," Aaron explained. "Being different, I was forced to look at the world differently, and I constantly questioned who I was. By the time you opened up to me, I was fully formed, if that makes sense. There were no more questions about my identity, about who I was." He did admit one thing: "I no longer look at people the same way anymore. You taught me to question those assumptions I made about people every day."

I continued to open up to Aaron, telling him other pieces of my story over those months throughout which we watched movies, chatted about them over coffee and brunch, attended block and housewarming parties, all the motions of a couple. He also opened up to me, telling me that my revelations had forced him to focus on his own struggles. He wondered why he'd fallen so quickly for someone he didn't know, why it was so easy for him to sacrifice his dreams for a woman, why he hadn't been single since he was fifteen. He returned to the promise he had made to commit to himself, not to a woman or a relationship.

Though he made room for me, Aaron's inconsistencies were consistent, and they supported the pit of dread in my belly that I was not worthy of love. His texts and calls and dates were intermittent. We'd spend a long weekend together here and there, growing closer, having sex, getting to know each other more intimately. I told him that I wanted to be brave enough to tell my story someday, and he encouraged me to retrace the steps I'd taken over a decade ago. He held me accountable to my truth, suggesting that I write down my story for myself and open up to those closest to me in New York.

One of the first people I invited into my life was my best friend, Mai. She was the woman who hired me at People.com, despite an HR rep's "professional" assessment of me as an entitled, incapable diva, which Mai attributed to my looks. Mai and I bonded over the fact that we were women of color in corporate America, over a silly devotion to *The Hills*, and over a mutual love of vintage shopping. Most important, we were both on the rebound, having left our starter relationships, longing for partnership.

There were moments of deep intimacy and sharing during our three-year friendship when I felt myself pulling back, withholding details that would reveal me. I remember that evening after her thirtieth birthday when we were placing her clothes (including a Minnie Mouse costume that still cracks me up), DVDs, books, and photos in cardboard boxes. She was sitting on the hardwood floor in gray sweatpants, weeping over leaving a man who was no longer good for her. "I don't know if I can do this," she said. "I don't know if I'm strong enough to do this on my own."

"You're not alone," I said, writing "sweaters" in bold print on a cardboard box with a black Sharpie.

"I know I have you, but I don't know if I can do this."

"You *will* do this," I assured her.

"How do you know?" she asked.

My heart was open, and I was ready to bare myself to her, to tell her that I knew she could do this alone because I once was a scared girl afraid of the unknown, of stepping out on her own. I pulled myself back and protectively squashed my instinct to share with her because I was too afraid that if I told her, she would think of me differently. Instead, I hugged her, grabbed another box, and filled our glasses with cabernet. A year later, we were in different places, and our friendship had grown constant, reliable, sisterly. Unlike when I was a teenager, I knew I didn't have to do it all alone. I had someone I could rely on, to share my anguish over the grayness of my relationship with Aaron. I called Mai wracked with fear. "I need you to know that I've wanted to share something with you many times but was scared," I told her over the phone.

"Janet," Mai started in her ever assuring way, "there's nothing you could do that would make me not love you."

"You know how you're always teasing me that you don't know why Aaron wouldn't want to be with me, that he's idiotic and all that stuff?"

"Yeah," she said.

"Well, he doesn't want to be with me mostly because of my past," I said.

After I told Mai my story, she yelled at me for scaring her: "You acted as if you murdered someone!" When we met that evening for dinner, she hugged me, acted just as silly as she normally did, and reiterated that Aaron was still idiotic not to be with me. Her friendship buoyed me as I spoke the truths I'd silenced long ago.

I lived in a world that told me in big and small ways every day that who I knew myself to be was invalid. I blossomed in spite of a society that didn't offer me a single image of a girl who happened to be born a boy, who was thriving in the world, off the streets, away from some man's wallet, basking in the reality of her dreams. As I typed away every morning in my bedroom before going to my office cubicle, I broke down those walls of shame about being a different kind of woman. I grew more confident, stronger, realizing that I deserved love.

After eighth months of limbo, I woke up at one A.M. on a cold February 2010 night to a text from Aaron: "Are you up? I can't take it anymore. Yes, I've been drinking but I'm not drunk. I'm just outside your apartment."

When I buzzed him in, he looked at me with puffy red eyes. He looked as tired and weary as I felt. We had a strong bond, a deep friendship that we had built over those months since I met him on that Lower East Side dance floor, since splitting that cinnamon roll, since he told me he wanted horses someday. But I felt myself giving up on any idea of there being an us beyond friendship. I thought that my being trans was a deal breaker, and I was growing to accept that.

"You know I love you, right?" he asked straight out.

I nodded, taking it as a final answer, a rejection of all my hopes for us. I didn't speak or expound on what we could be or rebut what I saw as his white flag of surrender. I'd been there, done that, with him. My love was proven, and I had nothing left to prove. My love was known, I was known.

"I left my apartment hours ago in search of something. I don't know what it was," he said. "So I went to one bar after another and ended up on your street."

I remained quiet, looking at him as we walked into my bedroom.

"As I stood on your street, I realized that, like that night when we met, I left my place looking for you. I've always wanted you, to be right here with you, Janet," he said.

I held my tears back, stubborn. I had cried too many times over him, over not getting a text or a call, over my unanswered invitations to hang out. I remained quiet.

Lying beside me in my bed, he said, "I'm tired."

I knew that his declaration of being tired was the moment I'd been waiting for ever since I had opened up to him. I knew this was our moment, the one that we'd remember forever, the one when we'd become that "me and you against the world" couple he once predicted we'd be.

"Make room for me," I pleaded as his head rested on my chest.

"Okay."

We moved in together in the spring, he met my family in November and I met his in December, and by the end of that year Aaron was beside me as I smiled from that stoop fronting Tompkins Square Park for my *Marie Claire* photo shoot, and he urged me from behind his camera to open my heart in my "It Gets Better" video. He was there with his camera, documenting my reunion with Wendi in late 2011 when she relocated to New York City for her makeup career. It was the first time she and I were in the same city since I was in college. Aaron and the friendship and love and partnership that we've built became my foundation, a platform that has fortified my own sense of self, giving me the strength to step out of silence and come forward fully as my own woman. I've found that Audre Lorde was indeed right when she wrote, "That visibility which makes us most vulnerable is that which also is the source of our greatest strength."

Speaking up about my experiences continues to be an incredibly vulnerable experience. I feel I am out there on my own, grappling with and sharing my truth. That vulnerability has also enabled me to connect to other women and plug into a wider network of narratives on our varying paths to womanhood. I have learned through the process of storytelling and sharing that we all come from various walks of life, and that doesn't make any of us less valid.

My assignment at birth is only one facet of my identity, one that I am no longer invested in concealing. Acknowledging this fact and how it has shaped my understanding of self has given me the power to challenge the ways in which we judge, discriminate, and stigmatize women based on bodily differences. The media's insatiable appetite for transsexual women's bodies contributes to the systematic othering of trans women as modern-day freak shows, portrayals that validate and feed society's dismissal and dehumanization of trans women. The U.S. media's shallow lens dates back to 1952, when Christine Jorgensen became the media's first "sex change" darling, breaking barriers and setting the tone for how our stories are told. These stories, though vital to culture change and our own sense of recognition, rarely report on the barriers that make it nearly impossible for trans women, specifically those of color and those from low-income communities, to lead thriving lives. They're tried-and-true transition stories tailored to the cis gaze. What I want people to realize is that "transitioning" is not the end of the journey. Yes, it's an integral part of revealing who we are to ourselves and the world, but there's much life afterward. These stories earn us visibility but fail at reporting on what our lives are like beyond our bodies, hormones, surgeries, birth names, and before-and-after photos.

Challenging the media tropes has been the most difficult part of sharing my story. On the one hand, there are through lines, common elements in our journeys as trans women, that are undeniable. At the same time, plugging people into the "transition" narrative (which I have been subjected to) erases the nuance of experience, the murkiness of identity, and the undeniable influence of race, class, and gender. It's no coincidence that the genre of memoir from trans people has been dominated by those with access, mainly white trans men and women, and these types of disparities greeted me head-on when I stepped forward publicly.

Initially, I was embraced by the stakeholders of the mainstream LGBT movement. I quickly noticed that despite the unifying acronym, the people at the table often did not reflect me or my community. These spaces and the conversations were dominated by men, specifically upper-middle-class white cis gay men. Women, people of color, trans folks, and especially folks who carried multiple identities were all but absent. I was grateful for the invitation but unfilled by the company. This was my political awakening.

I was tasked with speaking out about these glaring disparities, about how those with the most access within the movement set the agenda, contribute to the skewed media portrait, and overwhelmingly fail at funneling resources to those most marginalized. My awakening pushed me to be more vocal about these issues, prompting uncomfortable but necessary conversations about the movement privileging middle- and upper-class cis gay and lesbian rights over the daily access issues plaguing low-income queer and trans youth and LGBT people of color, communities that carry interlocking identities that are not mutually exclusive, that make them all the more vulnerable to poverty, homelessness, unemployment, HIV/AIDs, hyper-criminalization, violence, and so much more.

One of the reasons the gay rights movement has been successful is its urging that gays and lesbians everywhere, no matter their age, color, or wealth, come out of the closet. This widespread visibility has shifted culture and challenged misconceptions. People often transpose the coming-out experience on me, asking how it felt to be in the closet, to have been stealth. These questions have always puzzled me. Unlike sexuality, gender is visible. I never hid my gender. Every day that I stepped out into the sunlight, unapologetically femme, I was a visible woman. People assume that I was in the closet because I didn't disclose that I was assigned male at birth.

What people are really asking is "Why didn't you correct people when they perceived you as a *real* woman?" Frankly, I'm not responsible for other people's perceptions and what they consider real or fake. We must abolish the entitlement that deludes us into believing that we have the right to make assumptions about people's identities and project those assumptions onto their genders and bodies.

It is not a woman's duty to disclose that she's trans to every person she meets. This is not safe for a myriad of reasons. We must shift the burden of coming out from trans women, and accusing them of hiding or lying, and focus on why it is unsafe for women to be trans.

For a while I have had the privilege of being able to choose with whom I share my story and whether disclosure is necessary. I have based this decision on the intimacy, closeness, and longevity of the relationship. As for dating, rarely was I open with any guy the first time we met. I felt it wasn't his right to know that I was assigned male at birth. It was often irrelevant to our interaction. Not every date or hookup was worthy of me or my story. Some of those dates were best suited to drinks or dinner and maybe even my bed.

I've experienced varying levels of disclosure throughout my life. At thirteen, I told Wendi I was a girl. At fifteen, I told my mother and my siblings to call me Janet. At twenty-six, I told Aaron that I was a different kind of woman. At twenty-eight, I shed my anonymity in *Marie Claire* because I wanted to disclose an aspect of my identity that I felt was widely misunderstood, and often invisible. That catalytic piece moved people to think differently, disrupting the portrait of womanhood. It was the pivot in which I decided to invite the world into my life, when I chose to acknowledge that though you may not perceive me as trans, I am trans, and being trans—as is being black, Hawaiian, young, and a woman—is an integral part of my experience, one that I have no investment in erasing.

All of these parts of myself coexist in *my* body, a representation of evolution and migration and truth. My body carries within its frame beauty and agony, certainty and murkiness, loathing and love. And I've learned to accept it, as is. For so much of my life, I wished into the dark to be someone else, some elusive ideal that represented possibility and contentment.

I was steadily reaching in the dark across a chasm that separated who I was and who I thought I should be. Somewhere along the way, I grew weary of grasping at possible selves, just out of reach. So I put my arms down and wrapped them around me. I began healing by embracing myself through the foreboding darkness until the sunrise shone on my face. Eventually, I emerged, and surrendered to the brilliance, discovering truth, beauty, and peace that was already mine.

Acknowledgments

This book would not be possible without my parents, who gave me life and shared theirs with me. I'm equally grateful to my siblings, Chad, Cheraine, Cori, and Jeff. Without your love, there would be no me.

Aaron, my compassionate first reader, urged me to tap into myself and share my journey. He also ensured that I ate, scheduled TV breaks, and had someone to yell at when I was insecure and stressed. Without his care, this book would not be here.

My best friends, Mai and Wendi, were pivotal in helping me discover myself as a girl and woman. I love you. I was also blessed to encounter Ed, who first brought me to New York City, and Zach, who selflessly ensured I stayed. The companionship of Kristina, Nary, and Charlise made my first years in New York *everything*.

Many thanks to Farrington High School for welcoming me and bringing these critical people into my life: Mrs. Jean Chun, who introduced me to Zora Neale Hurston and *Their Eyes Were Watching God*;

Acknowledgments

Alison Colby, who consistently affirmed me; and the W. R. Farrington Memorial Scholarship Committee, who invested in my undergraduate education.

I'm indebted to Ryan D. Harbage, my literary agent, who believed in me and this book from the start; Sarah Branham, my editor and advocate at Atria Books, who wholeheartedly championed my vision with such tenderness and helped me sharpen it by asking all the right questions; the entire team at Atria Books, especially Judith Curr, Peter Borland, and Daniella Wexler; and Ellis Trevor, my speaking agent, and his team at American Talent Group.

Thank you to Lea Goldman and Kierna Mayo for making the *Marie Claire* feature come to fruition; my former colleagues at People.com for being there as I realized a dream; and the guys at Native Bean for welcoming me with smiles and lattes as I wrote my first draft.

The following people offered me insights, resources, and validation as I developed my mission and completed this book. Thank you, Marie Brown, Cecilia Chung, Laverne Cox, Michaela angela Davis, reina gossett, bell hooks, Isis King, Stephanie Laffin, Zakiya Lord, Kimberley McLeod, Monika MHz, Darnell Moore, Catherine Pino, Jen Richards, Monica Roberts, Angelica Ross, Kiara St. James, Jon Stryker, Chris Tuttle, Tiffany R. Warren, Bali White, and many more who may not be listed but aren't forgotten.

Many thanks to my online comrades. Your tweets, reblogs, likes, follows, messages, and comments have affirmed me, challenged me, and embraced me. I'm also grateful to every woman who contributed to #girlslikeus, showing the collective power of our stories, and those who told me my story moved them, resonated with them, and filled them with possibility. I am so humbled. Thank you.

Finally, this book is for my sisters, my siblings, my elders, and my foremothers (Sylvia Rivera, Marsha P. Johnson, and Miss Major

Griffin-Gracy) who lit the torch, illuminating a pathway to navigate a system not built for us. The only reason I am here today and am able to write is because you resisted, found your freedom, and showed me how to do the same. I'm in awe of your resilience *and* brilliance.

About the Author

J anet Mock is a writer who stepped onto the national stage in 2011 with a profile about her journey to womanhood in *Marie Claire* magazine. A believer in the power of storytelling, Janet writes and speaks about her experience of living at the intersections of multiple identities.

In 2013, she was featured in the HBO documentary *The OUT List* about prominent LGBTQ figures, discussed cultural politics on MSNBC's *Melissa Harris-Perry* show, and joined the board of directors of the Arcus Foundation. Her work has been recognized by the Sylvia Rivera Law Project, ADCOLOR, the Anti-Violence Project, the Center for American Progress, GLAAD, and the Women's Media Center.

A native of Honolulu, Janet attended the University of Hawaiʻi at Mānoa, earned her MA in journalism from New York University, and wielded her encyclopedic knowledge of pop culture as an editor for People.com, *People* magazine's website.

She lives with the man and the dog of her dreams in New York City. Follow her on Twitter at @janetmock, where she established #Girlslikeus, a movement encouraging trans women to live visibly.